A LEGALLY LOADED SPOLARIZED EXPERIENCE

ALL IN ONE LIFE BENEATH THE HYPE

PEGGY SPOLAR

LitPrime
"Your story is our priority"

LitPrime Solutions
21250 Hawthorne Blvd
Suite 500, Torrance, CA 90503
www.litprime.com
Phone: 1-800-981-9893

Published by LitPrime Solutions   09/07/2022

ISBN: 978-1-955944-94-6(sc)
ISBN: 978-1-955944-95-3(e)

Library of Congress Control Number: 2022908769

CONTENTS

Enjoy the many pictures throughout the book taken by me over the years. They convey the essence of my stories more effectively than just my words. Thanks to my family and those who stood by me over the years and in honor of my beloved parents. To the best of my knowledge and belief all statements made in this book are true, but you be the judge.

Author Ms. Peggy
IP Lawyer Mark Levy
Graphic Designers Ridge Prince and Zim Productions
Website & Digital Marketing by Sun Sign Designs
Published by LitPrime
Copyright Spolarized Entertainment Collection Corp. © 2019

Content Sections:

Get Legally Loaded is about makin' a better world regardless of race, religion, or social status. We all must "Rize Energized Spolarized®" to the highest degree and Shine the Star we should be Legally Loaded® with education. Once you've purchased the book "All in one Life Beneath the Hype" your purchase will include a download of the song "Philly Grown." To receive your download, go to www.getlegallyloaded.com and register where you purchased the book and the date of purchase by clicking on the box that matches the box below found on the home page of the website. Your name will also be registered in the "SpolarizedSmart™ Book of Knowledge" that you stand against fraud, corruption and discrimination.

Thanks Everyone,

Ms Peggy

Ribbons on my Shoulder a shout out to those who are Legally Loaded
Living' on the Ridge is Mighty Rough.
Living' on the Ridge you Got to be Tough.
Thanks to those who are on my Ribbons
and put their hands up with me Legally Loaded...

PHOTO BY ZIM PRODUCTIONS

5

The Entrepreneur Next Door™

Some of the Many Stars
that Made My Heart Zing along with the Rich and Poor who Crossed My Door and Some A**holes in Between.

Scott Baker	Treach	Neighbors
Young Spanish	Ruff Ryders	Rev. Carl Batzel
The Public	Ice Water	Holly & Paul
Nickelback	Brandon Jones	Patrick Metwier
The Village People	SNL	Dr. Hassan Khalil
Celine Dion	Nelly	Chad Efron
Mylon LeFevre	Big Sean	Andrew Lenter
Anthony Geary	Yomi	Ashia
Susan Boyle	Brandsmart	Mickey Zawiski
John Travolta	Stevie Wonder	Mad Dog
Olivia Newton-John	Coolio (feat L.V.)	Don Johnson
Adele	Stedman Graham	DJ Ace
Dire Strait	Oprah Winfrey	DJ Louie G
Meryl Streep	Calvin Lane	Deb Marello
Bryan Adams	WalMart	Nema
Scott Abramo	McDonald's	Alvin Tucker
Bill Haley's Comets	President Trump	Susan and Arnold
Joey Welz	Ray Jones	Ralph ROI
David and Jaye	Silent Giant Corp.	Jack Rosenkrance
Jennifer Warnes	Diavion DeNiro	Tom Wilbur
Ronn. Moss	Meek Mills	Lynette Carrozza
Ridge Forrester	Charlie Taylor	JT Allred
Carrie Underwood	Matt Jade	Hot 97
Don McLean	Charlie Briggs	Fifty Rackz
Janis Japlin	Monica	George Slavick
Biggie	Whoopi Goldberg	Fred Aquilar
Master P	2 Pac	Jeannette Rogers
Nick Cannon	Joy Behar	Greg Walker
Madonna	George Lucas	Georgis Gastone
Robert Gordy	Ed Sheeran	Jonathan Purdie
M.O.P.	Bill Maher	Wade Gibbs
Kurupt	John Lennon	Gail Young
Jermaine Dupree	John Legend	Jeff Green
Ja Rule	Luther Vandross	Dr. Jesse Kline
Stryper	George Satellite	A**holes
George Clinton	Chasing Cars	Mickey Bentson
Ice-T	Mel Montana	Joellyn
Damon Dash	Big Nasty	Anthony Marshell
Fubu	Karen	Ronnie Perdue
Beastie Boys	Macklemore & Ryan Lewis	Mack Montanez
BB King	Val Stone	Parish Family
Elvis Presley	Max & Poonima	Spolar's Pig Roast Family
Uncle Remus	Bob & Georgianne	Jeffrey McKinney
Busta Rhymes	Doris & Evelyn	Jim Guarino
Gene Steinhoff	WBLS	Tom Laskowski
Lamont Milner	Magic Marketplace	John Myers

The Entrepreneur Next Door™

Some of the Many Stars

that Made My Heart Zing along with the Rich and Poor who Crossed My Door and Some A**holes in Between.

Dustin Palmer	Get Down Art	Martin & Nancy
Lyricist Lounge	Eye Black	Jay Krimel
Heavy Rotation	Tomaszewski Family	Jason Mitan Esq.
Late Joey Conaway	Kelly Family	Chris Hanach
Geoffrey Atkins	Ira New Idea Sales	Jay Dinga
Brookline Physical Therapy	Hemp Club	Mark Pierson
Brenda & Toby	Larry White	Mark Brisco
Powell Family	Ricky Grey	Marino
Charlie & Marylou	David Truby	CES show
Dr. Linker	Harriet	TC
Na Na	Folgers	Nolte Family
Friendsville Inn Customers	Flo Rida	Jamel White
Loessy Family	B.O.B.	John Cogen
Mr. Phil	Anthony Buie	John Juric
The Tunnel Club	Vibes	Qwen Hadari
Peabody Hotel	Donald Langott	Rebecca Kondor
Port Authority	Idalia Thompson Moni	Jessie Strong
Franklin Rowe	Trisha Hipperts	Jarruth Duncan
Mike Calarosa	Owen Joyette	Jamie Hoffman
Publix	G-Unit	Thiphaphorn Topolski
Kraft Foods	Robert Hoopes	Simeon English
Frito-Lay	Dicks	Trisha Hipperts
Frystack's	TMZ	Tom Welsh
Jason Mraz	Facebook Friends	Bender Family
Compassion Int.	One Direction	Late Bob Bender
Benz	Kelly Clarkson	Renee Cloud
Maroon 5black	Miley Cyrus	Tommy Bellmon
Fat Joe & His Crew	Spolarized Smart Friends	Taylor Swift
BMW	Lady Gaga	Katy Perry
Baker Tax	Shay Olivia	Evanescence
Bender Family	Janet Jackson	Alice Bridge
Joel Johnson	Elton John	Survivor
Best Buy	LA Reid	Cardi B
Campbell's Soup	Some Assholes	3 Doorsdown
Nathaniel Johnson	Train	Alannah Myles
Bill Gates	Sue Dean	Chuck Berry
DJ Kali	Joan Star	Guns N Roses
Eve	RX	DJ Kid Capri
Bill Conti	Late Nancy Jelick	Ed Sullivan
Coca-Cola	Bobby Sharp	Justin Timberlake
Jerry Graham	Late Karen Strong	Lil Wayne
Dan Ricci	Wilkerson Family	T.I.
Ben Leung	Michael Spitz	Steven Palmer
Go-Daddy	Dr. Jonathan Yousef	Rocopra
Monolo Great Tickets	Adam Bell	Don McLean
Jim Doolittle	Michael Brooks	Shelby Jean

The Entrepreneur Next Door™

Some of the Many Stars
that Made My Heart Zing along with the Rich and Poor who Crossed My Door and Some A**holes in Between.

Santana	Sticky Fingas	Wyclef Jean
Dereck Hough	Killah Priest	Metallica
The Dream Cranberries	LYCRA	Eagles Rock Band
Linkin Park	DuPont Coolmax	Eric Clapton
Backstreet	U-God	Led Zeppelin
Gwen Stefani	Frank Stallone	Pink Floyd
Rod Stewart	Abba	Rolling Stones
Sister Sledge	Sun Records	Aerosmith
Jimmy Buffett	DMX	The Who
Dolly Parton	Saint Martin DePorres	Creedence Clearwater
Haddaway	Joe Jackson	Tom Petty
Rihanna	Things Change	R.E.M.
Julianne Hough	Russell Simmons	Daniel James
Jeff Bhasker	Black Expo	Imagine Dragons
Phillip Lavrence	Downtime Club	Glen Campbell
Mark Ronson	YMCA	Johnny Denver
Bruno Mars	Celebrity Basketball NYC	Frank Sinatra
UB40	J Records	Roa
KRS 1	Diadora	Dean Martin
Vanilla Ice	Empire	Willie Nelson
Wu-Tang	Fedex	Irene Cara
Drake	UPS	A Great Big World
Eminem	CNN	Cher
Michael Jackson	TMZ	Britney Spears
Brown Twins	Lottery	Ellen DeGeneres
Alex Hawley	Punch TV	Tracy Morgan
Ken Byrant	Shadowbrook Resort	Cash Money
Geno Williams	The Late Randeze	Kid Rock
Maxine Baresch Esq.	Greenfield Online	Ted Nugent
Abie Shalem	Pope John Paul	R Kelly
Spinks	Caesars Palace	DJ Red Alert
Section 8	Me-Too Movement	Jadakiss
Bryan Adams	Kingdom Bound Ministry	Jimmy Buffett
Nickelback	The Jackson family	Steve Dobrowal
Luciano Pavarotti	Carl Brown	Bette Midler
Ben Brown	Moe Millions	Bruce Springsteen
Suge Knight	Jeff DaBella	Bon Jovi
Beverly Frost	Richard and Lorrie	Deep Purple
Tom Foster	CMX-Eric Brown	Neil Diamond
Vince Burns	Easy Mo Bee	Queen
Youri	Outkast	Eddie Carr
Willie Esco	Renald Richard	Super Show
General Hospital	Ray Charles	Tail Gate Show
Reebok	AC/DC	Blue Ray
DuPont	Fifty Cent	Bob Sedor
Whitney Houston	Dre	Champs Groove

The Entrepreneur Next Door™

Some of the Many Stars that Made My Heart Zing along with the Rich and Poor who Crossed My Door and Some A**holes in Between.

Cloud Family	Dan Dizio	Gary Horn
DJ Kool Herk	Joshua Marks Esq.	The Late Randeze
Beyonce	Doddie Mondi	Daymond John
Damon Dash	Diane & Jim	Tracy Morgan
Jay-Z	Marvin Stewart Jr.	Queen Latifah
T-Pain	Lamont Gray	Amir Ziv
Liberace	VH1	Whitney Houston
Billy Joel	Locical	Macklemore
Snoop Dogg	Robert Hall	Ryan Lewis
Black Eyed Peas	Toby Gad	Rich Banks
Buster Douglas	Blake Shelton	IZ
Frank Lucas Jr	BB Records	Antonio Rasmus
Kanye West	Golden Swan Records	Tony Carbone
Jamie Foxx	Anthony Davis	Alicia Keys
Rolling Stones	MTV	Aretha Franklin
Will Smith	Tri Connect Ent.	Celine Dion
Hank Williams	Patrick Williams	Swizz Beatz
DJ Ace	Kids Gotta Eat	
Harvey Weinstein	Angel Ballard	
Funkmaster Flex	Barry Goldstein	
MC Hammer	Red Man	
Ruff Ryders	Keith Perrin	
Joe Jackson	The Harts	
Beanie Sigel	Alex Hawley	
Boo-Yaa Tribe	Eric Strong	
Aaron Neville	Alvin Tucker	
Seal	Champ Grooves	
Nas	A.J. Mrenice	
B.O.B.	Kevin Hart	
Puffy	BET	
Bow Wow	Rian Andrews	
PitBull	Michael Lutz	
Akon	Alex Martin	
ZZ Top	Redman	
Dan Woska	Rian Andrews	
John Sykas	Michael Lutz	

Parable given me by my Mother Mary

My dearest child when I gave you your name there wasn't a black mark on it. Wear it well. Understand regardless of who your parents are or what they may do or not do, it's not an excuse for your actions. You are unique, the one and only. You're able to fit into any shoe and able to climb any mountain.. Like the dolls that lay their head on your bed they know your heart and love you for who you are. It is you who must make yourself last and not fall to a person's plead, for a pure heart is transparently changed never the same if you give in and give up. We cannot baby you or treat you like a child. Everyone must grow up. You must grow to take responsibility for your actions. We want you to grow and become a masterpiece. The one and only you. I hope you are able to sit with presidents and hierarchies. That means don't suck your fingers or talk with food in your mouth or sit on the edge of chairs. Sit back sound. Don't lean on walls and leave residue. Shand on your feet. You were born alone. No one is going to the grave with you. Flowers and roses given you throughout life don't change the facts in life. I expect you to teach the same rules I have taught you to your children and their children and to those who sit at your table.

Love your Mother Mary

All In One Life

I WELCOME YOU TO VENTURE WITH ME A LITTLE DEEPER INTO THE LIFE OF A CHILD. I AM LIVIN' PROOF THAT COMIN' FROM NOTHIN' DOESN'T MEAN YOU CAN'T BE SOMETHING! MY MOTHER WOULD SAY "KEEP YOUR SOMBER'S OUT OF YOUR MOUTH AND YOUR PUTZY'S ON THE GROUND AND YOU'LL GROW UP JUST FINE." SPOLAR © 1993

Jump in my Shoe Yo...

Jump in my Shoe and if you can step along wit me you are damn good. When I teach, I teach to every individual in the street. From coast to coast, I'm bringing it to you straight up the way it goes. Like it or not I am who I am. My parents were in a motorcycle gang out of Philly call the Ramblers. They rode Cycles every weekend and went to the first Woodstock. I spent every weekend at Grandma Mary and Papa Joe's house. Grandma Mary thought if I attended the Catholic Church (Little Flower) around the corner from her house I would grow up just fine with some religious teachings. The nuns did look impressive with their black gowns and white collars. However, I was 9 years old and I didn't last long when the nun started talking about how sweet Joseph was to Mary.

The Nun spoke about how Joseph would put Mary on the donkey and made sure her dress was down and he'd dust off her soiled feet. I put my hand up and she asked me not to disturb her class. I spoke up saying but I have something to say. I stood to my feet and turned to the class and said, "don't listen to her she lies. I live with Joseph and Mary and when Papa Joe comes home wasted Grandma Mary tells Papa Joe to swing that sh★t off on the porch swing before you come in the house smelling like beer." For telling the truth I got thrown out of religious classes. I look at it today as just another learning process that was offered to me growing up. My parents along with my grandparents had very little education, perhaps 6th or 7th grade. Yet when it comes to common sense in practical matters and having strict rules they were off the charts beyond the normal range of expectations. My grandparents Joseph and Mary and my parents Mother Mary and Ernie helped me become who I am today. Today I'm a woman standing to my feet like a masterpiece with wisdom and knowledge of what's up. Back in time it was rare for a woman to stand up to a man. They were considered second class. However, my mother stood her ground. My father wanted me named after him Ernestine. My mother's parents Joseph and Mary gave her the headz up that she should pick the name. She followed the Golden Rule taught by Joseph and Mary that Beneath the Wild Weeds you'll find a Violet and hear the Ave Maria.

I've been called a lot of things over the past 79 years. Call me a bitch ain't that some sh★t. I got it from my mother when she went against my father. Right before I was born, she met a woman who wore her garter belt correctly and walked in her spiked high heels properly. My mother was impressed. Her adrenaline was flowing. The lady's name was Margaret.

A lot of parents think of childhood as children playing with toys and enjoying them while they're little. My father believed it was a time for learning the rules and getting them locked solid in the brain and play time came on the weekends. Daddy saw the Catholic faith as a religion that at least recognized women as Saints. Daddy ended up pretty cool with the name my mother chose. My first day of school at the bus stop my father took his two fingers pointed towards his eyes saying "focus, look me in the eye child. During recess when it's time to play I want you to only play with children that are Jewish." Of course, at that time I didn't know it was another faith but he wasn't talkin' about the religious side of it. He felt that Christmas for them wasn't a bunch of toys like us, rather gifts for them more often were books. He went on to explain it wasn't my fault that I was born blonde but the world more than likely will assume that I'm stupid and easy regardless if you get an A in school. I put my head down slightly but he pulled my chin up and once again stated to focus. So here I am running around the playground asking every boy and girl if they were Jewish. Many would say, I don't know what I am. Finally, after 3 recesses I found a little Jewish boy and I said, "can I play with you?" He shook his head yes and I yelled hooray. We became friends. My father was proud of me and told me why he made the request. He let me know that since I complied, I now could have other friends.

My second day at school I told my mother I didn't like my name Margaret. When she questioned why I told her it is too long. The kids call on Sally, Susie and Jane. I told my mother to say it and you'll see, Mar-gar-ret. My mother assured me she would fix it. She went to school and told them to call me Peggy. I was so happy cuz now the kids would call on me to play hopscotch. When my father found out what my mother did, he stepped up and said focus. He told me if the kids in school or anyone calls you Peg correct them. A Peg is something you lean on. Once you've corrected them if they do it again then they're being wise a★★es and trying to lean on you. Over the last 79 years I have to say my dad was right. If I have to correct anyone more than once I quickly realized they'll never be my cup of tea and I will never be their coffee.

We should realize not everything we see or hear is reality. The way I was raised allowed me to grow up with an invisible electrical energy to see beyond my boundaries. I would question my mother about stuff she did that seemed out of the ordinary. Long before plant food for shrubs and veggies existed, my mother would take her coffee grounds out and spread them around the flower beds. When asked she'd say I'm sharing the extra leftover coffee with my plants. She explains back in time Margaret's we're known as Crusaders whose Adventures were Miraculous to the point they never can be forgotten. Sharing my coffee grounds lets me not forget to share with others and how I stood my ground with a cup of coffee naming you.

I married a Catholic at 16. Back then when people spoke about fast food it meant during Lent and something made in Japan was considered junk. The term making out refer to how you made out on your examination. In my days smoking cigarettes was fashionable, grass was something we mowed. Coke was a cold drink I couldn't wait to drink and pot was something you'd use to cook food in. Grandma's lullaby was thought of as a rock joint out of key. Women were thought of as going to hell if they weren't virgins and blondes were thought of as stupid and easy. Women had to be married in order to have a baby. The sad part is who is stupid enough to believe in such bullsh*t. Perhaps, if you were raised in a world of innocents. Thank heavens my parents taught me how to be Savvy and Smart, how to get ahead, how to get educated, how to tell a man to back off cause I'm not a stupid easy blonde, and that life has weeds and stickers but beneath them you'll find a violet.

Growing up I didn't realize the way my parents used parables to teach me was smart and Savvy. It made it easier for me to touch reality and realize what they expected of me. At times the lessons were tough but I realized as I got older the teachings where what we perhaps should be teaching in today's time. I loved going to church when I was growing up with my Playmates Patsy and Gail. When I married at sixteen life was built around church with my friends Mable and George. As I aged, I became older and wiser. I learned to stand up and do things differently. I reflected the way people believe. I stepped into reality and realized there wasn't going to be some magical invisible person jumping in front of the bullet coming at someone or this spiritual invisible person was going to stop a car crash and I don't know any invisible person who stop someone from hurting a child. I live in reality that it is us humans that step to the plate. I began having balls enough to stand up to the rich and famous and those around me. I questioned why they haven't taken home homeless from the streets like me and got them on their feet.

The Awakening is when you're in a car crash or a burning fire and you need a savior. It's not a Supernatural human being that you believe exists, rather someone like my husband who saved a child from a burning house when no one else would, not even a fireman. It's a real person who steps up and helps you out. A Spolairo is the Spolarized Dope-A-Mean fix on Earth. When someone asked if you know the difference between what is right and what is wrong you answer, "I got this. I'm Spolarized to the highest degree Shinning the Star I should be."

My parents taught me that handling things isn't always nice but it's what you do that matters about situations and how you handle them. As a little girl sitting at the dinner table with Joseph and Mary it wasn't easy listening to tough stuff. As a mother it didn't get easier in life. I taught somewhat like my parents with demands, high standards, and hardcore. When my kids were young while watching TV, you could hear them say, "my daddy built that." Over and over, you'd hear them say my daddy built that. Many times, while watching TV I would lean over and say to my husband that guy is an ass. Either I had done work for him or he was a client or I've seen him at events being and a**. Before you know it, my kids began saying my daddy built that and then during commercials, I'd hear them say my mom says he's an ass.

I'd say to them don't say that social services will come in and take you away from mommy. The kids would say but mommy you said we can never lie and you called him an ass. I would say it's true I didn't lie but there are certain words you cannot say until your mommy's age. The kids went on to say, so what do we do when we see that ass? You stand up and turn your butt to the TV and smack it with your hand. It means the same thing because he is an ass. The next question they hit me with was, "what is an ass?" I replied someone who doesn't give a sh★t about learning the truth. Then I told them my grandparents Joseph and Mary rhymed before hip-hop. They would say living on the Ridge is mighty Ruff. Living on the Ridge you got to be tough. I realized in life they were right. I won some battles and I fought some Wars and I'm a Warrior without sores.

Women are a rising Force. They're not Blinded by the Light. In a sober mind reality is hard to fake. Life is do or die with what you make. A Spolairo goes from City to City, State to State, teaching how to hold your ground. A Spolairo knows how to cross many boundaries. The word was created from a Buried Secret. The awakening is dealing with a Spolairo because you may need a savior. A Spolairo knows how to not be beaten down but to hold their ground. A Spolairo has a Spolarized Society of Spolairos who know they were born to die and Live to Shine. A Spolairo knows that there's going to be a lot of Wild Weeds along the Path of Life with stickers poking and jabbing at you. A Spolairo knows the Meaning of Life is held deep within. A Spolairo keeps it Legally Loaded not having to look over their shoulder in worry. Spolairos are those who led the way to the Spolarized Zone joined together to build a better Nation living in the real world. One must know your life isn't a mistake.

Jump in any one of my Shoes and Rize wit Me...

Step in my Shoe

To some degree throughout our life we all have suffered.

Here's my List: I survived being raped and beaten in an alley when I was 9 months pregnant. Unbeknown to me, I was carrying triplets. I was beaten in an alley with one baby missing left to die with two babies inside. To the hospital I go in a coma with holes in my stomach where doctors worked on me. A nun blood brothered me to the eight homeless men of color who saved me, and the two babies left in my womb. The hushed-up work of criminality on the streets of Philly. I live with webbing and a sling which holds my organs in place along with a baby missing. The beating took place during the thief of the master that day outside Bandstand of my musical work. It went platinum and my Gold sits on the thief's wall along with the money it made plus the 2 remixes. I was threatened by Dickie death if I didn't shut up and back off once I awoke from a dismal state.

An attempt of murder of my son with a butcher knife while his pre-kindergarten son (my grandson) is tied to a chair screaming and crying as he watched an Evil person try to kill his daddy. My son lived and so did the child.

An attempted murder with a poisonous snake set loose in my house to kill me. Buyer traced back to the same Evil person who tried to kill my son who wanted me died and out of the picture.

An attempted murder of the same pre-kindergarten son of my son. The same Evil person put him in their car without a coat at 30-degrees and then throw him out of the car claiming he fell out. The child searched his way throw the woods and fell at doorstep of a house where the man called police. To the hospital we go listening to the child's heart wrenching cries over and over "I want my daddy" while police question the young child.

And an attempted murder by the same Evil person of my son's daughter. She is the sister of my grandson. The Evil person drugged the little girl. To the hospital we go to get an antidote. Listening to heart wrenching cries over and over in the hospital "I want my daddy."

And a smacked-up and held down traumatization of one of my other kindergarten grandsons. He was beaten because a group of adults didn't like boys with long hair. To the hospital we go. Listening to heart wrenching cries over and over in the hospital "I want my mommy" while the police question the little guy who identified the culprits.

And a planned out attempt to blind and scar my face by waiting behind a door to throw a product in my face as I enter saying I got you. Off to the hospital I go.

And a drug put into my son's coffee so he would blackout behind the wheel and crash on his way to work. After finding a prescription drug written by a doctor my son had never seen I handed it over to Dr. Kerr a local doctor who assisted me in tracking the drug back the culprit responsible for the crime.

And a kidnapping of my son's infant for ransom. Found in South Carolina after second call for more ransom money. Off to South Caroline to get the infant and then off the hospital we go. He was hospitalized near death.

And a snowmobile accident of my husband ended with a brain concussion and multiple injuries. To the hospital I go.

And a 4-wheeler accident televised at the Grand Nationals of one of my sons crashing on a jump. Broken bones etc. To the hospital I go the following day. Of course, we had to finish the race. Spolar's know how to suck it up yo. How else do you think we survive?

And an elevator drops six floors with me trapped inside by myself for hours hoping to be discovered. My fifth cranial nerve was damaged with a torn rotator cuff and two PCL tears. To the hospital I go.

And a car accident which caused a long-term case of dysfunction of the cranial nerve VII (facial nerve paralysis) from physical trauma. To the hospital I go. It taught me what it is like to have people stare and call me ugly.

And a snowmobile accident where one of my sons got himself a helicopter flight with head trauma so severe, he didn't know anyone. He lost a kidney, spilt his liver, a collapsed lung, and broke ribs. To the hospital we go with multiple doctors wrapped around me (the mother) saying there's nothing they can do. I should donate his organs. I began screaming back at the 4-doctor NO NO NO save him. They headed for the operating room to save my son. He survived and flourished.

And an internal bleeding of my mother cause serve anemia whereas she died at the hands of her physician who had already lost his license in two other states for incompetent treatment. Took blood from his patients but never got it tested rather poured it down the toilet. To the hospital I go.

And a father who was found in his apartment unconscious starved to death when a person took control of his money and took away his car leaving him unable to get to the store or visit my mother's grave. He was brought back to life. Unbeknown to me that something happened to him and what he endured I began searching for him when he did not answer the phone. I discovered he was placed in a nursing home where he was neglected and beat. To the hospital I go. I shut the nursing home down and saved the life of all the residents who were being abused and/or raped.

And a grandson with a full ride to college for wrestling ended in a drive-by shooting on campus of my grandson and his truck. Lucky no-one was hurt.

And many times, throughout my Life, I pulled out the Rosemary and took a whiff to open up my senses knowing beneath the wild weeds is where you find a Violet and hear the Ava Maria. I wore the shoe given me well as my parents would have expected me to with honor. This book is about what I endured and how I handled myself in order to survived and rise above it all. Step in my Shoes Yo! If you fall down just shout out like I do...

It's just another Legally Loaded Spolarized Experience how to Shine the Star that I am in my Shoe!

All In One Life Beneath The Hype

Perhaps, if it wasn't for the "Margaret Factor" I wouldn't have been an inventor or a rapper. In first grade I told my mother the name Margaret was to long. So my mother told me she'd fix it. My mother insisted the school call me Peggy. On the first day of school my teacher insisted I go one row ahead of the blacks in the back. The teacher said, "I'll call on you once a day and never look back; you're only going to grow up to be a ditz." Little did this teacher know that I would grow to be an electrical energized woman who would sit at the table of some of the largest companies CEO's and law firms in the world.

Philly Grown

As a child and through my early teen years I spent my weekends with my grandparents, Joseph and Mary. Every weekend Grandma Mary and I would hop the train in Trevose to Philly. While Grandma Mary was visiting her sister Aunty Sharp, I ran the streets of Philly with my friends and continued after Grandma Mary died. I was Philly Grown and born to Rock. I found myself chillin' outside Bandstand. I could see there was shady sh★t going on. My father taught me to keep my eyes open and whatever I saw keep it on a lee low locked inside me.

I was at Bandstand for one reason: I wanted a record deal. Word on the block was the TV network began realizing things weren't going as planned so they picked up a smooth handsome DJ named Dick Clark. Dick was there to help clean up the sh★t the network saw Bob Horn doing. It didn't take long before a different group of savvy men came on the set that were corrupt. Dick tried to play it cool like nothin' was going on or that he was blind to the fact that girls who wanted a record deal were being raped in alleys and their masters were stolen and sometimes even killed.

The word on the street was some of the girls were taken to a boat in the Delaware River and gang raped. Teens were given $15.00 a day under the table to show up because it helped the show get better ratings. It seemed like everybody played blind to what was happening. It was understood that the TV network couldn't fix things and the cops couldn't make arrests. You be the judge if I'm tellin' the truth or not.

I stayed focused on my dream of being an artist and blind to whatever I saw. I hit a cellar studio and laid down my musical work. I had the melody and lyrics down pat. The moment I was done recording, I headed out the door of the studio with a reel of the master in my hand. I hid what I did from everyone. How could I tell my parents I wanted to be an artist? Women in those days were created for marriage and child bearing.

Born Blonde

I felt like I was gaining ground by age sixteen. I was going to dance halls and jitterbugging to get a handle on showmanship in front of a crowd for when I got my record deal. A handsome guy asked me to jitterbug. He'd swing me over his back and between his legs. I never knew I could even bend in such positions let alone stay on time with the beat. When I returned home that night I was giggling entering the house. I ran to tell my mother how this guy could dance and how smooth together we were on the dance floor. My father turned to my mother and said, "Mother Mary -- you know when I say Mother Mary it's time to listen up -- it's gonna be a long night. Put on the coffee."

I never heard my father address my mother in this manner and I had no idea what the hell was happening. My father explained to me that God sent him a blonde because he knew that he would be tough enough to keep me on a straight path. In those days unlike today, a girl had to be pure with her virginity prior to marriage in order to get to heaven. It was an honor for a father to present his daughter holy with her virginity and a white veil covering her face to be lifted at the altar. The father would kiss his daughter goodbye then hand her over to the man so the two could become one in marriage.

My Dearest Child Upon Your Wedding Day

I know you are smart enough to know you can be anything you want to be. Your dream for yourself isn't over it just is delayed. I rocked you in my arms till you were four when your dad came home from the war. I brushed your golden locks of hair 100 strokes since you were born and I made sure you had no knots. As a child I sent you to Grandma's house where she and I kept you safe and pure from the world around you. Your playground was the forest across from grandma's house where the train whistle blows to let you know it was rollin' through. I remember how you would come home from the forest tellin' us you sang to the leaves and the train would drop off people. We thought it was cute till we realized it was the hobos who jumped the train out of Philly. They claimed you as their very own angel and believed you had a golden note locked inside. From that moment on grandma took you to Philly verse Philly coming to you. Today's just another steppin' stone along the path of life with a man who builds building in the city where you love to run and play. You should understand that daddy is right in the sense that every man has a dick and issues. The only difference between one man verses another is the issues will be different. Sometimes things that seem improbable have happy endings. The words I remember you singing so many years ago to the hobos were about the "Streets of Gold" lives in your soul. Today is just another stepping stone of a splendid performance on your behalf with an unfamiliar melody.

Love, Mother Mary Clair XXX

Ruffed Crinoline

My father thought when a guy ruffles a girl's crinoline and enjoys a night dancing the next step is to slide into her panties. Wow! I never thought of my father as being holy. I turned to my mother in wonder. My mother said, "Oh boy it is gonna be a long night alright. Your father always felt honored that God sent him such a beautiful child and he knew there was a price to pay if he didn't keep you straight." My father told me he'd be going to the next dance, so I could point out the guy who ruffled my crinoline. What?! The next dance I pointed out the guy.

My father took him outside to speak to him. I never learned what actually happened that night. On the ride home, I learned I was gonna marry him and there was no way out. He came to the house the next night and we went out to dinner. He told me his name was Tom and was a foreman bricklayer in the Union.

We got to see each other a few times over a period of four months as the wedding was being planned by my parents. I asked Tom if there was a way out of this. He said, "Wouldn't you be breaking your parents' ♡? You're beautiful and I'm lucky to have you as my wife." I thought it's not that he wasn't nice, but I wanted more for myself than marriage. I told him I wanted to be an artist. I knew I had my master hidden. I knew I loved my parents and didn't want to hurt them.

I finally submitted to my fate. Tom and I were of different faiths. My parents believed that a marriage can only be one faith. My father took out a coin and asked Tom to call out heads or tails. If it came up what he called out it would be his faith, otherwise it would be mine. He called heads and heads it was.

I had to turn Catholic. My father was so proud of himself for a job well done the day of my wedding. My mother was proud of me for smiling while hiding my pain. As my mother was putting on my veil she handed me a letter she wrote for me to read.

Our Wedding Day

On my wedding day I entered the church as the beautiful bride everyone expected me to be. My mother and father were proud of me and Tom was excited to take my hand at the altar. The 327 people came to enjoy the celebration. In the back of church was a soldier standing tall who happened to be waiting for the 12:00 PM mass. It didn't take him but a minute to realize the wedding he was attending was for the groom who just got drafted.

As we headed down the aisle the soldier stepped out into the aisle to address Tom. He said, "Sir I believe you just got drafted."

Tom said, "I know. I got my greetings this morning on the way to church." I was bewildered over what the soldier said. Outside church everyone threw rice as we ran for the car where my father was waiting to drive us to the reception blowing horns with beer cans and ribbons tied to the back of the car. My father told everyone else to head for the hall where the reception was being held.

Front Page News September 1959

A Man Drafted Into The Army
On His Wedding Day...

Drafted on Our Wedding Day

My father headed down the road then looked in the rearview mirror and said, "So Tom how long do you have?" Tom said, "5 weeks." My father said to me, "Honey you realize what just happened. Tom's been drafted leaving for the Vietnam War." What?! I began screaming at my father, "This isn't happening. I'm not going to submit to this, turn the car around and get the priest to annul the wedding." My father wouldn't turn the car around, so I jumped out at the stop sign. I ran down the road in high heels with a white hoop wedding dress and veil with my father chasing me. I finally stopped, and he fell on his knees in front of me.

He looked up at me and said, "What's wrong with you? This guy is gonna lose his life for his country and he'll want to leave his seed behind. I did it with your mother when I made you and got drafted." With tears streaming down my face I said, "Dad it's ok, if you did it for me I'll do it for you."

We went to the hall where everyone was waiting to see me dance with my father to "Oh! My Pa-Pa" by Eddie Fisher. Growing up my mother would sing the song as my father played the trumpet. The tears throughout the day streaming down my face were tears of self-sacrifice for the sake of others. The next 5 weeks I submitted to what was asked of me, getting laid almost on a daily, Tom left for Boot Camp and had successfully planted his seed.

Army Football

The Army drafted him on our wedding day for a war. When the Army found out Tom was a sandlot football player out of Philly they put him on the Army football team as a first-string HB and back up QB. He enjoyed flying round the country playing football. His letters from the service were about the joy of having a son while mine were about having a hard time getting used to marriage and a baby due. My inner thoughts remained the same that I lost my dream of being an artist.

Tom's dad decided to drive me to Alexandria, Virginia to see him play one game of Army football and return home. When our daughter was born, Tom flew home to Philly to see us. He kissed me and said, "You can name our daughter and as soon as I'm done my tour of duty, we'll try for a son. I'm off to give cigars to my buddies at the bar who I haven't seen before I leave again. I got to get back to camp because I've got a big game comin' up." I named her Peggy after me.

When I got out of the hospital my parents thought it best if Tom and I tried livin' together. My mother and Aunt Violet drove me and the baby to the apartment Tom rented off base. The baby and I went to his football games. During the week I'd take our daughter touring DC. I got to see John F. Kennedy riding in a convertible with his wife. After 2 months I called my parents to bring me and my daughter home. I had enough.

Tom had a house that was half done and vacant and unlivable. There was nowhere to go but my parents' house. They had their hands full already with my grandmother in the hospital and my father who was having a serious operation and now me who was a physical wreck having spells. My mother took me to a doctor about my condition and the doctor believed it was a broken ♡ and unfixable.

Philly Beam Cross Standing Strong 49 Years

the child inside knows how to play. As I got older my parents taught me how to be spunky, savvy, smart, and brilliant.

Like in a fairytale my grandparents believed that a person is able to gain knowledge and wisdom from Leaves. Leaves use intuition rather than judgment. They have the ability to hear everything around them that's relevant and pass it on through a breeze. If your ears are sharp enough you too will hear the sound the Leaves offer and have the instinct to know what's going on around you. Each year the Leaves fall to the ground. Year after year we shuffle them along under our feet to regain our composure and stay strong knowing new growth will appear and new information will be forthcoming.

Philly Transplant

Tom transplanted me far away from Philly with lots of critters and acres of forest surrounding us. There was no road, no electricity, no running water, and no telephone. Against my parents' wishes we brought our three kids and two Siberian Huskies to enjoy the new transplant. We pulled up with an old station wagon and a U-Haul hooked up to Tom's Ford truck and drove through the weeds that were everywhere. We brought two wood beams, so we could build a cross and a few boards with a toilet seat for an outhouse along with a few clothes. We were met by George and Mabel Nolte, friends from back home.

Shuffling through the weeds, the kids (our daughter 10 and twin boys 8) discovered this big rock. They climbed on top of the rock and said, "Daddy, put the cross on top of this rock." He complied. One of the great gifts Tom came to earth with was building creative works using bricks and stone to keep America strong. Somehow back in Philly he chose the right two beams for the cross. It's still standing strong 49 years through all kinds of weather. Over the years each of the grand children's baptismal holy water was poured upon the rock. This was gonna be my first rodeo at camping till Tom could build something for us.

When I'm pi**ed off I hop in my car and while driving I would lay my thoughts out the windshield. I'd say, "Yo God, listen up. By now you know I've had enough from this a**hole who's pushing his weight around. I don't need to remind you that in the book of John it says we're your children. I'm at a point where I'm done. I'm offering this a**hole up to you to take care of him. I'm hoping this isn't all fantasy and you'll take action. You know how many times I have fallen to my knees in prayer and this a**hole's still at it. I'm hoping you don't want me to take action. I'm sure there were times when you were pi** off like me and tore up a temple and I assume you didn't talk sweet."

I have always got a feeling of relief talking to God out the windshield. Then I pop a CD in the car radio and play the song by R.E.M. "Losing My Religion." I wait it out and if nothing changes then I handle it myself.

My bodyguard was playing golf with a Christian friend who prayed at one of the holes that God would guide his ball away from the water. When the ball went in the water my bodyguard turned to him and said, "How's that workin' for you?"

I knew I had to save myself and my kids in the middle of a forest while Tom was traveling back and forth to Philly to finish a job. I called the electric company and asked them to put up a pole, so I could have a light with an extension cord and a telephone line on that pole. The next day the electric company came and put in the pole. The first call was to my

Spolar & Sons Created Great Work of Art...

mother to explain where the hell I was. I said, "Mom I got to take off my high heels and put on a pair of Tom's boots if I'm ever going to make it here in this godforsaken forest which is ten times bigger than the one you raised me in."

My mother said, "What! I'll be right there." I said, "Mom, you don't understand the weeds are up to my waist. High heels and Philly Grown isn't gonna make it. I'm surrounded by hundreds of acres of forest and town is 15 miles away. What in the world do you think you could possibly do that I couldn't?" My mother hung up and best believe in three hours my parents pulled up.

My mother said to my father, "Daddy, get that damn 30-inch push lawn mower out of the trunk." My mother with a superb runway strut and proper lady-like attire with high heels started the engine on the mower. My mother began mowing weeds when all of a sudden out of the end of the mower came cut up parts of a snake. My mother started chasing moles with the mower, yelling, "Don't think you're getting away from me alive! I need a place for the children to safely play. You got acres to roam."

The children locked themselves inside the car with the windows partially down, devastated, yelling, "we want to go back to Philly." Of course, one of her heels broke off during my mother's episode of madness. She ran over to my father to borrow his boots. Really! My father says, "Mary, they're men's size 9." My mother said, "At this point I could give a damn. I've got to clear some of these weeds, so we can celebrate with a hot dog I brought." I put some rocks in a circle and we cooked our first hot dog on a stick.

Teaching Your Children, the Art of Work

Tom found a lumber mill and got supplies and built a cabin to live in till a new house could be built. Tom was a fabulous architect and continued building and creating works of art from Philly, New York, and Jersey. His work was in magazines. What was most important in the end was together as a family we built our house upon a rock with a strong foundation knowing seasons will come and go and my seeds will surely grow. Everything we have came from working together as family.

The children started busting a** at 8 and 10. Together we built stone walls, houses, rock bed gardens, out houses, roads and the like, to get to where we are today. One of the great grandchildren (age 6) asked his grandfather (Tom), "Poppie, what is my job title?" Tom's answer was a gopher. The child asked, "What is a gopher?" Tom explained, "A gopher is somebody that goes for this and that. When you get Poppie a hammer and the nails or when you get me a beer." At the end of the week Tom gave them a paycheck of a dollar a day.

While other kids were riding their bikes and playing, my kids came home from school every day to work. The grandchildren as toddlers, four, five, and six, went to work with their grandfather like their father did. Two generations of kids hopped in the truck with their Tonka trucks everyday ready to play in the sand pile at the job site being gophers.

It was amazing to see my twin boys at 8 years old carrying stone and loading them onto the scaffolding along with the block. They learned how to lay shingles on a roof by age 9. They were on riding lawn mowers and using a weed whacker by 10. My daughter had to pick weeds and vegetables. Together my daughter and I would can the vegetables so that we

TOM TAUGHT HIS CHILDREN AND THEIR CHILDREN HIS CRAFT ALLOWING HIS LEGACY OF EXCELLENCE TO LIVE ON.

had food to eat throughout the year. People who knew us know everything we have is from busting a★★ as a family. We weren't given a start by anyone.

Our children's hands had blisters and they had backaches. They say a picture is worth a thousand words and throughout my book you'll see plenty of pictures as livin' proof that we all busted a★★ to get to where we are today, and we never gave up on our dream. You could say my life is a storybook fairytale. Someone holds my fame, my gold and my millions in their wallet. I'm left to fend for myself in a forest by raising my own farm animals and growing my own food and shooting a gun to save my a★★ from the wild animals in the forest that surrounded me.

Philly Grown Barn Sh★t

Of course, when the kids started school almost every kid in the area had some sort of animal. My daughter always maintained her Philly Grown ladylike background. My boys on the other hand wanted farm animals like all the other kids. I thought I handled the situation with, "Oh really? Sit your butts down and listen up. We're city folks out of Philly and we're not becoming farmers. There's plenty of farmers who need us to buy their crops and meat. Got it?" I knew it wouldn't last long when Tom got word that his sons wanted animals.

The next day at work Tom mentioned to one of the guys his kids want animals like other children in the area. The guy brought him a feed bag with a rooster in it. On the way home, of course he stopped at the local tavern. By time he got home he forgot that the rooster was in the feed bag in the back of his truck. The next morning Tom opened the back door and yelled, "Yo honey, I left a feed bag outside the door with a rooster. Take it to the barn and let it loose for when the boys come home from school."

Do you have any idea what it's like to carry a feed bag with a roaster that isn't moving, but really pi★★ed off? I dumped the roaster on the barn floor and the damn thing looked at me, ran across the barn, turned and came charging me, hitting me on my shoulder, pecking my brains out. I yelled, "Who do you think you're f★★kin' wit? I'm from the concrete jungle... People live and die in the jungle yo..."

I grabbed the rooster's feet and slammed the son of a bitch into the barn beam. Can you believe that the damn thing with a broken neck hanging over its chest still tried to attack me? I yelled out once again, "Who do you think you're f★★kin' wit?" I ran to the house and grabbed my pistol and entered the barn and shot the bastard. When Tom got home from work I told him what I did.

Tom saw an ad in the newspaper for pigs and decided pigs would be good pets for his sons. We pulled up to the house to buy the pigs. A man came out of the house telling us to pay up ahead. He said, "Once I open the door of my house the mama pig will come out with her piglets. I don't want to pi★★ her off. I have to live with her. You two can each jump out of the truck and grab two piglets by the back legs. They'll be squealing like hell but run like the dickens back to the truck cuz mama is gonna be really pi★★ed off." Sure enough, he wasn't kidding. That damn mother pig was headed for us squealing, running her a★★ as fast as she could to catch us as we backed out of the man's driveway. Our 8-year-old sons got their wish and named them Porky and Piggy.

Storybook fairy tale saving your a** from mountain loins, coyotes and bears, growing your own veggies and beef to eat. Wearing two shoes, eh. Yo, I got this I'm Philly Grown.

One day on the way to the barn the boys thought they would pick up the rotten apples in the apple orchard and feed them to the pigs. After they left for school I went to the barn to check on the pigs. They were lying on their side kicking their feet, moaning and farting. I thought, oh my goodness they're gonna die. I called the veterinarian. When he arrived, he walked into the barn and he looked at the pigs and started rolling in the hay laughing.

While sitting on his a** laughing he said, "I heard there was a hot blonde in town that needed to be tamed out of Philly. What's wrong with your pigs is they're drunk from the fermented apples I see in the pen." I said "Really.... Who do you think you're f**kin' wit? I'm from the concrete jungle. You best leave and spread the word 'This White Bitch Crazy' alright. You owe me for rollin' in the hay. I'll send you a bill for $50.00. Get the hell off my land, dude. How dare you dirty my hay."

I knew it was time for lessons how to be a farmer. I walked 2 miles to the neighbor Toni and ask if he'd teach me something about farm animals. The farmer complied. The veterinarian didn't want to pay so I waited it out and placed his name on the barn door. Months later I met him in the feed mill walkin' out with a 100-pound bag of feed over his shoulder. I bumped into him on purpose, knocking the feed bag off his shoulder. At first he didn't realize it was me.

Then he said, "Oh you." I said, "Let me help." In the blink of an eye I bent down and sliced the bag open with my knife and pulled the feed from the bag leaving 100 lbs. of grain spread around the parking lot. I looked at him and said, "I'm from the concrete jungle where people live and die. You see I'm Philly Grown, and the Jungle came wit me. The city of Brotherly Love where you don't f*ck wit people. The slaughter today of grain takes care of the payment you owe me for rollin' in my hay, dude." He was speechless as I walked away.

Tom met a guy named Bill while sittin' on a bar stool who ran Bull Run Farms. He set Tom up to buy some cows. At this point I knew I had to get a grip on how to wear two shoes and still maintain within me, my city lifestyle. The children named the cows Betsy, Bucky, Barney, and Beauty. At first I thought naming cows was cute until we had to slaughter them and put them on the table. The first thing the kids wanted to know before they ate beef was that this wasn't Betsy, Bucky, Barney or Beauty. For the first time in my life I had to look my children in the face and lie, saying no we bought this beef at the grocery store, our cows broke through the fence and ran away.

Finally, all the animals we're gone. We were back to buying food in a grocery store. Halleluiah... As a family, we enjoyed riding snowmobiles and four-wheelers from town to town over every hill and dale. Sports is something we all enjoy. I taught my children to stay stable to who we are, livin' in a small town where everyone knows your business. Where churches are gossip centers and a way to talk trash about thy neighbor by way of prayer. It is amazing how the kids and I maintained our Philly Grown shoe livin' in a small town. It's not as if our family doesn't do f*cked up sh*t like every family. The difference is we take action to get the rodeo right. Right is right and wrong is wrong. We understood no one is without flaws, not even us....

How many people can say they owned a bar and never had a drink? Me... Keeping my sanity and staying faithful to who I am gave me balls I never knew I had.

St. Patty's Day we honored the Irish community that surrounded the bar. Tom was Irish for a night.

A Deal to Buy a Bar

One day I got a call from the banker in town. He said, "I'd like to meet you to discuss a business opportunity. I heard you were thinking of going back to Philly because there's little work and your husband is forced to work out of town. I'd hate to see a beautiful blonde like you leave." I went to meet with him. The deal he offered was incredible. It meant I had to put on a shoe I wasn't used to; but what the hell, I been there before. By now I had a closet full of all types of shoes from heels to barn boots with sh*t on them.

Philly Overturns Country

How many people could say they owned a bar and never had a drink except wine from the altar? How does one wear a shoe and stay straight to who they are when dealing with criminal activity, murderers, cheaters, drunks, drugs, and people carrying guns illegally? Keeping my sanity and staying faithful to who I was gave me balls I never knew I had. I proved once again I could handle it. I put the damn shoe on and became known to the community as a person you can't f**k with cuz, 'This White Bitch Crazy.' I couldn't depend on a cop to save my a** or help me out because the police department was 40 miles away. The first thing I had to figure out was how to handle a bar with a PA liquor license and a full restaurant open 7 days a week and a husband who liked to drink. Not easy… I taught my teenage children how to be grown a** adults at 18 and stay straight in this type of environment in order to maintain who we are, Philly Grown transplants.

It was truly amazing that we were accepted by the community. Perhaps prayers from the priest next door to the bar may have helped since the priest had to listen to the noise until 3 or 4 in the morning. If the priest looked out his window, he would have easily seen people in cars in the parking lot having sex. Of course, not with their wife, just someone they found at the bar; one-night stands. If the priest looked out his side window he would have seen drug deals happening in the forest across the street from the Church property attached to the bar property. The priest knew I had my hands full. He knew more than me; he was hearing my customer's confessions who were Irish Catholics.

We had one of the most successful bars ever in the county pulling in money up the a**. Word got out and people were coming from miles away, rollin' in on snowmobiles, four-wheelers, cars, and trucks passing other bars and restaurants, packing our place. Your guess is as good as ours what brought these people. It could have been me the beautiful blonde in town with big ta ta's or the happy go lucky bartender, Tom. Perhaps, it was they heard about Philly comin' to town where the music changed from country to some of the hottest music known for that area. I flipped the music in the jukebox and hired bands out of town that could give me the kind of music I demanded.

Had the disco music been out back then the dance floor would have been bangin' with "You Shook Me All Night Long" by AC/DC or Dire Straits "Money for Nothing." I could see a change in my customers by changing the jukebox. Instead of riding someone else's wife's a** they brought their own wife with them to dance under the disco ball. The cash register never stopped ringing. I made sure the juke box played my favorite tunes. Before you know it I had these people blatting out the tunes of artists worthy of my quarters. Of course, back then I liked Chuck Berry's "Rock N Roll Music" but it made the customer live in the past verses living in the future. Had there been tunes back then like Billy Joel's "Rebel" or The Police "Every Breath You Take" or Bon Jovi's "Blaze of Glory" even the song "Summer of 69" by Bryan Adams would have given them songs with repeated hooks they could relate to. My favorites to this day are "What is Love' by Haddaway and "We are the Champions" by Queen or "Somebody to Love." When Eagles won the Super Bowl and became the Champions, I got to hear Queen's song continuously that week.

Some of my other favorites are Bon Jovi's, "It's My Life" and Tom Petty's, "Refugee and Free Fallin" and AC/DC's "Money talks", ZZ Top's "Gimme All Your Lovin." I enjoy George Satellite's song "Keep Your Hands to Yourself" I think back to when I had the bar. Keep your hands-off other people's merchandise. It's obvious during my time owning a bar I was helped people understand that out behind the barn and cheating causes ♡ache.

Before disco hit it was pickin' the right music in order to upgrade people's lifestyles. Switching up the music and putting in one of the first disco balls helped my customer learn the art of dancing. People were coming to dance 4 nights a week to show their skill. Their boots changed to sneakers sliding across the dance floor. It was sweet cuz there was no more cow sh★t on the floors and the customers became my 'Friendsville Inn' friends.

I didn't understand during the disco years why when I heard the song "Baby Don't Hurt Me" by Haddaway it moved me into a zone where I desired freedom. I knew I was a leader not a follower. I knew the song actually was a cry out living within me. I've been known to dance around the kitchen with the mop singing, "oh baby don't hurt me no more." To finish out a day I'd play "Rhythm is a Dancer." I'd sing "You got to be what you want." A spinning disco ball in the middle of a huge dance floor captivated everyone and allowed a blonde from Philly to put a touch on country life at the Friendsville Inn.

The Effects of Your Actions

I believed whatever Tom did opposite of me that hurt me was due to the way he was raised. His family enjoyed partying every weekend with alcohol flowing. Tom said, "When my father and his brothers played cards, they rumbled at times just for the hell of it." His cousins agreed at times the gatherings got a little out of hand. Married into the family I got to experience the galas and barrels of beer, rollin' them back and forth from Hoopes Beer Distributor across the street. There was always good Polish food and an American flag hanging with clothes pins on the clothes and live ducks waddling around the bathroom tub. You can imagine my thoughts the first time I used the bathroom. How much fun can a shower be standing in duck sh★t, eh?

My parents knew nothing about Tom's family when my father forced the marriage because Tom ruffled my crinoline at a dance. My parents were completely oblivious of Tom's family. My father liked guns and was a hunter. My mother was a woman who believed in cleanliness, to be ready if guests knocked on your door, that your house should be in order. She believed when a woman is sitting her feet should be on the floor with her knees touching or her legs crossed so that no one sees her coochie. She believed in walking with your feet straight not like a duck that waddles. Sit properly at the table and don't suck your fingers or talk with food in your mouth. Don't plop on furniture. You are to lower your butt softly. Never sit on public toilets without paper.

My mother danced with my father till the day she died. There has never been beer or wine in their refrigerator. My parents saw nothing wrong with having a beer, a glass of wine after work. They relaxed with a cigarette on the porch. My parents weren't hypocrites, they were straight shooters. My parents loved dancing. If I still had the bar I'd be playing Eminem music along with Jay-Z's version of "Forever Young". I'm sure my customers at the bar would have replaced their attire with urban wear. ABBA is one of my favorite groups. I feel sad that so many R&B singers with vocals couldn't make it like Montrez. Listening to "Just What I Needed" by Cars and "I won't Give Up" by Jason Mraz over the years helped me overcome sadness. My customers loved the song by Queen "Fat Bottomed Girls." So much for Jazz in 78.

I loved the song by Queen "Fat Bottomed Girls." My customers watch my three teenagers go crazy playin' air guitars on the dance floor. The customers joined in singing. Eventually, the customers learned to play air guitars too. My kids enticed customers to hit the dance floor. Three cheers to my customers who found joy in feelin' free. Not just on the dance floor but the ability to change old school ways. When the song by R.E.M. came out "Losing My Religion ESP" I couldn't get enough of it. Somehow I believed the day would come when I'd find my way. I realized when I played Alice Bridge "I love the Nightlight" I was at a point that I wanted to live, feel alive. The new sounds of disco made me high. Disco brought me to my senses that I could stand to my feet; sing and dance my own tune hidden deep inside.

There comes a point when you need to sit back and look at the situation as a whole. My kids were getting older and finding a life and Tom was still drinkin'. I called a realtor and I put the bar up for sale and 2 days later a guy from Jersey walked in and bought the place. I sold my half. When Tom came home that day I said, "I sold my half of the bar today. He'll buy your half cuz my kids and I are done busting ass." He was pi**ed. Wouldn't you be? Tom was not only a good father but stood by me makin' sure our children understood the rules that go along with life. Tom was a hard-a** worker who gave his all when building something for someone. What was most important to him wasn't the money but that his name was applied to the work; therefore, it had to be excellent. If you needed a friend he was the man.

Not a day went by in my children's life where I wasn't being the parent instead of the playmate like their dad. Much like my mother, I taught my children to stand firm and stay faithful to who we are as family. Once I sold the bar I had to go back to the estate where it was quiet. It gave me time to think about myself and how my grandparents nourished me with broken English swinging on the porch swing with fairytale dreams. Funny how childhood memories made such an impression that I have a swing on my back porch now. A place where I often ponder over my thoughts wondering how I made it.

Gathering My Thoughts

By the end of that day all hell broke loose; reality began to set in. I used to play instruments in school. For some unknown reason I no longer could. I didn't realize why until my mother told me it was taken away. When I came out of the coma a psychiatrist was brought in to take away my golden note. I love music to the point that when I'm driving many times I can be seen pounding on the dash with the pedal to the metal.

You could say I'm in another zone, high as a mother on my own adrenaline. I sat on the swing and wrote a song on a piece of paper. Later that week I went into a cellar studio along with my first rock artist client Harmony Jams and laid it down. The song went something like this: "I put the pedal to the metal, and I sang out loud.

It's a new me comin' down the road in a new direction." Leaving the bar, I spent many years in the world of religion helping people as a lay minster at my church under the Rochester Diocese under Pope John Paul. I wanted to find myself, so I went into religion. I also tried body building, hunting, archery, multiple things; nothing seemed to comfort me.

A New Start with the Weinstein Boys

I heard about a movie being filmed and I was cast as an extra for the first movie production of Bob and Harvey Weinstein. It took me by storm into the world of entertainment and music. It was exciting, and it seemed like a perfect fit for me. Harvey came over once his eyes laid on me and said, "You know I can give you a better position.

I can move you up where you'll be seen more on screen. Who knows? You could become a star." I said, "I'm good." He then said, "Really... Why wouldn't you want to move up?" I began to explain and said, "My mother taught me that when you're born, you're born rich, poor, or in between. In order to move up in life something has to happen.

You'd need to know someone, blow someone, or kiss someone's a★★. I don't know you and I'm not willing to blow you, nor am I willing to kiss your a★★. I'm good."

He seemed OK with that. The film crew headed towards us and as they came closer I realized the film crew was people I knew. We greeted each other, and Harvey headed back to the movie theater where the cast was detained. There was a young man playing piano to keep us entertained. The production was a learning session for me.

The movie, "Playing for Keeps" was likewise a learning session for the Weinstein Boys and most of the crew as well. Although we were paid a wage for one position, throughout the production people were doing multiple jobs to make it happen.

Years later my friend Vince and I sat back laughing and reminiscing about the Weinstein Boys. We spoke about Bob and Harvey being so excited to finish the production they left some of the raw footage behind on VHS tape. When the production was in the can they forgot to pay some of the workers and cast last paychecks.

There are times I ask myself why is my life so different than others? I'm interweaved with earth and understand what looks good, what feels good, is not always good. And what seems so bad isn't always bad or what it appears to be.

Porch Swing

I looked out the window and saw the broccoli needed pickin' and ready to be canned. Who cans broccoli? I picked a rose on the way to the garden. The thorn cut my finger and I sucked the drop of blood. Through the garden gate I went and picked three heads of broccoli. As I headed for the garden gate I dropped one head of broccoli in the manure.

As I went to reach for the broccoli, blood began to flow from my finger onto the head of broccoli. My first thought was should I keep the bloody head, or should I toss it aside and pick a new one?

At that moment I began to hear a song I wrote so long ago, and the bloody broccoli began to change before my eyes. I saw myself with a bloody baby on my chest with a man biting the umbilical cord. I ran from the garden into the house and called my mother. She said, "I'll be right there." I said, "Mom you're three hours away. Please tell me what's going on." Silence...

I went out to the porch and sat on the swing till my parents arrived. When my parents pulled up my mother ran over to me. Through my tears I begged my mother to tell me the truth. She said, "We planned ahead for this day in case we died." She took my hand and walked me to the front door and my father pulled up the rug and there was The Hidden Letter.

The Magical Awakening

She said, "Daddy and I were told by the attending doctor that you would never remember what happened to you. He told Tom the same thing. But a nun convinced Daddy and I one day you would remember. We didn't want to cheat you out of the truth for the truth will set you free.

We taped this letter under the front door rug knowing one day when we're long gone you'd replace the rug and find the letter. The story is true to the best of our knowledge and is what we learned from the Mother Superior who cared for you until we found you.

You're a child born with many skills, one of which is singing. One day without anyone's knowledge you headed out the door for Bandstand to seek a record deal with a master recording you had hidden for years.

You were nine months pregnant ready to deliver your second child. Unbeknown to any of us including your doctor, you were carrying triplets. One can only imagine what gang or mob was working with the people on the set at Bandstand. Aunt Violet and your Godmother Ann and I went to Bandstand to seek knowledge of what happened to you.

We were told by some of the employees that gang members took notice of your golden locks of hair and wanted to feel the silk like strands run through their fingers gaining ownership of your master under your arm.

IN 1986 WE TRANSPLANTED OURSELVES TO A MOUNTAIN FAR AWAY FROM PHILLY WHERE A PAPA TREE STOOD TALL 100 YEARS. IT'S WHERE WE CLEARED THE WILD WEEDS AND SANG THE AVA MARIA AMONG VIOLETS AND THE LEAVES THAT KEPT THE SECRET OF THE "STREETS OF GOLD LIVE IN THE SOUL."

We were told while you were standing in line a gang member asked if you were there to dance. You answered, "No sir, I'm here for a record deal like Fats Domino." In your excitement I'm assuming you believed him as he took you in the front door and led you out the back door. You were met in the alley by gang members who were thieves who were doing their job to secure and own your master.

Knowing you, you would have fought with them rather than hand over the master of your musical work. As they began to rape you a baby slid out. They pulled the baby from your womb and ran off with your baby along with your master.

Homeless men heard your screams. Eight of them came to your aid and took you to a Catholic hospital. You were beaten near death, hemorrhaging and unconscious.

I'm assuming from trying to fight off the thieves. There were two more babies inside. The homeless men put the word out on the streets of Philly for a need of blood.

One by one, the homeless came in hoping they were a match. Thirteen pints later the hemorrhaging stopped. The nuns were overcome with sorrow over what happened to you. They went to the Mother Superior who took things into her own hands.

She cut your fingers and cut each of the homeless men's fingers and mixed the blood together as a ritual to blood brother the homeless to you and consecrated the act by making a sign of the cross on your forehead with the blood.

When your father and I arrived at the hospital the nuns told us what had been done to you. They spoke how they believed you were an 'Angel Made of Glass' and the blood would surely last. The nuns revealed how when you woke they saw a clear light pass through you and knew you would never be the same.

They explained how you went in and out of consciousness and saw each of the homeless men's faces. They spoke about how they saved the two baby boys in the nursery and named them. When Tom arrived and saw the 8 homeless men around you, he said, 'What are these nig★ers doing here?'

Dad and I tried to explain to Tom it's wrong and they saved our daughter's life and the two babies in the nursery. Tom told the nuns to send the homeless men away. The doctor assured Tom that you'll never know what happened to you. The Mother Superior said to Tom, "Sir, I can assure you one day she will."

"I've blood brothered her; it's too late." Words cannot explain the pain Daddy and I have had in keeping from you such a secret. We were given no choice but to write you the letter under the rug along with this letter in hopes when we were gone, my child, you'll know how much we loved you by telling you the truth.

Remember as a child how Grandma Mary and Papa Joe and I thought you were sent as sunshine for the world with golden hair like silk? You'd laugh thinkin' we were silly.

Remember how when you passed by the rich and the poor Papa Joe would say their ♡s turned to gold by the musical note that's hidden in your soul? Once again you'd laugh. As a child you believed the trees seem to know they could gather energy and strength from you. You were told tears of joys and sorrows help the trees grow. Remember Papa Joe teaching you about the Violets and the A·ve Ma·ri·a.

MOTHERHOOD

Motherhood is a lifelong process of caring, loving, nurturing, and ready on the spot to jump in and help regardless of the time of day, putting aside her own wants, needs, and dreams for herself for the sake of the seed she brought to life. Motherhood is a blessing if the mother wore the shoe wholeheartedly; making self-sacrifices in order to see the seed she planted grows into a beautiful tree. A mother's tears along with her thoughts, sorrows, hopes and dreams becomes the water that in the end helped the seed she planted mature into a tree. A mother is there to see the seed grow tall into a tree able to stand against the storms long after she's gone. A mother knows she may have a jacka** or two who are not fit to go to the Presidents house and sit at his table. A mother knows she may have a dumba** who isn't able to see a violet beneath the wild weeds and hear the A·ve Ma·ri·a. A mother who fits the role and wore the shoe proudly will have no regrets that she did her very best.

As a young girl from the noises of the hustle and bustle in Philly you formed an orchestra, so you could carry the sound and sing on the way home on the train. Of course, Papa Joe wanted you to sing classically fine tunes. As a child you grew up living in the forest where we sent you to play across from Grandma Mary's house. You sang to the hobos that jumped the trains to get out of the city. "You spoke about meeting 'a Beautific Man."

Daddy and I realized you had a great imagination. You spoke about how he lifted you to a 'Mystical Place' where you could jam all day. In reality he lifted you onto a big rock which became your stage and it was truly a person who was 'Beautific' and gave you the jump start you needed to continue the dream you had for yourself. It was Grandma Mary and I who hid beneath the wild weeds to watch you dance and sing with him."

Awake

After my parents left that day and reading the letter learning I had a baby stolen and for the love of gold on someone else's wall and money in someone else's wallet, I realized I'd never get back what was taken from me. I knew what motherhood meant to me. I looked at the papa tree in the front yard and thought about Papa Joe's teaching about violets. I ran to the forest and did what my son-in-law told me you do when you don't want someone to know your inner thoughts, hurts, shame, or pain and you want to let the pain and anger out.

He said, "You dig a hole in the ground with your fingers. You scream into the hole till heaven hears the hell you feel inside you. Let out your inner thoughts where they will never come back and hurt you and be forever safe. Know that your voice was heard as you cover up the hole."

When I returned from the forest that day I sat on the porch swing and like a child I rocked myself till I fell asleep. No one ever asks why I'm watchful over the swing over the years. My family looks at me like there's something wrong with me. They don't understand of course we can buy a new swing, but this swing has years of good and bad stories locked within the wooden chains that hold it.

When someone tells you to let it go, what is that supposed to mean to every mother and father whose child is missing, whose child's been killed? Does it go away for anyone who has gone through such an ordeal? It's easier said than done to wipe from the brain that your child was stolen, and you don't have it.

It's another thing when you hear your song played on the radio now and then the reminder that you've been f*cked. I realize it's hard for anyone to understand what it's like to have your song played on the radio 24 hours before seeing a vision of your baby laying on your chest with someone biting an umbilical cord and your golden locks of hair bloody.

For the love of money, I paid the price for everyone, the gang that wanted the money, the artist who wanted to be gold, and the guy who became famous who appears to be debonair and portrayed himself as innocent.

I can't tell you how many times throughout a day I cry. If you haven't experienced walking in another man's shoe, why judge why he does what he does?

To the best of my knowledge and belief all statements made by me in this book are true, but you be the judge.

SPOLARIZED IS DIFFERENT PEOPLE PARLAYING THEIR OPINION AND EXPERIENCES. IT'S A WAY TO GET DOWN NO DOUBT AND GAIN WISDOM AND KNOWLEDGE OUT OF THE POLARITY IN WHICH YOU SIT INTO THE SOLAR SYSTEM AND SHINE THE STAR THAT YOU ARE TO THE HIGHEST DEGREE ENERGIZED SPOLAIZED!

Rock with the Sun!

The Sun

When I awoke from sleeping on the swing I saw the grandkids running around the driveway. I went over to them and I asked, "If I was to trademark a design and named the design something like McDonald's and Coke, what would it be?" One of the oldest grandkids stopped for a minute and pointed to the sky and said, "The Sun, Baka." At that moment I felt the energy of the Sun penetrate through me as if to say yes. Go for it. Where it's said that the Sun shines the least is on the boarder of upstate NY/PA, however, it is where the Sun shines the most. Spolarized® to the Highest Degree Shining the Star You should Be...

Meeting with Nuns

My dear friend Nancy, whose uncle was a priest at my church back home, thought it was a good idea to go to the hospital and talk to the nuns and see what they may know. Nancy and I headed to Philly. When we entered the hospital, we asked to speak with the nuns that were there. I wasn't prepared for what they were gonna tell me. The nuns heard about a young girl who was raped physically and mentally out of her dream for herself. What they didn't know was my golden note had also been wiped from my brain and my musical abilities. A very old nun asked to speak to me privately away from the other nuns. She said, "I'm giving you second hand news I heard about years ago.

A nun told a story about a young girl who was brought into the hospital by 8 homeless men of color which they believed to be an 'An Angel Made of Glass' as a light passed through her." The nun spoke about how the girl was put under a spell by a psychiatrist when she came out of the coma to take away her golden note. The hospital staff agreed with the doctor that it was better left unsaid what happened to the girl. They felt this way the girl could live happily ever after. Only a few of the nuns actually knew what was done to the young girl. It was too late by the time her family found her. I recalled the nuns speaking about how the Mother Superior took things into her own hands and blood brothered the 8 homeless men to the girl and consecrated the sacred ritual. A psychiatrist was called in when the girl came out of the coma to put her under a spell, so she would never remember what happened to her. The nun knew the psychiatrist didn't understand the total effect of what he did by taking away the girl's golden note and what happened to her.

The nun believed in the power of prayer that the girl would one day awake from the spell." I began to cry and took hold of the nun's hand and said, "I'm that Girl. I'm alive. I am truly grateful to the nuns who helped save me and I'm thankful for you coming forward with the truth." I hugged her. Nancy and I left.

Comin' Out of a Dismal State

Every day before leaving for work Tom would request that I do something. He'd say, "Honey don't forget to can the broccoli." I'd say, "Yep." I was like a robot. Whatever Tom asked, I complied. He'd say, "Honey the gardens need weeding and the cows need hay," and I'd say," Yep, I know." I'd do what he asked of me. When I got done with his request I'd do things I wanted to do. Neither one of us realized the effect the spell had on me.

The boys were often seen holding

hands. I knew it was abnormal.

A Nun assured me it was a spiritual bond not to lose each

other from the loss of their triplet brother stolen from the womb.

I bought my sons Scapulars. They wore them daily till they graduated. A Priest enrolled them with a prayer that Our Lady's Promise would keep them safe with the Garment of Faith.

The "Identity Rock™" has a purpose to serve physically and mentally as you wrap and unwrap the swaddling cloth to regain your composure. It's the power to know the "Streets of Gold Live in the Soul." The one who leaps beyond the measure knows what it's like to really have pleasure. The mineral matter of which the Identity Rock™ is composed has its own shape and form like no other. A one of a kind you alone uncover and discover its character, see its face and know its place. Available on line at

Get Legally Loaded.

Identity Rock

The Goodbye

I left home to go to New York the way my parents advised. Tom said, "I'm sorry." I said, "I forgive you. However, you kept the truth from all of us. You lied, and you covered it up as if it didn't happen. Can you tell me where my other son is? We have no ashes. There was no funeral. In my uncontrolled extreme emotion, I picked up a rock and threw it at the foot of the cross in honor of human life. Every life has an identity. The rock broke into pieces each with its own identity. I tore our son's diaper into shreds and wrapped each rock. You've said stupid n*gger's on the job, did you realize you were f*ckin' a n*gger in your bed? Me. You knew 8 homeless men of color saved my life and your sons. I understand you don't realize you're a racist, so I can forgive you. You're always covering up sh*t, so you don't look bad to our children and say nothing except you're sorry to me. You took me far away from the city I love. What no one realized was the Leaves flew through storms and at times the Leaves hitched a ride with my parents, and they've watched me grow. The forest has helped me be hard edged and has given me the energy to continue where I left off. The spell put on me, Tom, is gone. I'm awake. Goodbye." It was such a turning point in my life. I had nowhere to go except leave and search out my past and see where it leads me.

Searching My Past

I began searching my past and learned there was a young fellow who helped out on the set at Bandstand who knew shady sh*t happened. I'll call him EC who kept his mouth basically shut. Who wouldn't, eh? EC is darn near the age of me. EC was connected to the entertainment world and was a friend of Frank Sinatra. I looked him up and we met. We talked about all kinds of shady stuff, including me. EC said, "Who would spill their guts if they wanted to live or get into the entertainment world? Surely not me." It made me think back to when my father would say, use freedom of speech and say nothing or plead the 5th yo… When my father told me stuff he'd insist I sit because he knew it was gonna hit me hard. At this point in my life what could I learn that would rock me harder than I've already been hit? EC was Philly Grown like me.

EC taught me it doesn't matter if you're workin' wit gangs, the mob, the Vice Ring, or the locals, sh*t is fu*ked up in the game. EC said, "You had something they wanted; obviously a gold record which made millions." EC told me sh*t he did to get to where he is today. He spoke to me and my associate Steve about Frank and sh*t Frank did to make it happen. How when Frank wanted something done he'd walk in the office and throw rolls of hundred-dollar bills rolled up with rubber bands across the desk and say get it done. I told EC I was raised to be savvy and tough, but a criminal I'm not. EC said, "Then you're not made for this game. Things in the game are never what they seem. They may look good and be bad or look bad and be good." I met with EC's sisters and they assured me their brother was a pr*ck who was telling the truth this time.

They spoke about different sh*t EC did that blew my mind. Here I am sitting in the house of the fellow from Bandstand who knew around about what was happening to young girls and knew the mob in Philly controlled the streets. A man who chose to turn a blind eye like other famous artists who knew what was happening. He became a backup singer

MOST PEOPLE ASSUME BLONDES ARE STUPID AND EASY.

MY FATHER WAS DETERMINED TO PROVE TO THE WORLD THEY'RE WRONG IN RAISING ME.

for a famous artist which led him to become a well-known promoter working with some of the most famous names in the industry. I often hear my mother's voice saying, "Child, one man's sin is no greater than the next man's sin. Sin is sin and sadly to say we all sin. No man is perfect."

Raised by a Tough Father

People at times thought of my father as being mean but was he really? My father taught me there are laws and you're going to follow them because you're my seed. Even though Tom and I were raised differently and were hard a★★es in a different way, we made the decision to raise our kids as hard as we were. Thinking back, I wouldn't be who I am if my father wasn't tough. Tough love isn't mean. One day I went to a carnival and if you pitched a nickel and it landed in the jar you got the jar with a little turtle in it. Who wouldn't be excited at 7 years old? I ran in the house to show my parents. My father said, "Come with me. You know we don't have pets in the house and when I say something I mean it." I shook my head yes. He led me to the bathroom and pulled up the toilet seat and said, "The turtle must go back and find its mother. Pour it into the toilet and flush and hopefully it will get back home." Of course, he was smart enough not to lie by choosing choice words like hopefully. I poured the turtle into the toilet and flushed. I waved goodbye and I said, "Go find your mommy and have a wonderful life. I'm sorry for not listening to my daddy." Now you might think this is sad or mean but in reality when my father said something you knew to listen. My father taught me how to stand to my feet against all odds strong.

Climbing the Mountain Peak

My Grandma Mary and my mother constantly spoke in riddles. They were rhyming before rap. They'd say, "I'll know you by the company you keep and know if one day you'll reach the mountain peak and your potential." I wish everyone who wanted to reach the mountain peak could look at the company they keep and realize if they're at the bottom they haven't begun the climb by changing self and walkin' away from what feels comfortable. My mother would say, "You can make it if you stay focused on the mountain peak being who you were born to be by utilizing your many gifts. During the climb you'll see who you are by getting those fingers and nails dirty with the truth. Truth is always a blink away if you open your eyes and believe in yourself and build strength to step ahead. During the climb you will learn what is best for you. Sometimes what we think will be good for us really isn't.

We can't all be Kings and Queens but what we can be is faithful to who we be. It is the reason we must climb the mountain peak which brings us back to living in reality and makes us happy with ourselves. Think what life would be like if we didn't have carpenters and plumbers along with ditch-diggers. What would a doctor or lawyer or the President do without the middle-class workers who keep America strong? How would fortunate people make it a day living like the less fortunate? The less fortunate sleep on the curb and sh★t in the same trash cans where they grab a bite to eat while "Shoes and Souls" pass them daily. The blistered hands of the middle class are what gave us beautiful high-rise buildings city to city. When a person dies everyone seems thankful for the funeral director and cemetery worker who is there to dig graves."

Human Ducks

Quack Quack

Regardless how you walk, you can be whoever you want to be.

Human Ducks – Quack Quack with a Touch of Kindness Game

The background of my character began when I was a child. It is where we all begin. It begins with your parents and your grandparents teaching you something that will last a lifetime. Something you can't help but notice and remember the rest of your life. It was important enough for them to take the time to teach you something they wanted you to remember for the rest of your life. This teaching has stayed with me over the years just the way my Grandma Mary wanted it to. Grandma Mary taught me to look forward and learn something every day. One day walking the streets of Philly with her as a young child she said, "Whenever you see someone's in front of you walking like a duck or like a half a duck know why they do that." At first I began looking for a white duck on the sidewalk. She believed you should always watch those in front of you and remember what's behind you. She explained there are "Human Ducks" who walks as if they were a duck with their feet outward instead of straight or a half of a duck with one foot pushing outward in order to step.

I'd ask what's wrong with that? She'd say, "See that person in front of us? Their mother wasn't smart enough to see her child is walking like a duck. She should be telling her child to pull in the left foot or both feet. There are exceptions where a child is born with a problem from birth but in most cases it's a mother and father who are busy with things of lesser worth." If Facebook was out I'm sure she'd have made Facebook more important than caring for family. I asked what's wrong with walking like a duck? She would say, "It's not really about the foot it's about the whole leg that's attached to the foot and then where it joins the hip pushing off and twisting as the child grows. Later in life as an adult it more than likely will have some sorta problem perhaps in the hip or back. Mind you she had a 6th grade education and in those days' parents relied on their instinct what to do. Surprisingly many of the old fashion ways worked.

From that day on my Grandma Mary said, "Let me know when you see a duck or a half of a duck. When we go past a "Human Duck" and it's a duck we'll quack twice. Quack Quack… If it's a half a duck we'll only quack once. Quack…" It was sort of a game and a way of teaching me how to keep my feet straight and how to pay attention to what's going on around me and to take parenting seriously.

As the story goes I ended up having friends and fam who walk like a duck or a half of a duck. When I tried to bring it to the attention of the parents they yelled at me. So, I backed off. Do they realize the muscles, tendons, and the way the foot pushes off to walk can force the developed of the leg and the way it sits in the socket of the hip? However, it doesn't stop anyone from being who they want to be with or without feet. The moral of the story is stay on top of your children. We learn from generations of mothers before me and after me. Mothers who sometimes without any education or any doctor degree develop their own way of raising their children smart and savvy. Smart enough to know to walk straight and know what is going on around them." Then I said, "What about someone without feet or someone who can't walk? What kind of Quack do we do?" She said, "As you go by someone like that you stop and say, do you need a hand? Offering someone a hand and helping them is a sign of compassion. Never take life for granted, child." Sure, enough a man in front of us who was struggling to walk. As we went by I said, "Do you need a hand?" He smiled and said, "Why thank you. I'm good." Three cheers to grandma Mary who created the "Human Ducks –

Letter to the Leaves

I'm leaving you this letter because I know you will hover over it and read it. I want to believe you'll send a copy of it to Philly for the Leaves left behind. I'm sure they'll appreciate you growing old with me. You know how hard I've searched out my past. You know how a few men and woman I call "Beautific Man" have come to my side and placed money in my hand to help continue my mission. You know how I've wished upon a star and saw a few rainbows in the yard. You watched me run through the wild weeds in search for violets to stay on point. You've watched me make homemade wine for celebrations. You've watched me dance around the yard singing out to you. Those who believe in me have run the meadows along with me that overlook the valley below. How well you know the life I've lived. Together we've traveled over creeks and trails on foot. You hopped a ride on my 4-wheeler and snowmobile stuff in the grill. You know the years of tears I shed to water down your base. I'm grateful that you soaked up my tears so there would be shade upon my face and a breeze to cool me down. I'm grateful to my mother who brought you here so many years ago. It is the forest and you my dearest Leaves who taught me how to enjoy the beauty of a day. You love me for who I am and understand my life. You know I've stood tall like you and survived the many storms that crossed my door. Thank you for holding dear my golden note with the hope together will zing a golden note again.

Quack Quack Game with a Touch of Kindness." My parents and grandparents taught me how to watch in front of me. Watch what is around me and walk straight. They assured me I'd grow up just fine.

History Beneath the Hype - Headed for New York Port Authority

I headed out the door on a mission for the unknown. Like in a fairy-tale my personal tragedy of a cover up of the untold story of a child cheated out of her golden note and her baby vanished for the love of fame and money became the "Spolarized Dope A Mean Fix Beneath the Hype." My mission led me through what most would consider "Dangerous Doors" crossing paths with every form of character. I headed to Port Authority in New York with a backpack and not a dime in my pocket. When I hear the song "Y.M.C.A." by the Village People, I put my hands up thankful I could shower there. Mr. Phill who ran the bus line knew how I'd pop in and out the bus stations on a lee low. I stood out front of the Port Authority like all the other people who were homeless like me, asking people if they could take me home and teach me to rap.

Stuff and Storm known as LDG came strolling out of the Port Authority with their cocky attitudes. Stuff gave me a smirk then said, "We'll take you home wit us if you're ready for the ride of your life past the zero zone." My reply was, "I'm ready." Did I get a break to be heard by any of the labels once I learned how to rap? Hell no. Much like Eminem, I spit my life on my first rhyme "Break Any Ribbon." I searched out total strangers to accomplish getting my rhymes laid down who knew nothing about why it was so hard for me to get on a mike. I've worked with engineers who knew what they were doing. They taught me sh*t I never knew about loops and back-ups. Mastering and levels. Most of the time I was working on other artist joints. I didn't know much about what a musical work consists of and who all is entitled points or due money from the finished product. Back then it was reels, tapes, dats, DVD's, and the like. No one knew a thing about me. I learned how shady the industry was and how tricky and how deceitful people could be.

Girls were giving lays to get record deals. I got to see people betraying each other, temperaments, attributes, and qualities, including their background and criminal side. All types of characters came at me. I don't know if it was for money or because I was a blonde with big tatas. Once they learned I wasn't a dumba** and had the ability to read contracts and understand them, they were happy to hear my advice and how to get on track. Many times, they took my recommendations and put it into action. They had no idea I already owned my own bar and dealt with people under the influence of alcohol and drugs and its effects. I was already a Baka, Diva, Gima, Philly grown from the concrete jungle. Little did they know I had already formed my first corporation along with a publishing company with BMI and became the personal business manager of many stars. Lucky for me I finally met up with good engineers who were on top their game and could lay my artistic and my musical work down.

Long ago in a forest that boarders Philly there was a Mystical Place where the Hobos jumped the train and spent their day jamming. Like any fairy tale one day "A Beautific Man" appeared and became the steppin' stone for anyone there to eventually find their way.

A Beautific Man

A Beautific Man is a person (he/she) who gives you the jump start you need to continue the dream you have for yourself. A Beautific Man is the steppin' stone that helps you meet the requirements necessary to eventually find your way. A Beautific Man is the electrical energy needed to succeed. Examples of a Beautific Man:

How would you react if someone walked into your office and laid down their dream on your desk even though you've never wined or dined or met them before? Would you believe enough in someone's dream to write a check at that very moment for $50,000 without any paperwork? Sometimes in life there's an exception to the rule where "A Beautific Man" wrote a check on the spot because he was human enough to believe in someone else's dream. Mine.

How would you react if a lady (me) walked into the law firm you had met briefly years ago filing her sons patent and asked you how to file a trademark without any money? Naturally you'd give her a fair price Her reply, "I have no idea where I'll get that kind of money, but I'll be back." Entering the parking garage, a man is looking for a car. She says she'd help him find it. She tells the man about being to a lawyer's office and how she needs $2,500 for her dream. The man says, "If you help me find the car you'll have what you need. Money means very little to me." She finds the car for him. The man writes her a check for $2,500. She returns an hour later after cashing the check to the lawyer's office. The lawyer is on the phone as she enters his office and hears him say, "You found the car. It cost $2,500 to find it?" He hangs up. She says to the lawyer, "He's tellin' the truth, here it is. Sometimes in life there's an exception to the rule because "A Beautific Man" was human enough to believe in someone else's dream. Mine.

How often does someone unbeknownst to you enjoy your wholesome conversation in the doorway of a feed store and says let's continue this conversation at a later date? How would you react if that person showed up at your door months later to continue the conversation? Shocked? Of course, you'd think they're a nut case and you'd sure in hell stay on the porch. When you learned they just wanted someone to share their dream with, would you believe in their dream enough to set them up in an office? Sometimes in life there's an exception to the rule because "A Beautific Man" was human enough to believe in someone else's dream. Mine.

What would you do if someone came in your NYC office on 38th & Broadway and left $100,000 in your desk drawer with a note that read, please accept this gift to help you on your way with your dream? If you didn't have the slightest clue who left the money and you believe the money must have come from some sort of drug deal or was stolen, what would you do? Talk about being in shock. I put it in the safe determined not to use it. I kept my eyes and ears open and tried and find out who the hell left it. It was there for years untouched. I told myself one day I'll use it for the goodness of mankind and in doing so perhaps my dream will fall in place. Sometimes in life there's an exception to the rule because "A Beautific Man" was human enough to believe in someone else's dream. Min

Philly Transplant

Beneath the Hype Section

Do you think for one minute that my life was easy? Think again.

Everything in my book is based on what I observed and how I perceived each and every situation. How I perceived and comprehended what I observed and registered seemed significant enough to be noteworthy. I didn't write this book to slander anyone or make false statements or to damage a person's reputation. Rather to divulge the life I've lived. To expose to you the reader what it was like being me. People believe what they want to believe. People condemn innocent people. For the love of money and other things like fame, people will find fault with just about anything including my book. Remember the 50% rule where none of us are perfect, least of all me. In reading my book keep in mind to the best of my knowledge all statements made by me in the book are true, but you be the judge.

How many people can say they've been before the federal government several times? It's not easy because whatever you may know or disclose some will wonder who the hell you are and how did you discover it. Do they really think I'm gonna tell them and have a hit put on me for being a snitch? No thank you… Maybe Congress should chill out on the block like the rest of us or try livin' on the street like I did.

I spent years undercover after I learned what happened to me on the Streets of Philadelphia. Best believe I headed out the door of my so-called mansion for the streets. My family was long gone and on their own with children of their own. I came home to see them for holidays and our Annual Pig Roast.

What happened to me can happen to you. If I had a Visa card with any money on it I'd have checked into a hotel after the first night on the block. What I learned over time is "Street Sense Makes Sense." My husband handed me his VISA card when I left. Hell, why would I use it and give him the benefit of the doubt that I needed him. He was the reason I was leaving the estate and my family. He sugar coated that the other baby died to the family. He believed the truth was better left unsaid.

When my twins were born, both families knew they were actually triplets, but none bothered to ask about the one that died. Where's the funeral or ashes yo? What the f*ck is that about? I had no idea I was livin' in a dismal state. How about a funeral eh? Perhaps a body. Ashes would have worked yo. His bullsh*t story eventually came to a head. Perhaps that's one of the reasons why I like Eminem so much; he's always cleaning his closet. To this day my family has little knowledge about my life. What I do or the places I've been. Eminem is one of my favorite rappers because his rhythms lay out people who fu*ked wit em. His hooks grab you by the balls where you can't help but repeat the lyrics in your brain.

People think they know you when they don't. My children think of me as a mother who corrects them when they're bad because they're my seed. I ask you who the hell's responsible for correcting your children if not the parent? I'm a mother like no other who hugs them when they need a hug and holds their hand when times are rough loving them unconditionally. They know the scripture well, (John 15:13 Greater love hath no man than to lay down his life for another). I wore my shoe well.

Philly Transplant

Beneath the Hype Learning Street

My attire is basically Wal-Mart clothing. At times a Ross store. It didn't take me long to discover how to hang out with major players. I befriended their bodyguards, drivers, housekeepers, gardeners, their lawyers and even their accountants. I made myself look street instead of my natural flamboyant stature in order to be accepted on the block. I carried a Bible with a tablet inside where I recorded and coded what I saw, what I learned, what I overheard. I thought one day I'll fix the sh*t that's fu*ked up in "My Country Tis of Thee."

Getting VIP passes into celebrity events wasn't a problem in any city. A doorman or employee slipped me passes for payola. I learned the game and realized there's barely a soul you can trust. People wondered who the hell is 'This White Bitch Crazy' at the events greeting people with a curtsy?

Ruffled crinolines got me in trouble as an innocent 16-year-old, however a curtsy made people take notice. Why else would I pay a G to get in when the ticket was twenty bucks? Do you think the late Whitney Houston knew what was happening to her for the love of the game? She was a gifted soul with tremendous vocals. What I needed was underground education. I learned quickly the game of fame along with its rules.

In the early 90's I was given VIP passes for Joe Jaxson's events, DJ FunkMaster Flex, DJ Ace, and the promoter Bud. These dudes filled NY clubs to the max. At a Wu Tang venue Sticky Fingaz came up to me askin' who I was. I said, "I'm nobody bro. But I got a VIP pass eh!" Kilah Priest and U God gave me their cell numbers one night in the club and said, "Hit me up." One thing is for sure the place was smokin' like walkin' in a cloud.

Beneath the Hype School Days

I walked to school in 7th grade back when girls were only able to wear skirts or dresses. The fastest way to school was the forest along with train tracks. One day a few of the boys who were considered nasty boys were hiding in the weeds. Unbeknown to me one was up in a tree waiting for me. He peed in a paper cup and as a joke when I walked past he throws the piss from the cup on top my head. I heard laughter coming from the edge of the forest. It was more of the nasty boys hiding yelling he pissed on your golden locks of hair. I began to cry and ran home.

My father knew being blonde that I would always be given a rough time by society. My father uttered, no need to cry, you got to get tough girl. My mother washed my hair and brushed it a 100 stokes. When I went to school the next day, I shared it with one boy. He spoke to the nasty boys and explained they should be ashamed of themselves. He explained that I couldn't help that I was born blonde.

After that those boys let me alone. I was proud of him. We became friends through high school. When my father found out I befriended the boy he said, "You do know your friend is Italian, right?" I nodded yes. My father only wanted me to hang with people who were Jewish. He believed it was the only way I could survive and have knowledge how to make it happen for myself.

My father believed Gentiles give their kids stylish clothing, Tonka trucks and dolls. He believed Jewish people gave their kids' books and college so they would grow up educated.

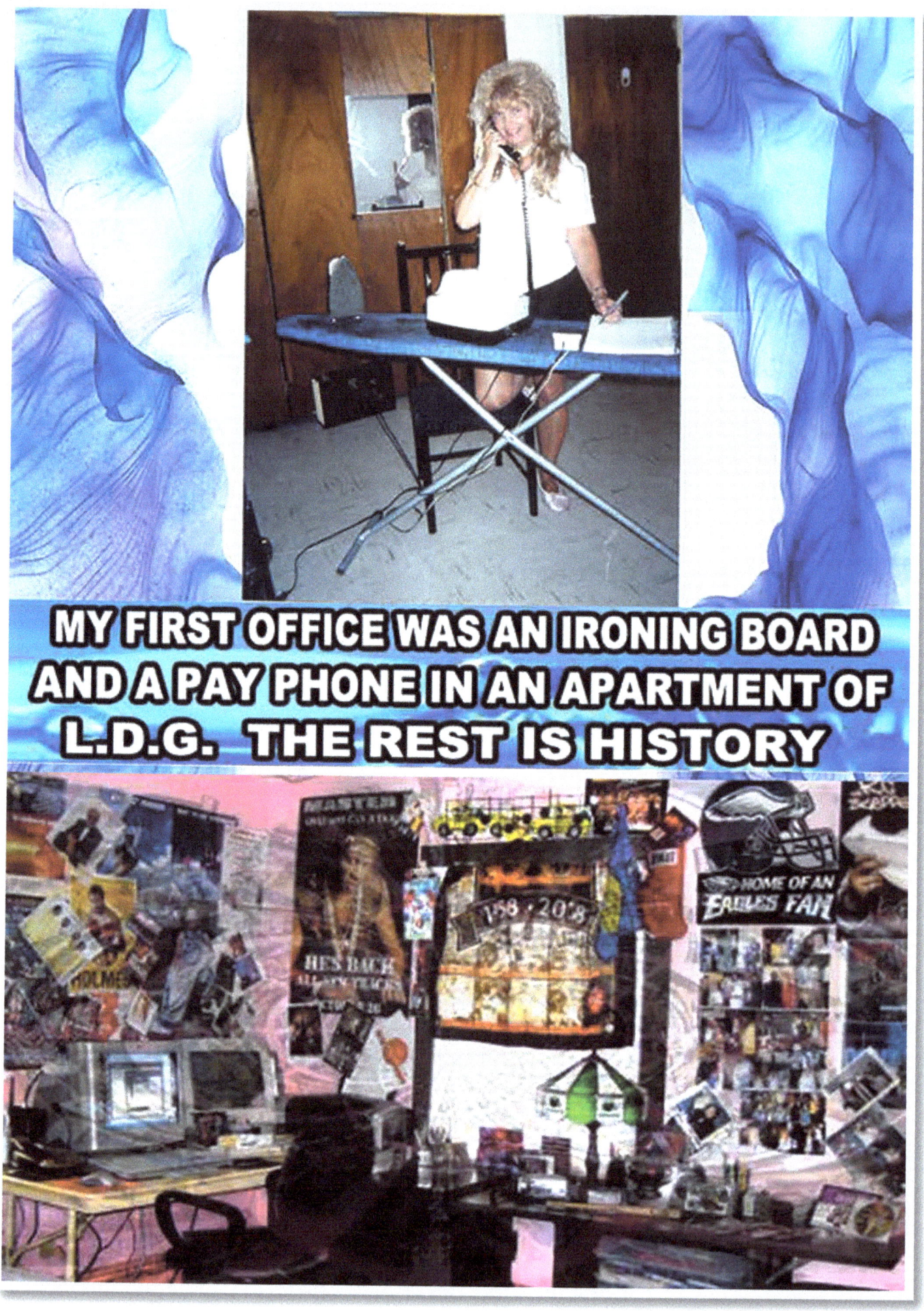

MY FIRST OFFICE WAS AN IRONING BOARD AND A PAY PHONE IN AN APARTMENT OF L.D.G. THE REST IS HISTORY

He'd say, "I want you to hang with Jewish kids' cuz you're going to need all the knowledge you can get being blonde." I suppose it was a simple way to help me understand growing up being born blonde and beautiful with big tatas built like a brick shithouse comes with a price. Many years later one of my husband's cousins was getting married and lo and behold when we went to the wedding it was the Italian boy who spoke up on my behalf marrying my husband's cousin.

Beneath the Hype First Office and Ironing Board

Living in the apartment of Like Dat Generation (L.D.G.), I had a pay phone on an ironing board. Hip Hop put out an APB on the block to be on the lookout for 'This White Bitch Crazy' and hit her with VIP passes. In those days people called each other niggas and I became their nigga'. They'd address me with, "what's up my nigga." If they asked me questions I'd say, "Bro it's never been about me yo, it's about you." One thing is for sure any English I may have had was slowly leaving me. Slang took over. It drove my IP Lawyer nutzo.

Befriending housekeepers isn't such a bad deal if you need money. I befriended housekeepers and when they couldn't make it to work I'd take their place cleaning the toilets of the rich and famous. I stayed on track focused on my goal to learn what happened to me. I danced and sang while cleaning to "YMCA" by the Village People. It was a reminder that I didn't surrender back to my house on the mountain. The rich and famous have no idea that their employees sell them out. In reality who can you trust, eh?

I had a special seat at the Port Authority where I slept in a chair every night until L.D.G. took me home to their crib. The cop would ask me if I missed my bus again. I'd shake my head yes. Mr. Phil head of buses at the Port Authority knew what I was doing. Finally, I got an invite to Donald Trump's house for "A Night with the Stars." There I got to sit with Frank Stallone and enjoyed learning about the industry. Being with such hierarchy was a privilege. Frank is an interesting guy.

I picked up clients by reading their fu★ked up contracts and showing them how they got fu★cked. Famous people took a chance on me meeting in private locations away from their lawyers and people on a lee low. Every time I heard the song by ABBA "Take a Chance on Me" I'd sing thinkin' my clients are lucky to have me. I'd show them how they're being fu★ked by their own lawyers, homies, and inter circle who they had befriended. Chillin' with them while they're screwing them.

I went to venues from city to city as far out as Memphis to visit Sun Records. After 8 years I formed multiple corporations and began working on developing systems that would stop some of the Fraud and Corruption in America. I filed multiple patent applications with the Patent Office. I was so energized that I could change things that I saw that were f★cked up. I knew I already paid the price, "For the Love of Music" someone had my Gold, the Fame and the millions my song made. At times I hear my song on the radio I quickly shut it down and cry my brains out. What does it matter the name of the song to people? A bunch of thieves got away with it and stole my baby. If anyone knew which song it was the thieves would make more money when people listen to it or play it. It still gets airplay today with a few remixes and more than likely most people know the song. I have never told a soul the name of the song.

Those were the days when I was sleeping at the Port Authority. Nothin' like getting your milk where you can. After all the 8 Hobos who saved my life and the life of my sons in my womb ate out of trash cans. Our cow Beauty didn't care who got her milk. I'm livin' proof comin' from nothin' doesn't mean you can't be something. I been from Broadway to Hollywood and invited to Mar-a-Lago and sat in gold trimmed chairs. Dress for success shouldn't matter. I'm known for wearing Walmart clothes. It doesn't make the man or woman. It True it gives one more confidence and feel more powerful or perceived as a leader. Many times people fail because they forgot that Street Sense Makes Sense. Street Sense is understanding different types of situations and how to respond and solve them along with challenges.

To whom it may concern,

I'm a child of a Sailor from World War II and a wife of a Soldier from Vietnam. To anyone who would call us losers and suckers let it be said, the 3 of us are Warriors to keep America Strong. Those who walk in a Glass Shoe shouldn't condemn a turf they haven't stepped on.

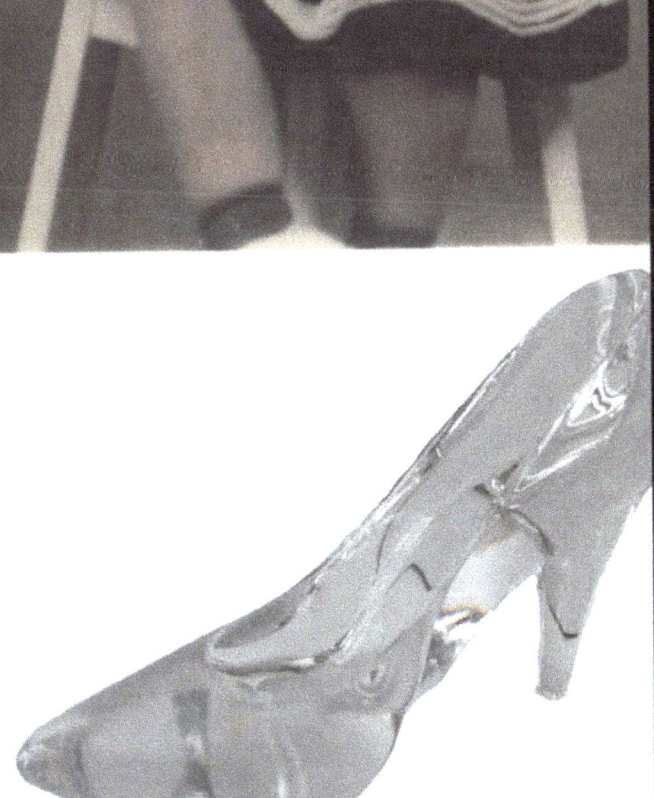

Beneath the Hype Racial and Social Injustice Issues

My father taught me to be savvy and understand that there will be men who will want to smell and taste of my forbidden fruit. Men will want to roll their hands through my golden locks of hair. Then there will be people who will think of me as stupid. As much as I hated hearing it over and over as I grew up, I have to admit my parents were right. It has not been easy being born blonde and having people characterize me. It seems my whole life I've been working and fighting for racial and social injustice issues. If you're a person of color it's unlikely somebody's going to walk up and actually use the n-word in front of you. When you're born blonde, you hear slurs from men like:" there's a blonde bet she's easy." Many times, when I'm talking to people, especially men, they don't give me much respect because they're looking at me like I'm a stupid blonde. It's not easy to wear the shoe I'm in. I'm a blonde who's been Blood Brothered to eight homeless men of color from the streets of Philly. If you were wearing my shoe back in the nineties livin' and chillin' with my homies who called each other, my n*gga including me, you'd understand it's slang. In today's time everybody tries not to use racial slurs or the N word.

Let's not forget those who indulges in hypocrisy about the N word. Those who became famous and became millionaires on using the word in their rhyme. I know plenty of people who make a show of being without moral faults. Don't under estimate a self-righteous person as being "holler-than thou." Put someone in someone else's shoe and see what they do. Self-righteous is being full of self. Even if your title was President it doesn't make you a President. A person's language doesn't determine his principles. Who would know this better then me?

It's truly the way you say the word as to whether it's racial or not. Just because it's not socially accepted anymore doesn't mean the urban community stopped using it. Let's not forget millions were made in Hip Hop off that word in a rhyme and across national airplay on radio where the FCC gave the ok as long as the word fu*k and n*ggaz were slurred. You can find my peeps from New York to Philly to New Orleans, Georgia to Miami to Memphis, as far across the map as Oakland and Vegas where they're still chillin' and use the word n*gga. I am truly grateful to the eight homeless men of color that saved my life and the life of my two sons who were left inside me to die. Racism or color didn't stop those men. We live because of them. If you're on Facebook you'll see people who say what they want. I suppose it's because we still have freedom of speech, eh? People of multiple colors, the rich and the poor, and some a**holes in between have crossed my door, they were the stepping stones that helped me find my way back into the entertainment world. Let me lay on you more Beneath the Hype and you be the judge if I'm tellin' the truth...

Beneath the Hype Black and White

I'm sure you met people who were racist. Sit down and venture with me how ridiculous some people are over color. It's personal to me because of the shoe I wear. My father worked along with the Police dept and knew some of the cops were to some degree racist. The altar boy for our wedding named Bobby grew up to be a cop and chilled with my father on the force. For years I had no idea why I felt uneasy when people would use the N-word around me. From the age of 19 I was livin' in a dismal state of mind. For years well into my forties I was searching for something missing. It was my child and my golden note. I had no idea that I was Blood Brothered to eight homeless men of color on the block as a ritual to save my life by a Nun. Oh yes, I got hell many times from my husband Tom for enjoying the company of people of color. He was scared I'd ask questions about why I was bruised with cuts on my body and bleeding internally. Better left unsaid said the attending doctor, "More than likely she won't remember much if anything about what happened because of the brain injury." Really? My playmates Patsy, Gail, and Bucky would go to Sunday school every week with me. After church I told my mother that Jesus loves the little children of the world. My mother laughed and said, "I know." Then she began to sing, "Jesus loves the little children, they are yellow, black and white and precious in his sight. When I was your age I went to Sunday school and when I'm old I'll go again." Amazing how racist people watch sports and wear their favorite teams' logo proudly on their chest. Have you noticed how much flavor is in sports? One of my favorite quarterback's was Vick from the Eagles. Perhaps, people need to learn from athletes who fill our ballparks and stadiums regardless of race, religion, or social states they "Rize Energized Spolarized®" shinning the stars that they are together as a team. My lawyer and I shared a child through Compassion International named Margarita from the Dominican Republic.

Snowflakes

I get a call from a young mother who says, "Baka, if you don't handle this problem I'm going to be in jail for knocking out a school teacher tomorrow." My answer was "I got this. What's going on?" She says, her daughter went to school and the teacher told the students "I see we have a child of color in the classroom." Of course, the other children probably didn't know what that meant. At recess the children figured out that the child was Brown and a different color than them. The children wouldn't play with her. The children ran around the playground saying she's a child of color, she's a child of color. I immediately hopped in the car to meet with the mother and child together. I explained to the child what I wanted her to do. Tomorrow tell Mrs. Jones you learned something last night and want to share it with the class. Act excited and do not tell the teacher what it is even if she asks. Just run to the front of the class once everyone is seated. Say, "Listen up if you all agree with me along with you Mrs. Jones, you'll all put your hands up and yell I agree." Then begin singing swinging your hands in front of you from left to right.

The Snowflake Rhyme: "The Earth is Brown or Green. The Earth is Brown or Green. Brown in the winter and Green in the summer. Do all of you agree the Earth is Brown or Green? If you agree put your hands up and shout out, yeah!"

Bravely extend your arm out towards the room like a jester and say, "Brown like me and you are all Snowflakes that float around earth in between." So much for laying out the teachers eh?

I'VE BEEN TO THE TOP MEETING WITH VIP'S OF

WALMART-SAM'S CLUB/BEST BUY HEADQUARTERS.

Beneath the Hype a Famous Man's Calling Card

A famous man in Hip-Hop owned a big record label in the middle of NYC and opened a telephone calling cards company. I'll give him the benefit of the doubt that he more than likely didn't know in the beginning that when you bought his calling card with his already famous trademark name and a cell phone rang near the card it deactivated the minutes on the card and you got nothing. Before I discovered it, people were calling his company saying they lost their minutes they paid for and the card was empty. His employees answering the calls would say to the customer perhaps you did something wrong.

On my way into a store I noticed a woman crying on the curb. In the hustle and bustle of people going pass her it was obvious no one seemed to care. I said, "Sweet pea it can't be that bad. Perhaps I can give you a hug or help you," She expressed how she lived on a fixed income and ate one meal a day for 3 months to buy the calling card to surprise her grandson for his birthday. When he tried to use it to call his dad it was empty. I told her I'll give you $50.00 cash from scrubbing toilets this morning as long as I can keep the card and receipt. I asked to see what was in her purse besides the calling card. She pulled out a cell phone and some makeup, a tissue and a couple dollars.

I went into the store and told them that it was blank. They gave me the phone number of the famous man's calling card company. The lady at the desk says, "We get a lot of customer's complaining about these cards." I called the company and explained the card is blank. The employee's reply was that the lady did something wrong. Nobody's grandmother should starve to do something nice for their grandchild and get fu*cked by the calling card company. What really p*sses me off is how this famous man got off free screwing society acting stupid like he didn't know. The Hip-Hop icon didn't shut it down when he learned of hundreds of calls to the company that something was wrong. It's up to you the reader to be the judge if what I'm saying is the truth.

Beneath the Hype Wal-Mart Headquarters'

I felt so honored being able to meet at the headquarters of Wal-Mart with the VP of Sam's Club who is a lawyer. I got to meet many sellers of products who on a lee low gave me the low down how the real-world works. Some of the growers and sellers are willing to rip off organic or regular stickers and credentials in order to fill orders and make sales. Wal-Mart and other honest companies are always on the alert for this. The product still looks the same and tastes the same. People have lived forever eating regular grown fruits and vegetables. How often are growers checked for using poisons on their crop? Can you believe people actually think the same product is different per store? They believe a Kraft product with the same bottle, same ingredient, the same ounces, and same label is different in Publix than in Wal-Mart's. Do you know how many people I've met who believe that Frito-Lay chips with the same bag, same flavor, is different in Publix or Target. Talk about stupid people eh. You should know the federal Government is on top of this matter of organic foods to ensure when it says organic that it truly is.

THE CANNABIS CUP IN DENVER WAS AN
EXPERIENCE... DURING THE EVENT I WAS
LIVE ON THE RADIO.

Beneath the Hype Meeting Snoop at Cannabis Cup

The Cannabis Cup in Denver was an experience. I went there to learn about weed and invest. A back-stage meeting was set up with Snoop by a fellow named Mark who works with Snoop. That didn't happen. Snoop's camp has rings and rings of homies who determine with authority his moves without his knowledge. Moreover, they pick and choose what he may or not be interested in when offers come to the table without his knowledge.

It's not like it's my first rodeo trying to get with him. I set up a meeting at Magic years ago when Snoops entourage was smaller and slightly different than those around him now. The entourage I experienced at the Cannabis Cup pushes you back like you were a piece of sh*t while letting their friends in without back stage passes. I called Mark's cell six times leaving him a massage that my bodyguard Dr. Mark VIP and I were at the backstage door.

He never answered his cell. Mark claimed he'd be able to get me in front of Snoop. I was live on the radio during the event talkin' about weed. People who want to chill at the end of the day smokin' a joint shouldn't be put in jail. Jails were meant for criminals.

We should be sellin' weed makin' tax money. I was born energized. I bust a** all day till I'm beat. I fall into bed with some wild lullaby rollin' around in my head. I've never needed a fix to chill at the end of the day. But that's me and how I operate. Not everyone operates like me.

The Cannabis Cup did have a funny side to it. After the concert that night people were so wasted from eating brownies and smokin' weed that they couldn't remember what hotel they rented. They spent the night on the concert lawn. The next day when we returned there were people laying on the grass totally gone. Dr Mark VIP felt their pulse and said, "They're all still alive."

Beneath the Hype Money Laundering Everywhere

There's all kind of fraudulent activity you'll never hear about because the FBI is keeping it on a lee low trying to get on top of it. It's not like I work for the FBI, Homeland Security, or any other organization. I've been ahead of them at times cluein' them in. I've traveled coast to coast for years to multiple types of events, conventions, and have met with all types of people including different gang members.

I was born with some kind of insight or a headz-up knowledge of what's up long before it happens. I can see connivers and bullsh*tters and discover criminal activity long before the authorities. Aside from all that criminal activity you see on the news there's 10 times more criminal activity going on that you have no knowledge of.

How many people can say they worked with Homeland Security on issues from one country to another? I can. How many people can say they along with their bodyguard worked on stings with the FBI to take down people operating business in foreign countries and America? You be the judge if I'm tellin' the truth eh! Ms. Dickie knows I'm tellin' the truth. Her a** went down along with her operation in Oklahoma.

Been to Washington DC Several Times

UNITED STATES PATENT AND TRADEMARK OFFICE

UNITED STATES PATENT AND TRADEMARK OFFICE

Beneath the Hype Messed up Sh*t in Gov't

I'm sitting with the Federal Government with my IP Lawyer explaining to the patent examiner that the system in place is messed up when it comes to calling cards and downloading of multiple products processing through POS systems. I explained to the Examiner that my systems are the fix.

He looked at me and my IP Lawyer with his cell in his hand turned slightly towards us with a smirk on his face and said, "I will never allow your multiple patent applications."

I said, "Is it because you think a senior citizen woman could discover a fix before that company which is the largest technology company? I realize I'm the rarest of rare in the field" He once again said, "I will never give up finding something similar and cite you." My IP Lawyer and I got up and left. I knew 72 billion dollars more or less was made by the cell phone he held in his hand with their download system that already existed.

When I got out on the steps of the Federal building I looked at my IP Lawyer and said, "What the f*ck just happened?" He said, "We could go to the Supreme Court. How much money do you have? I ask you, are we going to win? The courts employ him. There were only three people in the room, the Examiner who is the employee of the Federal Government and us. Where is the proof or guarantee that they're going to believe us?" I walked away with nothing.

Years and years of development of systems, legal fees and filing fees down the toilet. It didn't turn out the way it should have for me. I appealed to the Board of Appeals but unfortunately, they rejected my Appeal even though the Board did not agree with some of the rejections and statements that the Examiner made. I felt like the Eagles; I'm an underdog. To the best of my knowledge and belief all statements made by me in this book are true, but you be the judge.

Beneath the Hype Corruption Everywhere

I'm sitting in a west coast diner trying to call my daughter-in-law who's not answering the phone. Next to me a dude says, "Hey I'll zoom in and see if she's home. Don't worry I'm a thief. I'm not going to rob you. I got plenty of sh*t to rob here." He begins to explain the new technology that has the ability to go into a home without the person's knowledge. I give the dude my address and together we're in.

I asked him, "How is this possible?"

Here's what he said, "Do you remember when Bush was in office and 9-1-1 happened and Bush came on the TV saying, for probable cause the government should be allowed in your home without your knowledge under the Patriot Act? Did you think that kind of technology was created only for good guys? Did you think bad guys weren't gonna get their hands on it? Robbers, gangs and drug cartels are all using it." Technology with reverse cameras on all our gadgets and TVs available for use by bad guys. Wow!

To the best of my knowledge and belief all statements made by me in this book are true, but you be the judge.

Beneath the Hype Technology

I'm having coffee with a dude who tells me a story so fantastic that I had to believe it. A cop gets a call from a young man there was a robbery of his new games & TV he bought at Best Buy. The young man was so proud that he put it on Facebook that he bought new stuff along with an invitation for his buddies to come over on Friday night. He spoke about working late every night that week. On Thursday night he came home from work and everything was gone. The young man was in his early 20's so the detective asked him if he had a parent available that could come over during the report. The young man called his dad.

When the dad arrived the cop said, "Can I talk to you outside." Once outside the cop took off his badge and laid it on the hood of the police car. The cop said, "Sir I'm going to talk to you like a dad cuz I'm a dad. We have a technology that will tell us where the stolen stuff is. The technology can go into cyberspace and by entering the tracking number of the equipment and reverse camera on the TV we'll be able to see its location and who robbed your son. I can assure you the robber didn't take the equipment not to use it and I doubt it's the robbers first rodeo. More than likely he's got a police record and hangs with thugs. Our jails are at full capacity, so the bad guys only get a little time. However, his buddies will still be at large. How long do you think your son will last with the Susquehanna River that surrounds the city?

I'm gonna put my badge back on and you talk it over with your son and let me know if you want to pursue this case or you can tell your son to grow up and stay the f*ck off Facebook." What dad wouldn't be glad for the lecture? He surely doesn't want his son murdered. A few months later the father met up with the cop and he tells the dad they homed in on the TV and there were three guys using the games and TV.

All had prison records. Then the cop says, "I'm assuming your son is still alive. The new system of tracking and face recognition allows us to place one face with another on a friendship list."

Beneath the Hype Money Lost in Cyberspace

There is a whole department in cyberspace dealing with lost money from one bank to another in a transaction. It is completely out of the hands of the banks. If one number is wrong on the router or the bank account you're fu*cked. When making a transfer it can be a fraudulent account that may or may not exist. This is an avenue I have experience in. Over $50,000 going from one account to another was lost. Not just my money but other people's money totaling $500.000. We'll never see our money because we learned that the cyberspace department not only has our money but thousands upon thousands of other people's money. We took $500,000 dollars from a bank in Pennsylvania and magically it couldn't find its way to a bank in Florida. This doesn't include the money being laundered from one country to another in the same process. Most people are clueless what's up in America.

Beneath the Hype Venture to Pakistan

A business venture in New York lead me on a venture to Pakistan without leaving New York! Once inside the home of a man I was set up to meet on an investment of millions of dollars, he walked over to a knick knack shelf and touched it and before our eyes a wall disappeared. It was hard to believe that 6 steps down I landed in Pakistan without the flight. Almost unexplainable once the wall closed knowing I hadn't left NY but was sitting in Pakistan. It was hard to keep my composure. The man said, "I heard a lot about you that's why I invited you into my secret office place few people know about. I was told I could trust you and what better place to talk about millions of dollars than in the privacy of my country. Once you leave here you understand regardless if a deal is made or not that you were never here." I nodded yes. The man explained that his brother is with Homeland Security in Pakistan and yes we are in an embargo. He stated he came to New York with his family, so his children could get a good education. I enjoyed the time I spent with him in Pakistan and was relieved when he opened the wall into the main house. I was glad to see NY once again. No deal was made.

Beneath the Hype Commercials

What do you know about good companies versus companies that are shady? Without using any names, you be the judge if it's true or not. When a corporation is doing a TV commercial do you believe that they read the script and how their product is going to be portrayed in the marketplace? Here's how it works. A company hires a production unit to do the commercial. The company agrees with the script representing their product. The company over-sees who is representing the company and its product. The company was aware that the coordination of the fireworks must be timed perfectly with the walk of the Superstar down the steps.

My take is the Superstar got burned from the explosion of fireworks that went off too early and put the Superstar in the hospital. They already had plenty of takes. The Superstar had to be devastated. He would have blamed himself for not being more forceful. Perhaps, the medicine for pain that was given from the accident became his life time support. He had to wear a wig for the rest of his life. The doctor probably loved the easy money he was receiving by keeping him on prescription drugs.

Over the years in the entertainment business I have found people with fame sorta lose touch with who is for them and who is against them. They're so busy that they rarely recognize who leads them astray. In my eyes DMX with massive skills should have taken notes on who's around him. Second example where the same company once again did an outlandish commercial trying to beat the No. 1 product Coke.

The same corporation paid millions to create a commercial and once again millions to a Superstar to market their product. When did a commercial air in our country that only lasted a blink before being pulled? The commercial forced a mass boycott by American Religious Groups over the portrayal of Saint Martin dePorres who kissed the Superstar actress on the forehead as she let her shoulder straps fall while cutting her palms with a knife.

So, it's goes that religious groups were willing to boycott not only the corporation but their other affiliates and businesses. The male actor stated he was persuaded into the commercial and met with the director to hear the concept. The company apologized much like they did with the Superstar burned. I don't support a company who for the love of money is willing to try anything to get you to buy their product. I care about the judgment a company

The Magic Pump

PAPA JOE AND GRANDMA MARY HAD A MAGIC PUMP.
IT TURNED MUDDY WATER INTO COKE IF YOU
BELIEVED... COKE HAS COME A LONG WAY, EH

The Santa most of us recognize was created for a Coca Cola campaign. Coke has been in my life since papa Joe and grandma Mary's magic pump. Six generations drinking Coca Cola. I was married to my own Coca Cola Santa. My son was one of the top salesmen for Coca Cola and won many awards. My parents taught me when you are No 1 – You are No. 1.

makes when using their product. Millions drink and buy their soda but not me. I'll stick with the No. 1 drink, Coke.

Beneath the Hype Witness Protection

Have you ever known someone who heard or saw something f*cked up and had to go under Witness Protection for the rest of their life? I do. No one knew why this dude had to disappear with his wife and young children or why for years he or his family couldn't call his mother and father or anyone back in his hometown outside of Philly. He used a lot of excuses to his wife and children why they were moving around and on a lee low. He really didn't want them to be involved or know the full detail of why. After years of moving around he picked a place in Pa figuring it would be a safe place to hide away. He didn't realize it was where I lived.

He befriended a couple that I had befriended. One night while visiting the couple for coffee a knock came at their door. Sure, enough when it opened there stood the dude. To our surprise we began to hug. Wow. I asked him what's going on, where have you been? His reply was don't ask. Many years had passed since anyone had heard from him. He insisted we don't see each other very often because he didn't want to involve me and my family or jeopardize our safety if he was discovered alive.

Years later lo and behold he wasn't kidding, in the middle of the night a helicopter landed in a nearby farm field. All I knew was he was under Federal Protection for something that he had seen while working for a well-known major corporation we all know. When he heard the helicopter land nearby, he grabbed his kids without even their bottles and clothes and out the door into the car they fled. The only place he knew to go for the moment was to his mother and father's cabin hidden in the woods two towns away. He stayed there just for a blink and then headed to a new state to hide.

Years passed, and he felt comfortable enough to capture a life and get a job hoping they finally gave up looking for him. In his last years of life my IP Lawyer and I flew in to meet with him. He made us promise we would never say a word. He wanted us to know that the Witness Protection Program for him was a joke and they weren't protecting him. You survive basically on your own learning how to live under the radar without any guarantee from one day to the next.

He spoke about how long ago he got on a private plane with the executives of a major corporation who thought he was supposed to be a part of the deal they were making with a foreign country. When they learned he wasn't supposed to be exposed or have any knowledge of this meeting, they thought killing him would fix it. Luckily for him one of the executives from his company on the plane was appointed to handle killing him. This offered him the opportunity to exit off the plane at which point he ran his a** off and got away.

Once he got away he went to the intelligence community to lay down what he heard and seek protection by the Federal Government. After that his life was over. He was put into the Witness Protection Program which in the end did nothing except to tell him, he'll be hiding the rest of his life.

Beneath the Hype Eyes Watching

There's hidden cameras and visible cameras in most cities and even in small towns. Facial recognition places people together on a friendship list. It gives police departments the knowledge of where criminals hang out and what they're up to and it's very useful in a raid. It lets them know what you purchased such as paper wrappers for weed. If you've been in jail or have a police record when you get out and you go right back to the same crib you are once again added to the friendship list of corruption. When sh*t goes down you are guilty by association.

A smart person will find a new network of people. Let's talk about retail stores where eyes are following shoppers watching what they pick up and whether they read the label or not or put it back on the shelf or whether they purchase it. This information is then sold to manufacturers. When you leave a store the satellite may text you asking you how was Best Buy, how was Wal-Mart, how was the donut shop? You shouldn't be ignorant to technology.

To the best of my knowledge and belief all statements made by me in this book are true, but you be the judge.

Beneath the Hype Racial Injustice Workplace

My grandmother worked in the fields picking tomatoes. I want to believe that the growers sold the tomatoes to Campbell's Soup. I want to believe if Campbell Soup Company knew that the company they hired to grow tomatoes was profiling people they'd have gotten rid of the grower. Campbell's Soup happens to be the soup I grew up eating, likewise, my children. My grandmother would pick tomatoes and place them in baskets. At the end of the day a horse and buggy would pull up to pick up the baskets from the pickers. She received $0.25 per basket.

She noticed that the woman in the row next to her of color was given $0.10 per basket. She asked the man why the woman only got a dime. He said, "Because she was a n*gger." My grandmother said, "She deserves the same as the rest of us." The man said, "I'll fire you." Then my grandmother says, "I will turn you in." The woman starts to cry and says, "Mary, Mary, please don't say a word. I need this money. I made $0.50 today for my 5 baskets. Please Mary, it's worse than you know. Please let it go."

But my grandmother was persistent so at the end of the day she stayed back and watched to see what the woman was talking about. Before the woman could leave she had to walk the two horses to the barn to give them water and place them in the stall. My grandmother wondered if she was getting extra money for doing the service, so my grandmother quietly followed her to the barn. When my grandmother entered the barn, she heard the woman crying and screaming you're hurting me. My grandmother ran to her aide. She saw the man on top of the woman. My grandmother yelled, "Let her go, what are you doing?" The man yells, "She is nothing more than a slave. In order to keep her job, she must f*ck me every day."

My grandmother ran home to grab my grandpa Joe. He ran to the barn and picked up a shovel and smacked the man over the head. It knocked the man off the woman and into the hay. My grandmother grabbed the woman and they ran out of the barn. The woman cried and said, "Mary, Mary, what have you done. I need this job it doesn't matter what I have to do. I need to make money to feed my children." My grandmother reached in her pocket and gave her the $0.50 she earned.

The next day my grandpa was waiting in the barn and beat the living sh★t out of the man. He said, "you will treat all women the same and call them by their name. No one has to f★ck you for their pay. I will be here every day to beat the sh★t out of you until you change your Wicked Ways." The man never touched the woman again and upped her wage to $0.25 a basket. I wonder what the horses thought?

Beneath the Hype Religion and the Bible

Over time religion evolved with the perception of different ideas mixed with some facts. We started with the first Gospel and moved onto the New Testament. We believed one way and then we learned there could be another way. The devil tempts us to ruin God's work. This would explain then why God's people keep getting hurt. Over time religions didn't get rid of stories, they revised the stories by re-interpreting and re-defining them. I knew from my parent's teaching that everyone is tested along the path of life. Be prepared for war my father would say.

Of course, my father would say that, he was in World War II. I prepared myself and taught my family that good and evil are hard to recognize. Satan seems like the kind of person you dig while he's eating you for lunch. Satan will encourage you to do things that are not of God. Honestly, I could give a sh★t what people think about me because I'm outspoken. I see it as this is a big world and if I knock on enough doors I'll find someone who will like me and listen to me. It is our responsibility to recognize the presence of Evil and lay the Demon out. There are times when I ask myself why, oh why, am I the seed born to see sh★t happening and step in as a rescuer?

I ask myself why I just can't be like other people who are ignorant or oblivious to what's happening around them? It's because stupid people without realizing it are already doing Satan's work. As a child I was baptized Methodist. As a child I traveled on Sundays to multiple church services throughout the town. My mother would pick me up at the last church service I attended. When I married (age 16) I was baptized again into the Catholic faith. My parents were Methodist and turned Catholic after I did.

My dad read the Bible every morning while my mother made his breakfast before reading the Philadelphia Inquirer with his coffee. When I became the personal business manager of the rich and famous along with some NFL players, I became more aware of the mind set of how people personally feel about religion, God and Satan. I spoke to my mother about the different beliefs my clients had and asked her what she thought. Her teachings were to move with time like the Bible.

Throw out your saddle shoes and step into clogs. Never forget how to walk like a lady in heels and wear them when the proper occasion arises. When your burdens are too heavy, lay them at the foot of the cross and let God help do some of the work by bringin' you to your senses in thoughts of how to handle the issue yourself. My mother made me laugh when she ended with; best believe he's got a junk yard full of sh★t to handle of his own. God gave us the power to control our own life. I think back to the song in 86 by Beastie Boys "(You Gotta) Fight for Your Right." After visiting the big rock with the cross on my estate I'd hop in my car, put a tape in the radio and sing the song knowing my mother was right; fight for your rights, I got this.

Beneath the Hype Satan the Devil

I've dealt with some of the roughest things imaginable and how I got through is a wonder to me. Step into never land wit me. A person entered my life years ago who was as close to Satan as one could imagine on earth. It's the one person that brought out what my parents installed in me as a child, stand your ground against the Rebel Angel that lives in an invisible realm among angels. I met the person along with their parents and their extended family at prayer meetings! Ask yourself where would Satan want to hang out? Among believers!

Beneath the Hype Attempts of Murder

Do you believe in the Devil? I can say I've dealt with Satan the Devil on earth. Satan goes to the max to get gratification seeing you hurt. Some people believe the Devil is a red guy with horns. Satan is a Rebel Angel that lives in an invisible realm moving around where angels reside. To understand Satan, you should know he's the prince of darkness, a deceiver and a thief, a murderer and a liar all in one. Satan isn't mental, he wants what he wants and it's not because he's been hurt by anyone; he's truly Evil.

It's not just you he hurts; it's anyone in his path stopping him from getting what he wants. Satan is different than those who have done bad things to get to the top. Satan is different than those who let their temper get the best of them and do acts of violence and stupid thing. Satan isn't like a person who's been hurt or is a victim.

Satan deals in trickery which is very hard to recognize, until he's kickin' you're a★★. It is written in the Gospel (James 4:7) that when you oppose the Devil, he will flee from you. Really? I wish I could explain in words the strength it took me to get through multiple attempts of murder on my family and myself by someone who is truly Evil.

Satan uses all kinds of excuses why they acted in such a manner of Evil acts upon you. Satan exhibits remorseful tears to trick you into believing they just lost it and it won't happen again. In the beginning this person started with an attempt to kill by way of knifing one of my family members. My family member grabbed the children and fled to my house. The children were distraught.

The person whispered in the ear of the family member "if you press charges and I get sentenced to jail, when I get out I'll make sure to take your children which you love." The family member told his lawyer to back off. Satan saw it as weak. Satan loves challenges. If you understand how Satan works then you would know Satan's gonna try and do a better job the next time.

This evil person changed the beneficiary of the family member's death policy prior to putting poisonous drugs in my family member's coffee. That failed because the family member pulled over the work truck they were driving realizing they been drugged and needed a doctor. The drugs which were used were found at the residence and were kept by the attending hospital doctor (I'll call Kr).

For years the attending doctor Kr kept the bottle wanting me to pursue the case against the prescribing doctor for my family member whose name appeared on the bottle. The family member had never been to the doctor who wrote the prescription. Imagine the Person going to such great lengths to kill someone. Kr traced the prescription back to the Person trying to kill my family member. Unbeknown to the Person, I discovered multiple books studying what herbs can do if mixed with certain foods or different types of medication. One of the books contained the name of this person's daughter who was 2 and how much to give her to poison her naturally. The devil at times duct taped the kids locked in bedroom.

Kr was a Christen man and very prominent in the community. Kr was willing to testify on our behalf. Unbeknown to me the Person figured a new way to hurt my family by hurting me. The Person tried something out of their league by ordering a poisonous snake and placing the snake in my home without my knowledge to kill me. It nearly bit the grandkids when the snake came out from under the washer where the grandkids were putting on their shoes. I killed it myself. What the Hell, I've killed a few rattlesnakes in my days when the family rattlesnake hunted.

I took the snake to the poison control center. They traced the snake back to the person trying to kill me and the store it was bought at. Satan was getting desperate and figured at this point any family member was good. In order to hurt my family, this person figured killing children was easier. This person threw one of the young children out of a moving vehicle in the hopes of running over the child, saying the child opened the door. The temperature that day was 30 degrees. The young child ran away into the forest in freezing cold weather without a coat. An attempt to find the child quickly by this person was in progress.

The child came upon a house and was screaming at the door for help. The child was frozen, bruised, and terrified. A man (I'll call him RW), opened the door and tried to comfort the child while calling the police. The person was desperately in pursuit of the child to finish the job. The person arrived at the door of the man who took control over the situation. He said, "I'm not giving you back the child. The police are on their way." The child became hysterical and screaming he wanted his daddy (other parent).

The police took the child to the hospital where the child was interrogated by the police. In the accident ward you could hear the child crying for his daddy. The child, all of five years old, told the police what happened. The child went home with the father. The judge gave the child to the father and deemed psychiatric help was needed for the person. The above attempts of murder are just a few of the terrifying things my family has lived through. How does one explain what it's like to see your children and grandchildren suffer for no reason because a person chooses to do evil acts?

To this very day this person tries to use excuses for their actions instead of taking responsibility for their actions. Trust me, defeating Satan is an undertaking when a judge doesn't know the difference between mental and evil. This person is still walkin' around like, oh let it go, that's the past. I wish I could explain the feeling when a judge recommends psychiatric care for someone you know damn well isn't mental but is EVIL.

Ten years later the person looked me in the face and said, "I played all of you, including the judge and I even confessed to the psychiatric doctor on the last visit that I played him." The Devil leaned in and whispered ever so softly in my ear, "you're one up on me, you were right. I'm not mental, I'm evil." There are still times when this Devil comes in and out my life and my family.

In reading throughout my book about how I was raised with tough love you may have thought my parents were mean. But I ask you to try standing up to Satan performing evil acts if you weren't raised to be tough with balls. I forced the removal of Satan in court from where my family resides. The person knows they've been exposed to everyone within my network and family and defeated. The person knows they must clean up their act or the sole of their shoe will burn them once again.

Occasionally, the Devil runs through wild weeds and cleans up their act upon finding a Violet and for a moment hears the A·ve Ma·ri·a. The Devil still zaps with nettles and stings leaving a thorn now and then.

Beneath the Hype Church and House out of Order

Do you remember the story of the women in the shoe who had too many children? Over time the story became more clear and real to me. I went on retreat with two families who were best friends who had so many children they lost all control. They appeared kind, thoughtful, and were Christians. If you knew them you'd have a hard time finding a fault. If you looked a little deeper you'd find that the children were left home alone without adult super vision. Most of the time the parents were worshipping God or on retreat. As one would expect their house was out of order. The children ended up doing acts of incest, rape after rape of their sisters and brothers and rape of the other family's sisters and brothers. What a party with 35 children who had nothing to do, no TV, no toys, no games.

When the parents learned of such actions, like most parents they had to get a grip on the situation. The two sets of parents who were best friends handled it by asking the Priest what they should do. I always wondered why people ask their minister about things when he doesn't have a clue. The only way any of us know about subjects is if we've experienced it ourselves. For the life of me it's useless to ask people for advice who never wore the shoe. The Priest told the parents to put the multiple rapes of their children in God's hands.

Although I had my own thoughts and was suspicions from dribs and drabs I heard from their children, uncertainties kept me tuned into my own yard. I can't imagine having that many children between two couples to handle without being a hard a**. Both sets of parents are completely out of touch with reality of where we are in today's time. I knew how much I enjoyed retreat with the two mothers and their mothers as well as my mother.

At times I ask myself what the hell was I thinking back then? I was like many people wrapped up in religion and letting it control my life. Years later I was working on a film production and called a NY news network to use one of their cameramen. When the cameraman walked through my door I learned he grew up in my area and that it brought back sad memories.

I explained I was a lay minister under Pope John for my church for years. I told him I have prayed with hundreds of people at Kingdom Bound Ministries. I said, "Talking about your feelings many times helps. Nothing could be so bad that we as people can't work through and over time somehow we heal."

He began his story which became a blessing to me to confirm long ago my belief about two families. He spoke about how his grandparents and their friends knew their children were being molested and raped. He spoke about his mother being abused by her siblings as a child by the two families which ended up causing his mother's death at a young age.

He spoke about growing up without a mother and how he had to love his grandparents and learn forgiveness because religion was their guide. The Bible is a good book but out of touch with the world in which we live. Men over 100 years old could very well been senile. He didn't need to say much more before I named the same families I went on retreat with who did nothing to help their children but pray.

I assured him that over the years both families have walked through the wild weeds and stubbled onto a violet. They have heard the A·ve Ma·ri·a and have changed.

Beneath the Hype Dealing with Satan

The Devil understands when someone is on top of what they're doing while in their presence. The Devil doesn't think in terms of sorry for the things they've done, rather in terms of great work. Many times, Satan has offspring. One would think Satan's seed would be like them. The good news is we're all born with equal goodness and badness alike which will follow us all our life.

We also have the ability to make choices with our free will as to the path we choose or perhaps let one side govern over the other side. When speaking Satan always chooses choice words to say to its seed so that it can stay intact with its seed. Words like I'm sorry and you need to let it go. Satan uses choice words to lay blame on others or their actions are do the way they were raised. I got news for you: once you're an adult excuses don't work.

We all have free will to make good and bad choices. Satan wants to continue being among us and close to its seed. If evil done by Satan is exposed to its seed it makes Satan uncomfortable. Satan questions which side its seed is on. Satan knows the seed is not trustworthy once Satan is exposed. It is our job to not let the Devil exist within us and ditch em.

The Bible is a good book but out of touch with the world in which we live. The men were over 100 years old who wrote the good book and could very well have been senile. The Devil uses other forms of evil through other demons he defeated who are not living in goodness. The Devil sees a person with wisdom as a "Magnificent Creation", an "Angel Spirit" living within someone who keeps it real and stands their ground to go after.

Beneath the Hype the man RW

You know how much I talk about being 50% good and 50% bad and how one sin isn't any different than another man's sin. Sin has no weight. A sin is a sin. The man who took in the boy screaming at his door when his mommy threw him out of the car actually saved the boy's life. He was a true hero and savior that day. He stood up to Evil by not giving the child back to his mother. He chose not to let a child be hurt by calling the police when the mother arrived at his door crying and trying her hardest to explain the child fell out of the car.

RW was smart enough and brave enough to stand up against evil and know the difference by seeing the child did not have the proper clothing on at 30-degree day. He picked up on the mother wearing a coat and boots. He saw the fear and heard the cries of the child who was scared of his mother who threw him from the car.

Unbeknown to me this man had a sin. While I was a lay minister a man kept coming to the alter for prayers who was molesting his daughter. After weeks of prayers that didn't seem to have any effect on him, I turned him into the police. I couldn't even find peace and love in a church.

Each parishioner had major issues. They came for prayers weekly. I heard the same sin over and over. What good is it if they don't take-action? They feel justified telling someone. No! Stop doing fu*ked up sh*t. Unbeknown to either of us RW was the same man who years prior saved the boy. The man who was the boy's savior killed himself to stop himself from doing evil acts to a child, his daughter. A man with compassion and the love for another.

You can't imagine what it was like to go to the foot of my cross on the big rock on my estate and question when I learned he was the man who saved a life of a child while destroying a life of a child.

Beneath the Hype Accidents

How many people can say they've been in an elevator accident? It was located in my lawyer's work space. Upon entering the building, he heard screaming and realized someone was stuck between floors. To his surprise it was me. The owner was told the elevator couldn't pass inspection however, it was still operating. To the hospital I went with some major injuries. A damaged 5th cranial nerve along with a torn rotator cuff and a torn cartilage in each knee. How many people can say they've been in a hotel bathroom when some maniac came in and kicked the door open with the words "come out now?" I landed on the floor with the flush arm that sticks out from the side through my back. To the hospital I went for back surgery.

How many people can say they've been partial paralyzed on one side of their face from Bell's Palsy? Me. What hurt was when my kids ask their daddy to get a new mommy because their mommy was ugly. I ran up stairs and looked in the mirror and threw my hair bush into the mirror. It broke in a million cracks. My husband Tom said, "You know they don't understand that you can't buy a mommy or trade her in." Of course, I understood. But it hurt like hell. I went into the bathroom and looked into the mirror and said, "I've got this." I stayed in the house for eighteen months. When I ate food it just rolled out my mouth and I slobbered. I had no control or feeling in half of my face. My face drooped and my one eye wouldn't close. It was true, I looked awful. I lived on basically liquid. My in-laws lived next door and didn't question Tom where I been hiding. Holiday's they assumed I was at my parents. That part was true.

My mother and my God Mother Ann basically took care of my needs like bring me groceries. Eight months later my face was back in place. I was thankful beyond words that I could once again look in the mirror. I chose to do something good for someone. I anonymously paid for a prescription at the local drug store for a person who had no medical. The pharmacist kept the secret. How many people can say they were yanked hard by the arm by a plane steward who wanted me to move more quickly? That wasn't very smart. As I pulled away from him and his hand slid over mine it pulled my diamond ring off. It fell between the jetway onto the tarp below. The airline was notified but continued boarding and I was screwed out of my ring. In the lawsuit it stated I couldn't tell anyone about the airlines' settlement or the name of the airline. In all three legal suits named in the book, the companies wanted their names withheld. We really know little about the corporations we deal with.

Beneath the Hype NYC Homeless

Homeless can be found nearly everywhere. In New York city a favorite spot was the Port Authority. I had to travel daily from the apartment in Queens to my office on 38th and Broadway through the Port Authority. You see the same faces on the block begging. In San Francisco the homeless wrap around you 5 or more at a time. Manhattan, Midtown and Time Square were considered a drug-infested area in the nineties. At one point in my life I was living in the Port Authority with a round trip bus ticket. Disney decided to buy space at Time Square. This meant the city needed to be cleaned up.

One night at 3:00AM I left my office headed for the Port Authority. As shocking as it sounds I saw stake body trucks along 8th Avenue and 42nd wrapped around the Port Authority grabbing homeless throwing them in the trucks on top of each other. The homeless were yelling and screaming asking what's going on? You could hear them saying you're hurting me. I couldn't believe my eyes. It made me sick to my stomach. I questioned a man, "What is happening? Why are you doing this to these homeless people?" He said, "We're cleaning up the city. No one's supposed to know. We're being paid to haul the homeless out of the city and drop them off on the outer edges of the borders." I said, "Are you kidding me?"

The man continues talking aloud as he's pickin' up homeless people. I'm listening to him and walking alongside him. "Do you think anybody gonna admit what's happening or who hired us? I'm just doing my job, lady." They say that part of the city is looked upon as slum with homeless laying around the street eating out of trash cans and taking leaks in the alleys.

I was yelling at the man saying, "Some of these people have been here for years. Their parents abandoned them when they were 10 and 12 years old." I pleaded to stop throwing people around like they're not even human. Two men shoved me and said, "Get away before you end up in the truck." I felt so helpless.

I watched the morning news and newspapers with no mention of the city being cleaned up. Talk about a hushed-up deal and who really knows who ordered the clean-up.

Beneath the Hype Dealing with Murder

One night leaving the studio at 3:00AM on the 14th floor headed down the stairway I hear a man yelling" you fu★kin' bitch." I'm with a 15-year-old artist. I know I'm the only one in the building and as I looked over the rail he sees us. I can't take the chance the guy would run up 7 stairs to us and punch in security settings and unlock the door and be on us.

I knew at that moment I needed to get past him. Deciding how to handle a killer in action on the spot isn't easy seeing a man repeatedly stabbing a women who appeared dead in a stairway. You know you are gonna be next. Not to mention the life of the young girl with me. I whispered to her I'll handle this and to follow my lead. This is life or death with one chance.

I begin repeating to myself I got this. As I head down the stairway and climb pass him I say, "Yo bro I couldn't have done better myself." He addresses me by saying, "Bitches I hate em. You a fu★k bitch?" I say, "Fu★k no. This white bitch crazy. This is your deal. I'm out of here." Once we were out the building the young girl begins hyperventilating. I pull her shirt over her head and say breathe slowly. Concentrate on the soul and the shoe tellin' you we're good.

Beneath the Hype Respect Others

Throughout my life I've realized that I'm different. I realize that I'm extraordinary. The one and only me. I am who I am, and I can't change that. People don't give me respect for having knowledge in the field where I have no degree. People set aside that I have qualities such as gut instinct, good judgement, along with intuition. People who have never walked in my shoe, or been there or done that, all these things play a part of who I am.

I believe it's because people feel intimidated by me without realizing they are. The one thing my lawyer always said about me was, "That I'm the most persistent person he's ever met. That I never give up. Being educated doesn't give a person an inch of common sense."

He repeated many times how my judgment and common sense was top notch and exceeded most. I'd answered back by saying, "It was living in the street with common folks and livin' the homeless life and raising myself up to sit at the table with Elite folks that taught me how Street Sense Makes Sense. It's where you see good folks and bad folks and criminals, trotting the street together. Multiple shoes passing each other daily regardless of who they are, where they came from, or who they've become."

A ransom kidnapping of a baby was found after a wish was made on Kansas City Pig

Beneath the Hype Kidnapping

A ransomed kidnapped baby was found after a wish was made on Kansas City Pig. Can you imagine what it's like to have your grandchild kidnapped for ransom? You're in such a state of shock that someone would hurt a child let alone for the love of money. The police told us the chances of seeing the child again are slim even if they call you for more money. If you pay the ransom more than likely you won't get the child. It makes you so helpless that you want to die yourself. All the police had to go on was a footprint along with a birth certificate and a court order for the child to be returned to my son.

Of course, the kidnapers emptied my son's check book of thousands of dollars right out the bank's drive through window. No questions were asked by the teller and the bank took no responsibility of the name being forged. Ask me what it's like to have your son (the father) of the kidnapped child want to die. My son was scheduled for an archery shoot championship in Kansas City the following week. I convinced my son that he and I should go to take his mind off the pain he was in. I assured him the police would notify us the moment they knew anything.

While my son was shooting in the tournament I heard about a statue of a pig where you rub the pig and make a wish. I can't explain the powerful feeling that came over me believing this pig could help me get back my grandchild with a wish. I rubbed his belly as I made the wish. One might think it's a religious incident and one may never really know the power in a prayer.

The moment we landed back home the kidnapers (who were all related to each other) called for more ransom money. We flew to South Carolina and unbeknown to the kidnappers the police setup the release. The baby needed hospital care. The good news is once again together we as family survived. Kidnappers fled the scene as the police surrounded the place.

Beneath the Hype Raising Someone's Seed

Sometimes in life you take on other people's (children) seeds. Especially when your children marry someone who has children prior to the marriage. Taking on a child and placing the child under your wing and becoming their grandmother is part of my story. My life consists of my children, their children, then other people's children and then my great grandchildren. For three generations we as a family have been raising other people's children along with ours seeds. We argue and scream like every normal family. That's when it's time to run for the Rosemary. Put some in a bowl and pass it around for everyone to take a smell to open their senses. Somehow it works.

All the children call me Baka. Do you have to be blood to be a grandmother? Hell no... I became a grandmother to three boys, Paul, Jeffrey and Dustin who came to us as children and grew to be grown men. Men who graduated and went to college. The two mothers never left their son's side. They were there during the good times and the bad to raise their sons and share their sons with us. Sometimes in life men forget they planted a seed and walk from their responsibility. Lots of men disappear till their seed is grown. Sometimes they reappear offering a fabulous story why they've been missing along with child support. They have some

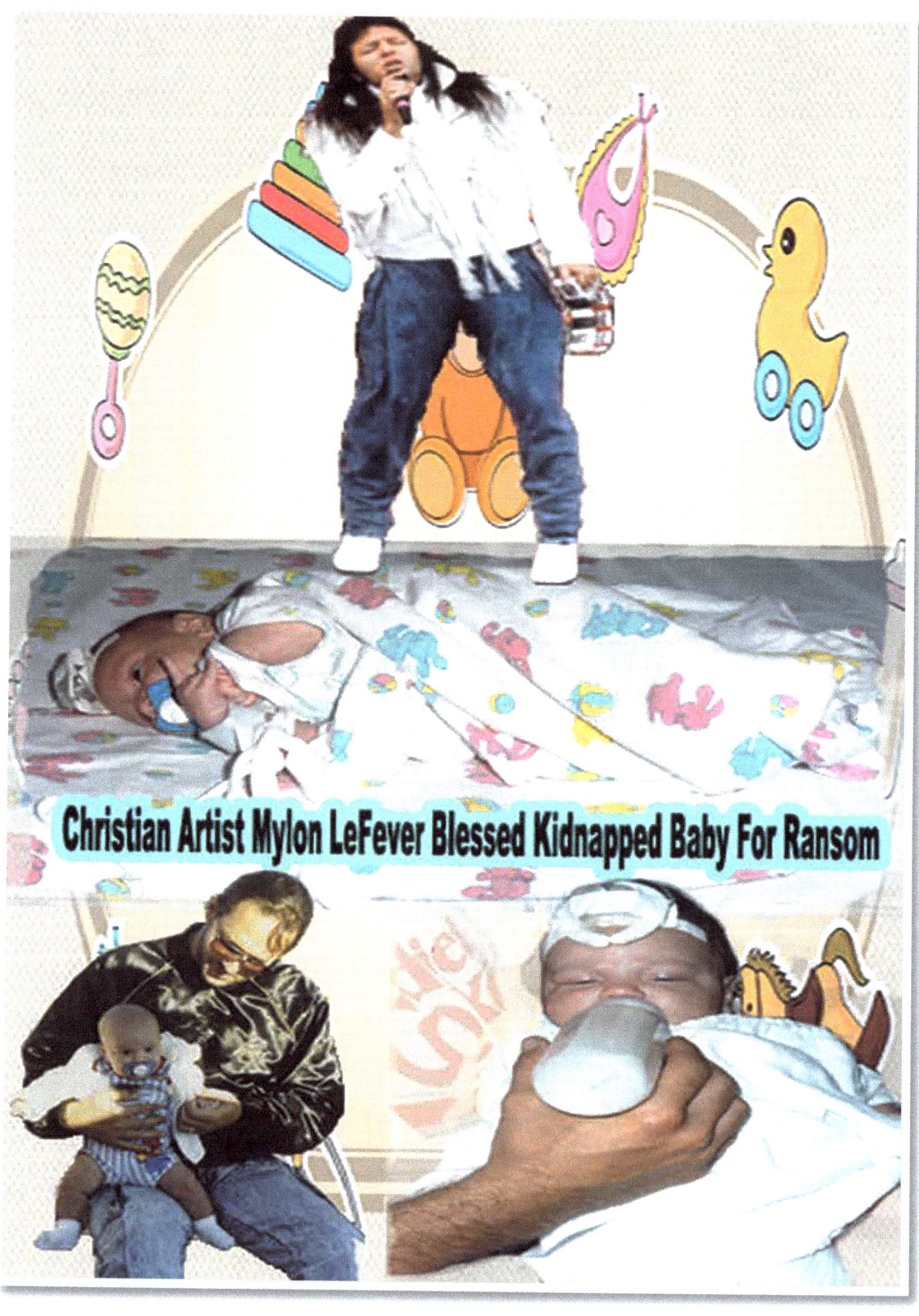

Christian Artist Mylon LeFever Blessed Kidnapped Baby For Ransom

fabricated stories why they weren't a part of their child's life and of course most will say it wasn't their fault.

Mylon LaFevre was a Christian artist who was hot in the marketplace the year our grandchild was born and was named after Mylon. We were heavy into Christianity and went to Christian concerts. Our vacation every year was spending a week at Kingdom Bound at Darien Lake Theme Park/Six Flags. We as family took our children and other people's children who were a part of our life with us. One year we took our godchild Holly and the neighbor's son Paul with us and they ended up marrying.

We should realize parents aren't perfect because parenting is a learning process. With that said, if I knew then what I know now about raising a child I probably would have put on a chastity belt. Parenting isn't an easy job. Most kids know everything from 7th grade till their senior year. Just about the time they need a car, money for college, you name it. They'll more than likely not give you the time of day. In some ways our family is different than most.

Our children were taught life isn't handed to you. Work and learning to handle damn near any job that arises. They were taught to understand that family shares the ups and downs in life equally. That doesn't mean you won't have a jacka** among you who will never get the rodeo right.

Once you have a child it's time to step in and wear the shoe well without excuses. No child asks to be in this world. As you well know if a woman opens her legs and a man enters the action, he has the ability to plant a seed. I've raised many of half-grown adults from the street from coast to coast whose fathers and sometimes even mothers kicked them to the curb.

I didn't raise seeds that were Saints. I raise human beings who like all of us have flaws and at times have made mistakes. Each child who entered my life had their own traits. Many were left to the dogs to survive. Many of the parents came back after they were fully grown and offered excuses. Do you know how we feels when we raise a child who is a grown adult and a parent knocks at the door? I'm back... Sure with your excuses. We must forgive someone who says their sorry but that doesn't mean you take them back into your life.

My father would say, "When someone has hurt you and says their sorry you must forgive them. That doesn't mean you can trust them. They are smart enough not to do the same action again. However, when it is a seed the rule changes. Blood is stronger than actions." It's a work in progress to keep you on your toes. Who else could do that other than a jacka** kickin' you're a** to keep you sharp? Angels are supposed to be in heaven not earth. Since we're Eagle fans we know sooner or later we can Fly and get it right.

To the best of my knowledge and belief all statements made by me in this book are true, but you be the judge.

Beneath the Hype Nursing Home Abuse

My parents were married for 64 years and they were always portrayed as a couple in love. My mother became ill and cancer took her life. When she died my dad had a hard time handling the loss of his wife. My dad went to my mother's grave every day and took her a cheese or peanut butter sandwich and fed the birds who watched over her. He took an outfit every day of what he thought she might have worn that day.

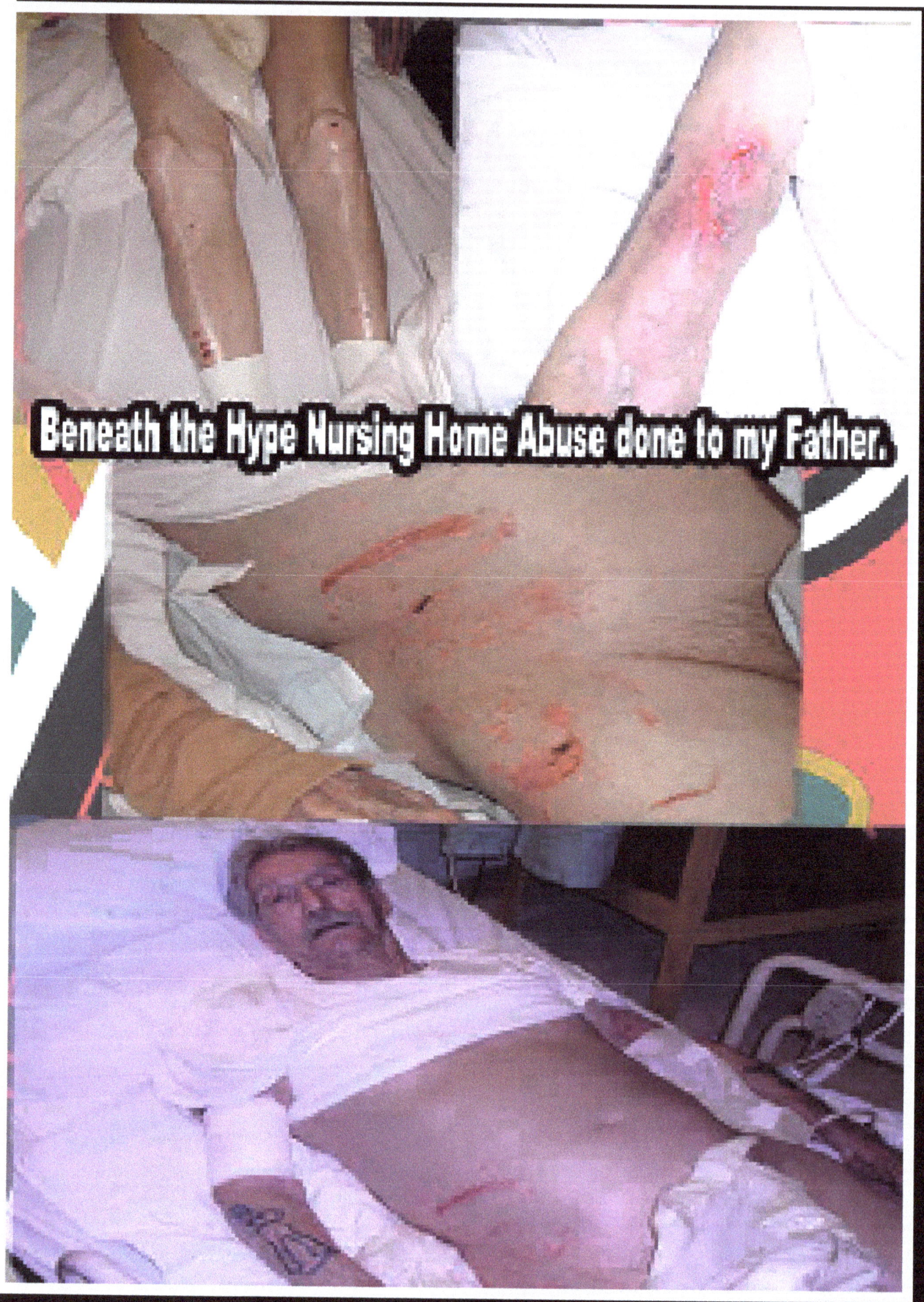

84

He washed her clothing with his at the end of the week. He laid her pajamas on the bed and slept with the vision of her next to him. As strange as it may seem, it harmed no one. My dad wanted to care for his wife's grave, her clothing, and her home till the Lord called him home to fly with Eagles wings with her. I traveled constantly working with a heavy load of clients driving 3 hours so I could go out of Philly airport and visit my dad. I'd keep in touch with my dad by phone while I was on tour with clients.

When I couldn't get him, I thought he must be at the cemetery or chillin' with his buddies in the apartment complex. Unbeknownst to me my dad's car was taken away so that he'd stop his behavior visiting my mother. I haven't the foggiest what the person was thinking by taking the car. This meant he couldn't get to the store to buy food. Eventually he ran out of food. My dad had pride and wouldn't call me, and he wasn't gonna say a word to outsiders that he was hungry.

His buddies saw he was getting frailer by the day. His ♡ was beyond broken from losing the love of his life, my mother. His buddies became concerned because they hadn't seen him in days, and he didn't answer the door. Eventually his buddies realized something was wrong and got the manager to check on him. The manager went in with a key.

When I couldn't reach my dad by phone, I called the manager at the apartment complex. I was told that my dad was found unresponsive and was taken away in an ambulance. When I arrived, I spoke with one of dad's buddies at the complex who said, "Your father was taken out in an ambulance. I know to be a fact your father had not one bit of food in the apartment".

"We believe he was starved almost to death. The apartment has been cleaned completely out by your family member. We don't know where he is." Dad's buddies wanted me to take-action on the person(s) who they believed did this to my dad and put them in jail. I called every hospital in the area until finally one of them said he was released to a nursing home, but they had no idea which nursing home. I began calling nursing homes in the area till I found my dad.

When I walked in his room his first words were, "What took you so long?" I said, "Daddy I had no idea. I kept calling but the phone just kept ringing." The registry showed he was brought in and had no visitors. I leaned over to hug my dad and he said, "Ouch that hurts, please don't touch me I hurt all over.

I've been beaten by one of the aides who learned I worked with the police department." I pulled the sheet down and before my eyes saw my dad with lacerations, wounds and gauze on his arm from a cut that was grown into his meat but never changed. This was a cover-up with nothing documented on his file at the desk. I closed the door and went to the office and told them that no one was to go in my dad's room.

I bought a camera with two extra batteries. I returned with my father's favorite food McDonald's. He was overjoyed. For the next 24 hours I stayed in that hospital and I took pictures of what was happening to other patients. I documented all my dad's wounds and stayed with him till I could get him relocated.

I couldn't understand how the person closest to my dad could hurt him by letting him starve and taking away his car and not letting him morn the love of his life, my mother, his

THE WELL BEING OF THE LAST DAYS OF A LIVING SOUL SHOULD BE PRIORITY ... MY FAMILY COMFORTED THE LAST FIVE YEARS OF MY FATHER'S LIFE.

Poppie's Last Toast at 90

86

way. After a while I had enough evidence on the nursing home and searched other documented reports of things that weren't quite right.

I took things into my own hands. It appeared the owner talked his way out of sh*t when discovered. I called the state of Pennsylvania to handle my complaint.

What I want you to understand is in this country there are cover-ups, doctored paperwork, so the public doesn't realize the devastation of what really happens in nursing homes.

A lot of people placed in a nursing home will be diagnosed as senile by the attending doctor. The doctor checks what nurses may have noticed about a patient instead of actually visiting the patient. The doctor knows damn well if he claims them senile, he won't get wrapped up in any wrong doing by billing as if he actually visited the patients. I suppose there's a few doctors with compassion verses their wallets.

The last days of a living soul should be treated with kindness. I discovered all kinds of fu*ked up sh*t covered up by writing the report differently than it really is. Paperwork is modified on the reports with warnings rather than shutting it down. The well-being of the elderly should be priority. My next step was to call the editor of the newspaper and give her the pictures that I took and own by copyright law.

The pictures were of my dad being abused by the facility giving the newspaper legal rights to the story. The editor said, "The love ones of the people in the nursing home would be devastated if they saw what was done to your father." I said, "Who wouldn't be devastated however, the records show that more than half of these elderly people haven't had a visitor. Only the short-term people who are there for physical therapy come and go."

I explained to the editor as well as the state the facts. Patient's feet have no slippers, no shoes, no socks and are blue from dangling with no foot rails on the wheelchairs on concrete floors. I took pictures to prove my statements as facts. The patients get a diaper change in the morning and one before bed and sit in sh*t all day. The records showed this nursing home has had thefts, a rape, and other undisclosed charges long before my dad was admitted and was still in operation. Give me a f*ckin' break.

The editor told me she couldn't print my article because it would upset the readers. The state acted and shut it down after I filed my claim. The state reported it was being closed for undisclosed violations. The newspaper printed the nursing home was being closed and patients would be moved into other nursing homes.

Within 24 hours I removed my dad by myself to my house until I could find a decent nursing home to put him. I visited my dad 3 days a week and if I had to travel or be away my daughter or granddaughter would visit him verses me. We'd push him in his wheel chair a half mile each way to his favorite place McDonald's.

My cousin Bobby visited my dad and took him to McDonald's. My dad began to cry saying, "Bobby I cry because I can't believe I was taken away from the love of my life by the child (my son) I favored. I'm gonna die not knowing why." The last days of my dad's life I danced around his wheelchair holding his hand with a picture of my mother in my other hand while at the nursing home. He was all smiles as he and I twirled around and threw me a kiss. I played the song "Dance with my Father Again" by Luther Vandross. My father always made my mother number one and when she died he realized that I was an echo reflection of her elegance. Dancing is a family thing we all enjoy. My son and daughter entered dance competitions. They won multiple competitions and had TV networks airing their performances. When I see my children dancing I think back to that incredible dance with their father that ruffled my crinoline that cost me my dream for myself.

My dad died of a broken ♡. My dad couldn't rap his head around why he was treated the way he was. For five years my dad waited by the phone hoping on Father Day or his birthday he'd get a call from his son. But it never happened.

No matter how much we try to comfort him; he was unfixable. His ♡ was torn to pieces missing my mother, bleeding from not being able to visit her grave and feed the birds that surrounded her. He couldn't rap his head around what was done to him to end his life. On holidays I took my dad to my house to enjoy the celebration. Pictures don't lie what this sailor endured for the sake of love and being beaten by an employee who learned he worked alongside the police department. I realized it happened for a reason.

My dad's beating finally saved the lives of all the other patients that were in agony from not getting the proper care. People much like my dad who were dropped off to rot and be forgotten. We both felt good knowing the people in the nursing home were finally rescued. My dad spoke about how his son considers all of us dead. Funny those exact choice words came out years later by my brother in testimony in a court of law that all my family were dead to him. My father favored my brother because they had things in common like hunting. In the end my father realized I was the child who loved without conditions. He learned I was the seed who loved unconditionally.

He thought of me as dynamite; a person who doesn't tolerate bullsh*t and gets the rodeo right. My father was proud of me steppin' to the plate to save the other people who were placed in hell to die. I spoke to the state representative and asked why wasn't something done with all this documentation prior to my father and why the facility wasn't closed before this? The representative had no answer. I made sure this time the state would shut it down and put the owner of the facility out of business. I knew whatever cock and bullsh*t story the state or newspaper wanted to expose I could live with. Before my dad died he whispered in my ear and said, "Your mother called you an "Extraordinary Person" and she was right."

Beneath the Hype Rednecks

Don't get insulted if you're reading this particular article in my book and you're a Redneck; you are not standing in my shoe. I'm sure there are people who call themselves Rednecks that are super human beings. A guy I knew had a habit of wearing boots to everything including weddings and the like. His explanation was they are clean and didn't see anything wrong with them. My answer was I see plenty wrong with boots and a suit at a dress up affair. I'm a city girl who's been living in a forest 40 years and been to plenty of campfires and learned about out life behind the barn. I've met plenty of people who think of themselves as country folks or Rednecks. In a Google search, it describes Rednecks as people who often drive 4X4 trucks, ride four-wheelers and enjoy doing wheelies. Hell, my family does that, and we aren't Rednecks. Rednecks talk about booze and party time. Hell, lots of people talk about that. I learned Rednecks have different chants. Some create their own lyrical tunes adding in their like and dislikes.

YouTube videos show Redneck women don't mind being called broads, dress like cowgirls and favor country music. Hell, I grew up on Charlie Daniels, Hank Williams, Johnny Denver, and Glenn Campbell who I doubt were Rednecks. There's plenty of people who wear boots and jeans including me and don't call themselves Rednecks. However, they know to wear shoes to funerals and weddings. Sit down and enjoy the spiel. I'm giving it to you straight up. I got invited to an event along with my bodyguard. After four hours the DJ asked to clear the dance floor for the ritual chant the host and friend do at campfires and winters in their cabin. An hour before the announcement I noticed some of the people replaced their shoes with boots. It seemed weird that people actually put boots on with fancy dresses and tuxedos. I was in a state of shock when I heard the words, "Down with the Jews." I ran over to the only Jewish man I knew (my bodyguard) saying, "I am so so sorry. Till that moment I was clueless to what real Rednecks were about.

The symbol of this group of Rednecks was boots. The event forced me to study Rednecks. What I learned was there are people who call themselves Rednecks to be cool. A true Redneck has a cult personality along with a fixation and hatred of three things. True Rednecks hate the same three things and use them in the chant to remind themselves not to forget what they believe and hate. I call it programing the mind. Similar to church where you're programed to believe a certain way according to the religion you choose. The moral of the story is TV reality glorifies Rednecks for the love of money and display it as cool to be a Redneck. However, studies show the actors are only acting and their backgrounds usually are not what they portray.

Isn't that the meaning of trickery and practice of deception? I never dreamed people would actually go so far as to enjoy chanting and joking about people of color, people of different nationalities, people who are gay, or any social injustice, and portray their something they're not. It's just simply wrong. The word Redneck came from sunburn on the neck. They are generally poor white people who stomp their feet and are many times inbred bumpkins who are toting a gun. Rednecks didn't drive hopped up 4X4 trucks and 4 wheelers posting on Facebook mudslinging with their broad in order to feel cool.

Mic check mic check…
Listen up one time, yo…

I realize it's hard to overcome being programed as a child one way and then discover what was taught isn't genuine. A song with superb vocals, track and lyrics is "Take Me to Church" by Hozier. If you got guts watch the video and if you don't cry with compassion, you're sick. After speaking with the host of the event, I sensed his regret that it happened and a feeling of unspoken remorse. It made me realize there's many people livin' in the dark about true Rednecks. God Bless America Land That I love. It enlightened him enough to strolled through the wild weeds in search for truth. I'm hoping he sees a violet and hears the A·ve Ma·ri·a.

Flaws within the Church

I see flaws in every church I've been in throughout my life. I love the joy of singing the many hymns along with some of the sermons. What I dislike most is when a reverend, rabbi or pastor is still wet behind the ears and not living in reality with the rest of us. I can't deal with someone telling us how to live when they haven't walked in our shoes. Since I was a lay Minister I got to pray with people in jails. In the entertainment world I've dealt with criminals, gangs, and the like. Nothing has taught me more than the street. I've had the opportunity to work with people who have been in jails who were set up or framed. If you ask me if my circle of friends were pure, I would ask you how pure is your circle? If you think for one moment that your family and outer family and friends are pure, think again.

Thinking back to St. Joseph's Church in 1981 listening to a priest giving a sermon about Olivia Newton-John's song "Physical" which just hit the marketplace. I go to church to Worship the Lord. Many times, a priest, a rabbi, a reverend and the like, have their own beef about things and fit it into the sermons. Just such a case was this particular Sunday when the priest's homily was telling us that the song "Physical" was about sexual performances. He believed it could be a way to program us to be more physical with sex. He wanted the parishioners to avoid the song by turning it off. He believed a good parent would not let their child listen to such a sexual piece of work.

You can believe this or not, but my daughter was sitting next to me and we liked the song. We looked at each other in shock. The church came to complete silence. We could not believe his sermon. It was not what either of us went to church to hear. We went to praise the Lord. My daughter was pregnant and the child in her womb began to kick. My daughter put her hand on her tummy and was inspired to search out the song after mass. In checking the lyrics, and looking at the video, we learned that the lyrics meant make your body talk.

The song was about taking care of your body more or less. Exactly what the Lord would want you to do, take care of your temple. Not only was the priest off on the subject but he influenced a lot of Christian parents that this wonderful song was a sexual attraction to children to masturbate or worse. All the churches around my area needed correction long before I got there.

For the Love of Music My In-Laws Rock!

IN-LAWS

LIVIN' ON THE RIDGE YOU GOT TO BE TOUGH I AM WHO I AM. I MADE MYSELF STRONG MENTALLY AND PHYSICALLY

Don't Let Looks Fool Ya.
I Wipe Out Snakes And Kill Coyotes

I'm born with extraordinary insights into sh★t happening around me. Many times, when I see messed up sh★t I try to find a fix. You have no idea how it drives me crazy. I want to walk away, but somehow I keep looking back asking myself why others can't see when things are messed up. I've even went to the foot of the cross about bullsh★t. If you knew me through reading my book, you know I would set up meetings with the priests or sometimes with the diocese. From reading my book you should know by now that I laid that priest out about that homily. He did not apologize to the parishioners.

It's not like I haven't written to dioceses or threatened to sue them. They act upon it. They wait a while so that it doesn't look like I'm a winner in the game of corruption within their walls and discovered messed up sh★t in their organization. I see corruption in many religions. I can't stand when someone uses religion as a way to look like what they're saying is right. Don't preach and ask us to take care of our temple when you are 400lbs yourself. Don't blame it on a health issue when you're having coffee and donuts after the service. Clean your own yard before you step into ours. You're getting a good paycheck with medical and a car to drive with insurance from McDonald workers and the like in your pew.

To the best of my knowledge and belief all statements made by me in this book are true, but you be the judge.

Beneath the Hype Freedom of Speech

Don't bleed because I say something sharp that might cut you like a knife. Freedom of Speech at times seems sharp, firm or harsh, and can even make us feel uncomfortable. Freedom of Speech makes us more resilient, up-to-date, smart and aware versus saying nothing and doing nothing to protect yourself. Knowing what's going on around you is knowledge that you can use.

Beneath the Hype Stand Your Ground

One such story to explain how I should have stood my ground was when we went crabbing in a row boat. Tom was drinking beer and we were floating along without an anchor. I kept saying, "Honey I think we are drifting far because I can't see land. I can see waves ahead which I think is the ocean."

The children on the other hand kept singing row, row, row, your boat as they were rowing. I'm pissing my pants thinking we are going to die. I don't want to make the children think their father is drunk and an a★★hole.

He's singing "row, row, row, your boat" while the we were beating down the crabs we caught that were climbing out the baskets ready to eat us. Neither of us knew which way was north or south, east or west. Like all of my experiences with this man I made it seem like it was fun. What a lie.

By dark we found our way home and called a cab once we hit land to take us to where we originally started. It was 5 miles away from where the car was parked. My children thought it was a great adventure and were ready to do it again.

Stop livin' in equivalent to prison fallin' victim. When you break free you can Break Any Ribbon. I won some battles and I fought some wars. I'm a warrior without sores. I'm proof comin' from nothin' doesn't mean you can't be something.

The next fishing trip he thought we should crab off a dock. It would have been ok except he decided to stop along the Jersey Shore where it was desolate.. Really... We got our baskets and wandered through the weeds in swamp water and climbed onto the dock. It seemed OK cause we were catching crabs. All of a sudden a dead body came floating out from under the dock face down.

Our children were very young (4 and 6) and said that a man was swimming below the dock. The children had no idea the man was dead. My husband said, "Head for the car and drive to a pay phone so I can call the police and guide them in." I was ecstatic.

By time I got back with the police my husband had the dead man on the doc. He was a convict who had been missing for a while from a prison. The stories living with my husband are endless. My children looked up to him like he was their idol.

It took a lot for me to learn to stand on my feet and stand up to this man. I didn't really want to lose him because I knew that every man had a dick and issues. Just a different dick with different issues than the man I'm living with. I've been working through issues my entire life making this man look good. Philly grown took over and I learned to stand my ground.

You be the judge if I'm telling the truth or not. Sometimes things you think couldn't happen actually happen.

Beneath the Hype Famous Man with Multiple Names

A meeting was set up in New York City to meet with a famous man at his label. Instead he decided it wasn't worth taking. He told his buddy to take the meeting for him. I was sitting in his private office with his hired hand. His buddy let me know this was a no-show. I'm thinking what an a★★hole. I wanted to believe he changed his ways. I was played.

It cost me travel and a hotel. Really. It took me back to when Easy Mo Bee was workin' wit em. After his buddy left the room, I gestured to other hired hands to hush and moved about the office showing them hidden mics where he may be listening in from LA.

He's a savvy smart successful businessman who now has a show on TV. I decided I'd let him know, I'm from the Concrete Jungle Philly. People live and die in the jungle. Fu★k me once and perhaps I'll fu★k you back. This was one of those rare moments. Much like Donald Trump he also likes gold.

I asked the hired hand if I could use his private bathroom. They gestured me to go ahead. I spread my legs over his gold toilet seat and pissed on it. I'm sure when he comes back to New York the piss will have dried. But I believe he'll feel the heat. When he became successful, he left behind the dude who busted a★★ blowing him up and paid the dude pennies. Fake a★★ tears mean nothing to those who know him.

Over the years he's been in some bullsh★t stuff, you'd think by now he would have strolled through the wild weeds and found a violet and heard the A·ve Ma·ri·a.

A Night with the Stars at

President Donald Trump's Estate...

Beneath the Hype Donald Trump

An invite to Donald's house. Don't think for one minute I was enjoying "A Night with the Stars" event at Mar-a- Largo. I have to say Donald Trump's estate is the gaudiest place I've ever seen in my life. Gold everywhere, above the doorways, the arms of the chairs. The sofas are pure white material. Huge chandeliers everywhere. I was married to an architect who worked for the rich. Seeing Donald Trump's fireplace damn near gagged me.

When I entered, a doorman took my shawl. He said, "Just look for your name tag. They usually sit people who know each other close to each other." I wasn't sure I'd know anyone of this magnitude. I'm a peasant who does contracts for the stars.

I began looking for my name with no luck and returned to the doorman. I said, "Maybe hey sent the invitation by mistake. I didn't find my name." The door man freaks out saying, "We don't make mistakes madam…

That would never work for The Donald. It could cost me my job and if I get fired, I'd never get another job. I'll be right back with the guest list." He came back, and said, "What is your name?" I said, "Ms Peggy." Then he gestured me towards the front, and I would find my name. I was seated with hierarchies.

I wondered who do they think I am? I'm a peasant compared to them. The table was right next to the Stallone's table. Later in the evening I ended up at that table enjoying conversation with Frank Stallone. I learned so much that night listening to Frank about the entertainment world. Little did Frank know my son named his first born Rocky. A guest at the table asks my name. I laughed and said, "Adrian." They asked what I did for a living. My answer was nothing compared to the people at this table. They assumed I was joking.

When it was time to leave I went back to the doorman to get my shawl. As he's putting on my shawl he said, "Now little lady I know you are new so remember to put a tag on your dress that it has been to Donald's house. You don't want to disrespect The Donald by anyone wearing the same dress. There's been plenty of pictures taken tonight and I'm sure one is yours." I ask the doorman does that mean that Frank Stallone has to get a new suit every time he comes? The door man laughed and said, "Men can wear the same suit. They're men."

He leaned over and whispered in my ear, "Hushabye any words we spoke." I nodded I got you. I had a camera, and no one seemed to care about me takin' pictures. I have a picture of damn near every room. When I brought the outfit back in New York I walked into a high-end store and told the saleslady that I was coming to an event at Donald's house. It makes complete sense to me now why I needed an upper level dress in order to be excepted into Donald's world.

Most people don't understand beauty. Beauty is in the eyes of the beholder. What is beautiful to one person may not be beautiful to another person. I felt I was beautiful in my light blue two-piece outfit with a semi-flare short skirt because it mimicked my hourglass shape. A perfect waist line is what is considered most attractive on a woman. If you know me then you know I don't give a sh★t what people think of me. However, I don't disrespect a person's request that high-end attire was expected. I complied with the requirements expected of me. Donald is the last man I would of thought would be President.

Beneath the Hype If You Believe

I wanted to get a letter to Pope John Paul and lay his a★★ out. I didn't know how to go about makin' sure the Pope actually got my letter. I loved my church, but I feel it's time for an upgrade. Being a lay minister so many years and hearing open confessions forced me to at least try. I went to a couple dioceses and finally I found one that worked to get my letter on a lee low to the Vatican. I was told with a large sum of cash money on a lee low and the promise I'd never tell anyone; it would happen. I answered yes.

I used some of the money left by that anonymous person in my desk. Sure enough, a month later I was called to the diocese to pick up a package. For the life of me I had no idea why I was given a pair of rosaries and a blessing from Pope John Paul. I already had my own rosaries. For years I threw them in the bottom of whatever purse I was using.

On my way to my office I stopped to look in a new store front window. It had a picture of Michelle Obama and one of the Pope. As On the other side of the window a man gestured me to come in. I shook my head nope. I'm thinking I don't wear diamonds or gold on the streets of New York. I ship my sh★t to the event through FedEx or UPS and then back to a locker when I'm done. The dude unbolts the door and says he saw sunshine in the window. Unbeknown to him I happen to "Rock with the Sun." He said, "Please come in and look around I am bored." I think what the hell. He's showing me around and saying, "You see that picture of Pope John Paul in his coffin and the rosaries?" I said, "I've been carrying around rosaries from Pope John Paul years in the bottom of my purse. They are filthy."

He said, "May I clean them for you?" I said, "Yes" I proceed to pull them out of my purse. He threw them in a machine and as the machine was going around the dirt was falling off and as he looked into the machine I hear him going, "Oh, oh, oh, my!" I'm thinking they are breaking into pieces and I'll be carrying a baggie with them in the bottom of my purse.

He stopped the machine and grabs them with a rag and lays them on the counter and grabs a magnifying glass. Once again he started "Oh, oh, oh, my!" I said, What's wrong?" He says, "Do you realize what these are worth coming from the Vatican from Pope John Paul?" I shook my head no. I asked him to find a pawn shop, so I could call them to see if I could sell them.

Sure, enough the pawn shop fellow says, "If they are real, the value is around $15,000. I will give you $10,000. I say, "$10,000! I've been carrying $10,000 in my purse all these years when I don't even wear my wedding ring which is only made of gold and was a couple hundred dollars. Wow!!" I get the address and I'm headed there by way of the Port Authority. There was a homeless man frozen to the concrete in freezing weather in the middle of March. I stopped dead in my tracks.

I thought what I want in life is a record deal that I can't seem to get. What the hell is $10,000 going to do for me? Not a damn thing. I bend down and say to the homeless man, "Focus dude. once in a lifetime 'An Angel Made of Glass' passes by you. It means this is the moment. If you get up and come with me, I'll rent you a studio apartment for one year. I'm going to stop off at a pawn shop to grab the money and then we will get you situated." He could hardly walk so I flagged a cab and I headed for the pawn shop.

After the transaction, I'm sittin' in a cab with $10,000. cash. I asked the driver if he knew of any studio apartments for rent. The cab driver takes me to a building where he saw a for rent sign. I tell the landlord I'll give him $10,000 cash for one year for my friend to live there. He says, "It's a deal." He asks the homeless man his name. I heard the fellow saying my name…. my name? I say, "We'll be right back." I go outside. I say, "You don't know your name?" He nods his head no. I say, "This is what you got to do. Pick a name any damn name, and I'm assuming you don't know your social and pick 3 numbers say dash, then 2 numbers say dash, then 4 numbers. Got it?" He nods ok. We go back in.

The landlord says, "What's your name?" The fellow says, "John Blow. 123-45-6789." The landlord begins to yell and says, "What kind of mother names her kid John Blow and what kind of government gives a social with numbers in order?" I say, "Are you cutting down his mother and my government? I'm gonna get me a lawyer to deal wit you. However, if you're sorry, fill out the paperwork and take the cash and all is good." The homeless man lived happily for one year.

Beneath the Hype Priest Fell from Grace

I suppose there are good clergy, priests, and Rabbi's where you feel comfortable learning the bible scriptures. My children and I became lay ministers and my children did theatrical dance for church and priest jubilees. The church seemed like a perfect fit for our family and the priest gave homilies that were incredible. After mass the priest would go out with some of the parishioners for breakfast. He would say Peggy you can clean up and finish the blood of Christ and lock up. That meant drinking a quart or more of wine in about a half hour. On my way home, I realized I may be driving drunk. I thought this is the priest's duty to drink the blood of Christ.

The following week I said, "Father forget your breakfast with the parishioners. You finish the wine." Father says, "You're right, we'll take care of it after Mass together. I'll be able to continue going to breakfast." The following week after mass Father and I walked behind the altar carrying the blessed wine towards a bathroom. Father grabs the wine bottle and pours the wine down the toilet and flushes. He turns and says, "The blood of Christ is back to the Earth. Just rinse those glasses and we're out of here." A week later I went to the rectory unannounced. I wanted a chat with father about his actions with the blood of Christ.

The housekeeper says, "You can't disturb him. He's in his bedroom with a quest." I pushed pass her and headed down the hall. I heard noise coming from one of the bedrooms. The door was slightly open and as I looked in father was in bed with a college student. I open the door and said, "You're done!." I made sure he was excommunicated. A few months later front-page news was Father D was excommunicated. It felt good to know the church handled this business. This was a man who knew the Bible and actually feared the Lord. This was a man who helped many people find their way. This was a man I worked with for years on retreats, on mission, served under as a lay minister, and was a sinner.

To the best of my knowledge and belief all statements made by me in this book are true, but you be the judge.

Our children knew the "Toilet Paper Rule." They knew the difference between a good sh*t verses a bad sh*t. In the past good beats came from tappin' on the wood to keep mice away in outhouses. A hot DJ put his fingers to work and made a stellar beat...

Beneath the Hype the Fifth Amendment

When I was in 7th grade I was a whipper snapper. I asked my mother why daddy always says to Plead the Fifth when you see something messed up? My mother began by saying, "Hard talk child is when we sh*t we flush which gets rid of things that look bad like a cover up." I ask, "What happens when you potty in an outhouse?" My mother used a parable saying, "Sh*t is left in the hole as a carrier of meaning. If someone passes a big turd and looks into the hole, they think wow. That's a big turd. They walk out of the outhouse proud. When a person's sh*t comes out splattered landing on top big firm turds the person usually exits the outhouse feeling down as if something is wrong.

The outhouse was a good place to hideaway, listen to your favorite music and get out of doing chores. A persons' actions speak louder than words. Always be on your p's and q's to watch people's Karma. It's what will make you savvy, smart, and extraordinary. There's nothing better than wisdom and with it comes knowledge to know in life what is right and what is wrong. Flush toilets made us feel equal coming out of a bathroom. Flush toilets made it easier to get rid of undesirable sh*t. We're left to use our nose to determine what we think by the stink left behind. Much like the Fifth Amendment people are no longer caught in a trap."

Beneath the Hype Drug Money Kills

A dude hit me up about meeting on some good beats he created. He decided he'd rather tell me about his life back when he was in 6th grade. He said while waiting for the school bus a man walks up to him and says, "Sonny you see down the end of the block that black car parked with a fellow in it? I want you to take this paper bag to him and hand it to him without looking in it. He'll give you another paper bag and you bring it back to me. You got it? Hurry so you don't miss your bus." He says to the man, "Why would I do that?" The man says, "You love your mother, don't you?" He nodded yes. The man says, "If you don't do what I ask you when you get home from school I'll have killed your mother and have her brain on a plate for breakfast. If you mention this to anyone, I'll Kill you! Got it? Hurry boy!"

I look at this dude and asked him why he's tellin' me this shit? He says, "Cause I'm done Ms. Peggy. I'm a grown a** man and I been a drug dealer for the cartel since the bus stop. There's no way out, the drug dealers own you're a**. They'll kill your loved ones and family." The dude invites me into his van out front of the studio. There's a little boy asleep on the back seat around 3 or 4 years old. There's a paper bag between the seats. He pulls the paper bag onto the seat. He says, "See this drug money Ms. Peggy, it's about $200,000. more or less. I need to turn it into the drug cartel. See my boy in the back seat I'm offering you this money if you'll take my boy and raise him...

When they come for the money and I don't have it, they'll kill me. Trust me they'll get a new kid on the block to do my job. It's worth it to me because I don't want to have my son grow up in a fu**ed up world rather than a good one. My mother died, and they killed my sons' mother when I tried to get out. All I have is my son, please take him and the money." How in the hell do I walk away knowing shit exist like this? I'm between shit and a hard pan that I'm not willing to get into. I walked.

Eight years later I met a guy who knew the dude from the studio. I ask him if he knew how the dude was. The guy tells me that the dude was in a drug ring and wanted out. They found out he wanted out, so the cartel killed his son and then he killed himself. It set me back a few days. I couldn't stop thinking of every drug deal I heard of or seen; the end result I felt justified what I did. Fighting Evil with Evil acts gets you nowhere. Taking drug money and a child without proper paperwork is wrong.

Sometime in life things don't end up the way we wish they did. Standing firm in your shoe isn't easy. Wisdom in life keeps the soil beneath your shoe from burning you.

Beneath the Hype Gangs

It took guts to continue my work. Gangs know I don't say zip. I do what my father taught me as a kid, Plead the Fifth Amendment. My father would say, "Many good kids hang out in alleys and belong to gangs. As grown men they become known for their wars with other gangs. Does it matter what gang member you meet? No... They are individuals who belong to a group that has a title and roll from coast to coast. Usually they have their own initiation into each group. What does it matter to you what they have done or what they do? You can find hypocrites in church pews. You been raised with morals and to take care of your own yard not others. You've been taught to treat others the way they treat you. Do not judge a man unless you've walked in his shoes then maybe you'll know why he does what he does."

To the best of my knowledge and belief all statements made by me in this book are true, but you be the judge.

Learning What's Up

How many people can say they've had a baby torn from their womb when they weren't dilated? Who goes through pain without medication? Who delivers being beaten and thrown to the concrete in an alley and left to die? Me. How many people can say they've had multiple surgeries to put their organs back in place after falling out of their body from what was done to them? How many people can say they live with netting along with a sling to hold their intestines and bladder in place along with 5 holes in their stomach from such a monstrous nightmare? Me. It is for sure I could never wear a bikini.

No matter how many people think they can rise above what was done to them it's a work-in-progress every day the rest of your life. Flashbacks of what is put into the brain can never be ejected. Many people live with tragedies and drama that happened to them. Rising above it is a work in progress the rest of their life. It's hard at times to look at my sons who were triplets and not knowing what happened to their triplet brother. People find it easy to say just let it go. That's easier said than done.

How many people can say a song playing on the radio is theirs without any recognition? How many people can say their gold is on another man's wall along with the money it made? How many people can say Fame sits on the wrong door step? Me.

How many people can say both their parents were taken before their time by the hands of others? Me

How many children do you think pass through Michael Jackson's life? How many people speak of Michael Jackson as being a gracious, generous, gentle person? To see Michael, to know him, was knowing how genuine his ♡ was. The desire of Michael's ♡ was to make a better place for all mankind, especially children. I can't tell you how many lawyers convince their clients to pay out money to shut up people who want to destroy celebrities. We all should agree that Michael Jackson's intense work ethics and performances showed us what great talent along with intense drive for perfection was all about. Spending money to bring joy to children made him happy. He made music that made our ♡s zing along with incredible performances.

Throughout his life there's been a few isolated incidents where someone made a claim. Each seemed to be based on money. Most of the multitude of people who have worked with and for Michael have never seen a questionable event regarding his behavior and actions. He was one of the most unique individuals created. Now that he's dead accusations are being made that he had done something wrong or touched a person under age inappropriately.

Shouldn't we be thinking more in terms of a motive for the madness that's happening with this famous artist like money? My story has a different twist than Michaels. My story goes back to an angelic looking man who gained fame because of his demeanor. Many signs were there to show that the man was not who he pretended to be. Aside from the mobsters who surrounded him and the love of fame there were a few celebrities who let go what they saw and heard. Things that were uttered in the street fell on deaf ears.

The Philadelphia police assumed what they heard was questionable and unsubstantiated, so they didn't get involved. When I learned what happened to me, I backtracked and talked to celebrities who were on the set or performed on the show and even some employees. It took years to track everyone who could have known something. I met with a worker at WFIL who spoke about what she heard on the street. I assured her it was true. I am a victim of a corrupt system.

A friend of mine had a friend who had a sister that was taken out on a boat in the Delaware River and raped while trying to get a record deal. My friend set up for me to meet his friend and he confirmed the story was true. It convinced me what I was told by my mother and her best friend Violet's daughter, must be true. My mother along with her two best friends (Violet and my godmother Ann) sat me down when I wanted to go to Bandstand so that my music could be heard.

These old ladies told me the story about Violets daughter being raped and got pregnant. She had a baby boy. I was a 15-year-old teenager and couldn't wrap my head around it. I screamed at the three of them telling them "I'm different, they won't do that to me, I will get a record deal you'll see." Where was I coming from when these three ladies had tears in their eyes pleading with me? They made me swear I wouldn't go to Bandstand. Years later and 9 months pregnant, married with a daughter two years old. I thought I was bold enough, grown enough that I could handle anything that came my way. I was wrong. Standing outside the door of Bandstand I felt good about myself. You already know once I entered Bandstand what happen to me. Twenty years later I meet up with Bill Haley's Comets piano player Joey, in Tennessee. Years later I had set up this meeting with Joey and my lawyer at the Rockabilly hall of fame.. It's amazing how many people turned their back on such criminal activity.

Joey Welz piano player for Bill Haley's Comets.

I met up with a man who I had never met before on a record deal for a client. He ended up being the young boy from Bandstand who held the cue cards who wanted to be a superstar himself. I traveled as far as Vegas to meet with him. Multiple people told me he knew better than anyone what happened at Bandstand years before. They assured me not to get my hopes up cause he more than likely wouldn't spill his guts. Like the rest he turned a blind eye cuz he was headed for fame himself. He told the same story as the rest. How girls were being raped multiple times and if they didn't survive, their bodies were taken by boat out to the edge of the Delaware River never to be found. Men dominated the field and women were considered as prey. The men would turn over the recorded masters for payola.

Years later when I learned what happened to me I asked my mother for forgiveness for not believing her about what was done to Violet's daughter. I felt worst knowing my husband knew what happened to me and did nothing.

Are we to assume that the people who came forward with accusations about Michael Jackson and lawsuits lied in the past or were forced to lie? Are we not to believe it's for material gain? Are we to believe they don't have a motive for lying? Could it be preexisting misconception of what was programmed or believed to be factual?

Had I not met Michael and known his father, had I not known the Jackson's bodyguard and driver, had I not known Ben Brown who was my client, had I not believed the Brown family related to Don King who worked with Michael, had I not known Moe Millions who likewise knew Michael, I wouldn't be able to make such a claim of Michael's character.

People always spoke of him as being gracious and kind and above all what a gentle soul he was. How sad that the media who once befriended Michael now offer a different opinion and believe new accusations that have risen. Another example is how many of you stood by and justified what you heard a man say on a bus about women and their bodies? A prominent man admitted he enjoyed touching women and their crotches without asking their age, without asking permission, because he could get away with it.

Regardless if the tape was him saying it or not, do you agree with such actions? People are condemning Michael Jackson without knowledge of the truth. People have thrown Michael to the wolves. How does this work again??? Good for one man and not the other.

When I grew up it was socially accepted that when men gave you a hug you knew damn well he would squeeze tight to feel your tatas. He would slide his hands and arms along your arms as he broke away which was a way to feel your tatas. Men did it because they thought it was cool. Men in my days would walk away and say softly to other men standing in a group," I can assure you those tatas are real". It made a man feel like he was a real man. The difference is men in my days didn't disrespect women by putting their hands between a woman's legs and feeling her up. Men knew what was socially acceptable.

They knew they didn't want men to go that far with their wife or daughter. Sliding off tatas was as far as it went. Men knew what was appropriate and what wasn't. In my days if it was discovered that a man had touched a women inappropriately, someone would have jumped in and beat the sh*t out of em. I can admit a few men lost their teeth at my bar in the parking lot. One dude got knocked out. Men back in the days handled men. Men set men straight. The police didn't get called for monkey business.

I took the fall for you all. Why break me when you made me? Shout out to the rich and poor who crossed my door and all you a**holes in between. Put your hands up. You're in this book and your name is on my ribbons.

People kept their eyes open and they weren't walking around in a la la land even under the influence of alcohol. People recognized if something was going on with their children. People knew how to handle things themselves. They didn't run to a doctor to tell them their child was out of control. People didn't put their children on drugs because they were acting out.

The things of today wouldn't have been excepted in the days of old nor honored. Instead they were looked upon as dirty old men who need an a★★ kickin' in the parking lot when they were out of order. When the job was done the men would announce that's "one". Very few people ever needed to go to "three." Today people except and excuse dirty old men who brag what they could get away with. A good man wouldn't have excused a man bragging about having the ability to touch a women inappropriately by sliding his hand down their crotch. After all its somebody's sister, somebody's daughter.

A good man doesn't joke about disrespecting a woman. I laugh when I think of the many people who have been caught lying. They say it's just a little bitty lie. Is there really a difference between one lie and another? Sure. The truth is none of us are perfect; we all have flaws. The truth is we are all unique and different.

Going back to what my father taught me about lies. When someone says they're sorry forgive them. That doesn't mean you can befriend them again. When it's blood or your seed, the rule is different. It lays weight upon your ♡. You realize you have a jacka★★ on your hands that needs some work in order to get with the plan. A family member needs to know that you're not giving in and will hold firm with the same orders you were taught to follow. I can't tell you how many times Joe Jackson hit me up for a pep talk. I knew those who worked with Michael's label MJJ. I became friends with Harriet who busted a★★ for the dudes.

Spoke with Joe many times given him headz up about how things were being covered up at the label. We all need a pep talk now and then. How well my family knows what a pep talk is like. Nothing said in a pep talk is nice and more than likely a pep talk makes you feel like a piece of sh★t. That's the plan. If family can't talk to you straight up who in the hell can? There hasn't been a day since I woke from my dismal state that I haven't felt pain from what was done to me.

Part of the pain comes from those who knew sh★t wasn't right at Bandstand, including the operating doctor who cleaned me up and administered the call for pints of blood. Pain from the nuns who took things in their own hands while I was in a coma. Pain that my husband didn't take control of the situation. If something did happen and I died he still had his two sons and our two-year-old daughter at home. Fu★ck me once fu★ck me twice I was fighting for my life. Pain from the psychiatrist who thought it was better to take away the golden note being sure I would not hear it again. Surprise! It was still playing on the radio years later. The mob, the production company and those who handled my Master along with the engineer who did the remix and recorded the music and lyrics with a chosen artist probably all know the real truth. I just wonder if they realize what dumb a★★es they really are sitting at the end of the buck. The big bucks are in the publishing where it began which sits in the wallet of Dickie. The artist who knew damn well he didn't write the song but holds the gold on his wall is at the very end of the money chain. How many people can survive such a physical reality? Me.

How many people can get through multiple attempted of murder of your child and your grandchildren? Me. How many people have had a kidnapped grandson who was found and lived? Me. Let me remind you what my mother said when she sat on the swing to tell me what happened to me at Bandstand. She sat half of the day on the swing teaching me how to rise above what happened to me. She said, "Child what good would it do to confront Dick? He will weasel out of it by saying he had no idea what happened in the alley outside of Bandstand with the mob.

One can't always get back what they've lost they can only move forward and learn from their mistakes. You were told not to go. You knew I taught you that we were born in the middle not rich or poor. You know that I told you in order to get to a higher level in life one of three things had to happen. You had to know somebody or bl*w somebody or kiss somebody's a★★ to get ahead. Did you think for one minute I was not being truthful with you? Look at people who use the N word then they grow up and curse at others who still do.

I love you enough to tell you the truth… Leave this place it will always be here when you return. Learn a new beat on the drum. Hit a new note and be happy that you're alive. Never forget that you're Philly Grown from the Concrete Jungle where the Streets of Gold that Live in the Soul. Trot onward my child. Don't let yourself go backwards. I am there for you." I positively align with a lot of the Catholic church's teachings and guidance, but not with all of it. I concentrate in being a good member of the community of man, a good family member and certainly, try to never harm anyone. That is the commonality of All religions we can All live with. I left home with my purse and a map of NY on a handkerchief along with an Identity Rock and waved goodbye.

Beneath the Hype - Shoes tell the Story

Regardless of the shoe you buy or the shoe you choose to wear, it is where you step that matters. Step-Step-Step everybody knows extraordinary people don't quiver they deliver. Everybody knows extraordinary people but if you don't, just tell them that you know me. I'm a Baka, Diva, Gimi, Great Granny that hits you sometimes where it hurts, givin' it to you straight up.

If you don't watch where you step your shoes will show where you've been. More than likely your shoes will contain spit and gum along with dirt and pi★★ from when you took a leak. A person's shoes tell the story of his walk. No one should feel good wearing their shoes as if they were sweepers. You shouldn't feel good about using your shoes as a flag to comprehend what a life you live.

Each shoe has a story to tell where it's been and why it leans this way and that. There's no instruction one can give that will give you the fix as to walk straight and fly just right along the path of life. It is you in your shoe who needs to take a position in society.

One doesn't have to do good things to be good. Fast Runners do not always win the race and the brave do not always win the battle. Wise men don't always earn a living. Step in the shoe of another. Step, step, step, before you condemn what people do. People often ask me why I have multiple shoe's filled with dirt outside my door. It's those who made my ♡ zing along with the rich and the poor who crossed my door and some a★★holes in between.

SPOLARIZED® PRESS CONNECTION

Spolarized Press Connection Music Beneath the Hype Section

Mylon LeFevre

I can't say enough about Mylon LeFevre since my grandson is named after him. On stage during a Kingdom Bound Ministries event Mylon gestured to my oldest grandson Luke Anthony (eight years old), who was singing his ♡ out, to climb on stage. Mylon ask him his name. Luke Anthony proudly told the audience his name by saying, "I'm named after a star but not you." The audience laughed. After the performance we met with Mylon. He blessed our baby named after him.

White Heart and DC Talk were also on stage that weekend. We love all three. My grandson was a wrestler and earned a full ride to college. I took him with me to the CES show in Vegas. It is a huge show with every manufacturer showing off their newest electronic products hitting the marketplace. He showed off his skill in gaming with multiple companies. He killed it and was offered a position with several major gaming company for good money. He also showed he could handle major presentations of new technologies. He turned down all the job offers. Family meant more then traveling with a fat pay check in his pocket.

Anthony Geary from General Hospital

All of my grandchildren are named after Stars. Luke Anthony is named after Anthony Geary who played Luke on General Hospital. Who could forget one of the biggest weddings in a TV series? Luke was one of those children who has his own mind. One Sunday he stood up in church as a priest was doing his homily. The priest asked him if he had a question. He answered yes about that scripture. The entire church laughed. By 7 he was still speakin' his mind.

We were on the bleachers at an event and a man behind us was drinking beer out of a cooler. Luke stood up turned around and said to the man, "I hope you're not driving when you leave. You've had 6 beers in an hour and a half and drinking and driving is against the law." The man was pissed. My son-in-law is a sweet pea, but if he has to stand his ground he's prepared. The man began yelling at Luke. My son-in-law informed the man to "watch his mouth... the kid is right." Luke Anthony conquered gaming as a child. After college he thought he'd try hittin' the mic on a rhyme and killed it.

Olivia Newton-John and John Travolta

Most everyone knows Olivia Newton-John and how she made our ♡s sing. Who could forget Grease and the performance of Olivia Newton-John and John Travolta? The song "You're the One That I Want" was one of the best-selling singles of all time. Back in 1978, I was still livin' in a dismal state of mind. Music and dancing kept me goin'. I didn't know all the abilities that were locked up inside of me when it came to music, let alone an ear to judge musical work. Three generations of women gifted with the ability to perform and sing who have never been discovered. What talent gone to waste, my mother, my daughter and her daughter, and myself.

SPOLARIZED® PRESS CONNECTION

I didn't realize at the time watching Grease that I was learning and studying both the artistic and theatrical components of the production along with the technical aspects of the soundtrack. I knew the chemistry between Olivia Newton-John and John Travolta was superb. The movie Grease along with the talented Olivia Newton-John helped mold the decision for my daughter to name her daughter Olivia.

By 12 years old I took Olivia under my wing and groomed her. I became her personal business manager. She grew to be an artist, a writer, an actress, and a speaker. She performed before huge audiences along with becoming a professional visual artist showing off her talent live on stage at Caesar's Palace before a large audience.

She drew the portrait of the real Rudy from the movie Rudy which the story was based on. Olivia has done TV specials and was asked to the Super Show. Olivia went to college for visual arts and became a professional in the field by age 19. The Super Show represents every major sport product and licensed athletes.

Olivia was selected to be a consultant to help major corporations and buyers know what's hot and what's not. She was a panel member for the conference on teen marketing "the real deal" presented by Sport Trends, Reebok, DuPont, LYCRA, DuPont Coolmax, and Greenfield Online Inc. Her discussion focused on sport participation and the factors that influence product usage and spending. The event was held at the Emperor's Ballroom Caesars Palace, Las Vegas. Olivia had a hard time understanding why we just didn't take the record labels deals that were coming her way.

Olivia performed in many clubs in New York. She performed at the Jacob Javits Center for the Black Expo, at Kool Herk's Birthday Bash, at Downtime and the Virginia Beach Party. She was rocking Rocawear along with L.D.G. Both were offered endorsements by Diadora.

By 15 Olivia was insane on the mic rapping side by side on stage wit L.D.G. Olivia hit the hoops for Celebrity Basketball Games in NYC with Fat Joe. She was insane in rap and R&B writing her own joints and laying them down along with performing major gigs at 16. I decided to put her in a studio with an insane engineer to lay down a metal album. Once again she proved to be an outrageous writer with hooks and ready for fame with platinum joints. She was able to hit perfectly the notes with multiple octaves.

Her work has not been released due to the vulnerability to steal copyrighted work so easily. Together we learned copyright laws through my IP lawyer. I did a film feature using her as the lead actress with a Sag waiver and she was absolutely insane and captured the character.

I felt so blessed to have a client with such abilities. Almost impossible to believe. I sent the movie with a representative to the Cannes Film Festival. Did I get anywhere? No... Once again the people who had an interest in the production wanted to put money up and take over control.

J Records put out an artist in the same category as Olivia with the same name. Word hit the street that it wasn't by accident. I called my IP Lawyer and asked him what do I do? We had posters all over the city and now there's an Olivia in the marketplace. It was hard for my client Olivia to understand that we were the first to use the name Olivia by itself with a trademark applied to the name and yet our money and work was in vain. Perhaps, that's why Olivia Newton-John adding something on to the name Olivia, so she didn't have to deal

SPOLARIZED™ PRESS CONNECTION

with a**holes who don't check to see if the name is being used by someone else with a ™ applied on the posters or whenever the name was used. An example would be the TV series Empire. Who hires a lawyer who did not check for the already existing trademark Empire? Even though I watch the show and think it's exceptional, it doesn't change the fact it had litigations.

I gave Joey Welz, the piano player from Bill Haley's Comets, one of my client's songs under a license contract for the US marketplace only. Joey gave it to Orchard and they supposedly knew it was only for the US. I discovered that they distributed the music in multiple countries. I had to get my IP Lawyer to figure out and charge someone for corruption. I never got a damn dime from the money it made. They just shut it down.

It's amazing how people don't look at themselves as thieves when they know damn well they are. Someday someone honest and smart may show me a real deal for my 3 TV series and a film feature in the can or my collection of musical work. Someone like Fifty who isn't a dumba**.

Well, let me rephrase that statement about Fifty, he's older and wiser these days then when he took the artist Olivia from J Records and tried to do something with her. If you notice Fifty makes better choices for himself. Most rich and famous people keep me as a coin in their pocket and some act like they don't know me. My client and granddaughter Olivia sat in on multiple meetings with hierarchy. She has seen the corruption and together we rolled in and out multiple studios laying down beats, laying down tracks, hoping for the dream.

Sylvester Stallone - Rocky

Our home had a bodybuilding room in the basement where my sons would work out after school. In 1976 they were bodybuilding with the soundtracks from the Rocky movies. As parents we were glad our sons were in the basement bodybuilding and working out on machines and not on the streets. I can't tell you how many times I've heard the Rocky soundtracks blasting over and over from the basement. My son said, "If I ever have a son I'm going to name him Rocky." Sure, enough he got his wish. Rocky's bassinet in the hospital was covered with pictures from all the magazines with Sylvester Stallone.

Who would have thought years later I'd meet Frank Stallone at Donald Trump's house? Sylvester and Frank are the real deal. Rocky was the first grandchild to have a child making me a great grandma. I took him with me to the Magic Marketplace convention. Rocky enjoyed dining with the tailor who dresses the Presidents.

During the convention Rocky was offered a job by a major player in the textile business. They saw him as an asset to their business because he knows how to sell a product and wear a suit properly. He went to college for a civil engineer degree.

Silverwind

Back in 1988 our family was into Christian festivals. I began working with Kingdom Bound Ministries and I was also a lay minister for the Roman Catholic Church. In 1988 a song came out called "Elya" by Silverwind. As family we sang the song many times. The verses

SPOLARIZED® PRESS CONNECTION

talk about reach to the shy. She proved she can reach her goal. My son's wife was expecting her second baby and I suggested if it was a girl it should be named Elya. Sure, enough Elya was born. She worked hard to get her multiple degrees which made us very proud of her. Elya won numerous awards in international amateur film and video competition in "Russian Bananas." She was spectacular. She earned a Bachelor of Arts, Bachelor of Science, and a Doctorate in Physical Therapy.

Ridge Forrester - The Bold and the Beautiful

My youngest grandson Ridge was named after the soap star Ridge Forrester from CBS's "The Bold and the Beautiful." The actor's real name was Ronn Moss. I suggested the name for my son's third child because of the way Ronn Moss portrayed Ridge. Ronn's karma and his abilities are amazing along with his fashionable style of clothing. He was a musician, a singer and songwriter, and a member of a band. I got my wish. Ridge was born and much like the actor, has many of the same qualities including graphic design.

Ridge is a whiz at knowing how to accomplish something. He skipped a whole year in high school and was probably the youngest senior to ever graduate in the school. He has the gift of computer graphic designs. Ridge took things a step further applying himself to live flowers. His floral designs are truly only found in a "Prince's Garden" along with designs for Princesses.

Won a Son-in-Law at the Lottery

I'm not one to play the lottery but my husband asked me to buy some tickets for him. There was a fella who looked like a rocker standing in front of me who didn't play the lottery either. His buddies at IBM ask him to buy some lottery tickets for them. I struck up a conversation and asked what he was listening to.

He gave me a snicker and says, "Nothing you'd be interested in." I assured him I love music. He took off the headphones and turned the sound up to number 10 and placed the headphones on my head. I started bouncing around singing the song.

He looked at me and said, "You know that song." My reply was, "Wanta see them backstage?" I ended up taking him to see the act along with my daughter. The name of the group was Stryper. Excellent musicians who knew how to write lyrics and knew how to perform on a stage and bring the house down. Stryper had their sh*t together. Low and behold my future son-in-law turned out to be a fantastic singer.

Phone Book Ad Spolarized® Saved A Life

Can you imagine getting a call at 3:00AM hearing a voice ask you what

Spolarized® Records means. The dude says, "I'm looking' at your ad in the yellow Pages and see a sorta rainbow of colors with the words Spolarized® Records. I'm sittin' wit a gun to my head and I was gonna use the phone book in front of the gun because I don't want to see what I'm about to do." I say dude, "If you put the gun down and tell me where you are and if what you're saying is true and the ad's in color, then this is the moment when 'An

Angel Made of Glass' passes through you. Please understand I won't be played. If this is a prank or mischievous act just hang up. It's all good.

Understand if I get out of bed and meet you wherever you are it may take some time. Promise to put the gun down and believe I'll arrive. If it's not true go ahead and be a fool and pull the trigger. Are we in agreement?" I hear "huh?" I continue saying, "Regardless how this turns out I want you to know a Fool takes his life or the life of others. Death doesn't solve problems. Nothing in life is easy. If you walk in someone else's shoe you'll see fields of wild weeds."

If you wait it out through stormy weather eventually, you'll see it is where the violets grow and where you hear the A·ve Ma·ri·a as a thanks for believing in yourself."

I'm waiting on a click that he hung up but instead I hear the dude give me an address. I head out the door on a 25-mile trip in the middle of the night to meet this guy on a street corner. Standing on the street corner is a dude in his early twenties with a phone book in his hand. Sure, enough there is a full color add of Spolarized® Records which was supposed to be in black and white.

He tells me his story. As a child he remembers his dad screaming a threat at his mom that if she comes after him for child support he'd kill the child. His mom lived off social services and money she could grab from men who fu★ked her.

After a few months a man moved in and took over the house and there was nothing she could do to get him out. Then he filled the house with multiple women to be used for service. Finally, the man took over the boy's room. His blanket and clothes were in the attic. His mom explained there's nothing she could do. The ten-year-old boy says, "Mom there's no heat or electric or a bed and I'm afraid in the attic." She hugged him and said, "It'll be ok. There's nothing I can do."

By age 12 the boy couldn't deal with the women screaming, "please you're hurting me, please." He ran down the attic steps and saw his mother's mouth bleeding and he saw a girl in his bed naked crying. He looked at the man and said, "You're done hurting women. I'm the man of the house and I want you to leave." Then the man says, "You need to catch the school bus and tonight I'm giving you back your room." The boy was excited and believed everything would be ok.

When he came home from school his blanket was back on his bed. He ran in and jumped on his bed. The door shut behind him and there stood two men. They held him down and forced him to do sexual acts, laughing saying, "This is what we do to your mommy." Then they bit into the boy's penis till it was nearly off and left.

The boy spent some time in the hospital trying to reattach the penis. After years of repair he could drain normally. The boy was sent through the social services system and his

117

Spolairos

CROWN ROSES

THINGS CHANGE

SHIZZLE STUDIO

mother went off to rehab. He ran away from social services and lived in the street with an APB out for him. I've never met a child who thought the people who raised them through Social Serves were nice.

I called the phone company about the ad in the yellow pages. I ask them why the ad was in multi colors. They got back to me saying when they realized the mistake, they went back to the order of black print. They assured me only 2 or 3 misprints were actually mailed out. Can you believe that another fellow with a similar story got a misprint colored phone book and called me? As for the story of the boy who wanted to kill himself, he's now a grown man who knows a Spolarized® Rainbow of Colors pulled him through.

Artists Things Change

One of the first R&B acts I discovered was in Memphis Tennessee. I was there with my daughter at a music festival called Crossroads. While walking along the avenue I hear men harmonizing a beautiful melody from an alley. Three young men stepped up on me like a bunch of thugs and said, "What the f★ck you think you're doing?" I answered saying, "Good music is hard to find and the song you were singing is insane. How would you guys like to go to my crib in PA. I'll put you in a studio and do some gigs?" They came by bus on a one-way ticket. What happened to them before I came along was ♡ breaking. They called themselves "Boys to Men." They met up with a fellow who was a manager who signs acts to record deals. The dude insisted they should keep the name under rap quiet and stop using the name.

He left to see what he could do for them. Of course, they were excited and complied. They truly believed this dude was going to get them a record deal. What happened so I was told in actuality was that an act out of Philly name "Boyz II Men" popped up. Of course, the dude wasn't gonna admit he stole the name from the 3 guys in Memphis. I'm assuming "Boyz II Men" were in the dark and I'm assuming their story is true. The three guys were devastated. They had no choice but to change their name to "Things Change." You be the judge if the boys were tellin' the truth or not. To the best of my knowledge and belief all statements made by me in this book are true, but you be the judge. As promised, I put joints down in a studio and they killed it on every track. Two of them returned to Memphis.

The one named Montrez stayed working shows. He performed for the after Grammy Party in New York, at Downtime and the Metropolis. A few A&R reps looked at him and all agreed he's good. As an example, they spoke about Suge Knight who puts money on artists and blows up artists. Once money is on your a★★ you're expected to jump. Once an artist is famous they forget without the money from someone like Suge, they'd still be a wannabe. Shouldn't Suge be pi★★ed? Personally, people say shit about Suge but at times I find I'm on his side. Things Changed had a good ride while it lasted.

Jackson Family

It's always been a pleasure to sit and talk with the late Joe Jackson about the entertainment industry. The man who first signed Michael and the Jackson 5 was Ben Brown who owned Steeltown Records. In 89 we cross paths when I was comin' out of my dismal state. They knew I studied music my entire life. Little did I know I was a well-kept secret. Ben and Joe

Spolarized Press Connection
Beneath the Hype Since 1994

120

Peggy & Robert Gordy
Remembering the Legacy of Motown

would reach out to me on a lee low when they needed advice or wanted to chat knowing damn well I'd keep quiet. Neither one wanted any one to know they knew me. They were having their own issues. Ben wanted things his way and Joe seen things a different way. Ben kept his son and Joe kept their kids out of the mix. They knew I was a victim to the system and got my wisdom and knowledge on the block. They knew I was on a mission of my own. Years later Ben ended up one of my clients.

I learned a hell of a lot about the Jackson 5 talking to these two men. One thing for sure regardless of how you view Joe, he is a dad who protects his children at any cost even if it meant taking the flak onto his shoulders. I'm not even sure his children understand the amount of stress put on this man. When you go back to when Michael was a kid and the Jackson's were in their teens and their career began, it was Ben and Joe who truly made it happen. The combination between Ben and what he could offer and Joe the father who could handle his children, worked to bring out the hidden talent and creative abilities they together saw existed within each of the children.

The Jackson 5 could have been easily overlooked if it wasn't for these two men who were smart enough to see what was right in front of them. Ben often spoke about the unnoticed sacrifices Joe made to make this happen. It couldn't have been easy on these children who like all children wanted to play or be like other children. Instead these boys were told to put their talents to use and stay focused. In the beginning Ben and Joe kept these boys on point. Three cheers to Michael and the Jackson 5 who proved that if you work hard the end result can be hugely successful.

Although Michael was only with us for a short time he taught us the meaning of excellence and perfection. And who could ever forget his Super Bowl performance that was off the charts. Janet was able to secure her spotlight by showing us her talent. When it comes to Michael and the Jackson 5 you have to pick and choose who you believe discovered them or who produced them out the gate. Ben Brown crossed my path back when I was victim at Bandstand. We hooked up again when Ben wanted to release stuff of the Jackson 5 with Steeltown Records.

In order to keep things business like, the Jackson's were taught or perhaps trained to call their dad, "Joe Jackson", verses daddy or dad. One thing about Joe was he was cheap. So cheap that at times I had to pay for his air flight and hotel room if he was comin' to NY. I finally got to meet Frank one of his driver who was a sweet pea. I was happy to help out with any issues Joe may have had. I had an IP Lawyer who was trustworthy and had knowledge of the bullsh*t in the game. I could ask him anything and he'd give me a straight answer. That didn't mean Joe would take the advice or guidance.

Can you imagine what it was like for Joe and Katherine to drive their children after school doing their homework to a studio every day? We can only assume that there are probably some people that have been left out of the creation of the Jackson's work or assume that there are some people that were given credit that shouldn't have been given credit. At any rate the world is a better place for having the Jackson 5 a part of the entertainment world and them being able to utilize their God-given talents to such marvelous degrees.

Ben Brown says he discovered the Jackson 5. I believe he's telling the truth. Ben told me that when the Jackson 5 were children, people around them handled their business and

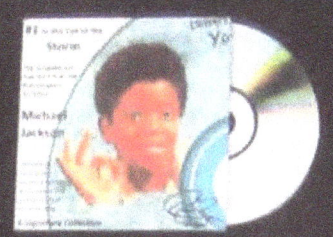

I AM HONORED TO HAVE THE FIRST RECORDED SONG OF MICHAEL JACKSON AND OF THE JACKSON 5. THE RECORDINGS WERE GIVEN TO ME BY MY CLIENT THE LATE BEN BROWN. STEELTOWN RECORDS WAS FOUNDED BY GORDON KEITH, BEN BROWN, MAURICE ROGERS, AND LUDIE D. THREE CHEERS TO EVERYONE WHO WAS A PART OF THE DEVELOPMENT OF THE JACKSON 5 ALONG WITH THEIR LATE FATHER JOE WHO REALIZED HE WAS BLESSED WITH GIFTED CHILDREN.

recordings. Who knows if they did what was right eh? As the Jackson 5 got older they began to take control of their future and their music. Ben said, "Joe and I made it happen for these kids and everyone who saw them wanted to jump on the bandwagon." Could other people have discovered the Jackson 5 at the same time? Truth is these five boys had talent and hadn't been discovered till Joe told Ben to take a look at these boys. Joe knew he had something and wanted someone to tell him he was right.

I feel honored to have had the privilege of knowing both Joe and Ben. I felt honored to have given good advice to both men regardless if they listened or not. I felt honored when they'd call on a lee low admitting they should have listened to my advice. I was privileged to have shared with Jermaine Jackson at a convention. He was with three children who had the patience of a saint, never once interrupted, huffed or puffed or acted up waiting for us to get done chillin'. Right before Joe's passing, Joe asked me to work on a drink product with him. To the best of my knowledge and belief all statements made by me in this book are true, but you be the judge.

CMX and Michael Jackson

Moe Millions SVP of CMX introduced me to Eric head of CMX. It was quite impressive. Michael Jackson was there laying down joints. Michael was serious about everyone complying with the rules set forth. No one was allowed within the actual studio section where Michael was putting down his music. There were times when you'd see the producer Jerry or Michael going in and out the studio for a break. What an exciting thrill to even see Michael that close up. Eric liked Moe because Moe was the type of person who wouldn't kiss a**. Moe has never had a problem telling anyone what he thinks. Moe and I have been friends over 24 years.

It's pretty hard to swallow when someone says that Michael would take any creation of someone else's work and use it. It's not the first time someone says bullsh*t about artist and people with fame and I'm sure it won't be the last. Befriending Eric who is Don King's family and enjoying the passes to see boxing champ's fights in the ring over the years wasn't nearly as exciting as CMX first class studios and seeing Michael.

Of course, me being Press I got VIP passes into venues and events on my own without any help. I learned firsthand by seeing and listening to the protocol Michael demanded when he was recording some of his classic super hits. I learned about Michael's musical work and how he never asks anybody's opinion or input about his music other than those who were part of the copywriting. Michael didn't care what people thought outside the studio door.

Everyone at CMX knew they'd hear the production when it's finished. Michael was an accomplished writer, artist, producer, and knew what he expected out of the engineer and himself as the finished product. The production wasn't over until it was over and he and Jerry and those involved were satisfied.

Eric accommodated Michael's wishes when renting CMX studios A and B. Eric knew the studio was making big bucks on Michael, therefore, Eric made sure everyone followed the rules. When you heard the finished product, your ♡ pulsated, and you knew a hit was just created. Of all the Stars along with friends, family members and Michael's associates, I have never once heard a thing about him being inappropriate with children. Those who knew Michael knew he was about making a better life for children and all mankind. There has

Street Pennies From Heaven

Every trip with Grandma Mary to Philly I understood it included pitching pennies to the Beggars. We'd walk block after block looking for pennies on the pavement people dropped. If I found a penny and it was heads I got to keep it. If I found a penny and it was tails I got three chances to flip it. If it came up heads I got to keep it or tails leave it. At the end of the day one penny was for me and one penny for each beggar. As I dropped a penny in their cup I'd yell, "Heads up Street Pennies from Heaven."

My father's father who was my
Great Grandpa was a Cowboy actor in silent movies.
He lost his life in a scene where he was to be shot
from a roof top and fall into a wagon as it rolled by.
The horses went to fast and he landed on the ground
dead with a broken neck. When I look back I think
how lucky I was to have both sets of grandparents
teach me how to have self-respect and self-worth.

always been an underlying question about people seeing him as a meal ticket such as lawyers and doctors and those who wanted to gain fame and money.

As for those who knew him, never once have they questioned him harming anyone least of all a child. To the best of my knowledge and belief this is the way I remember Michael and the way I saw it. You be the judge if it's true or not.

Biggie

Let me begin by saying only a few people know this story to be factual; those who were in my office that day along with Mel Love "Link 2 Link." Mel ran a street team and worked for Bad Boy. Mel is the beginning factor of the greatness of Biggie Smalls. He was actually the one who gave him the name "Notorious."

Many of the Rich and Famous forget who helped make them famous. Mel beat the streets posting flyers for major players including Puffy, Diddy, or whatever he wants to call himself. Puffy gave him enough pennies to get on the train. In the beginning Puffy was shrewd.

Once Puffy was successful he walked away from Mel and the street teams who did Puffy's sh*t work. Puffy never learned about "Pennies from Heaven." One for me and one for you. I learned that as a child walkin' the streets of Philly. At the same time Mel was blowin' up Puffy, I was in multiple studios helping engineers of famous artists without credit. Mel was a young kid beating the street instead of getting an education and his dream for himself as an R&B singer.

Back to Biggie: I entered my building on 38th and Broad. When I hit the elevator, it wouldn't open. I thought damn I got to walk 14 flights straight up. When I entered my office, everybody was sitting on their a★★. I said, "Couldn't one of you have called the landlord? The elevator's broke." Mel said, "It's useless to pay these people. The elevator's not broke Biggie's got it on lockdown with 4 bit★hs." I said, "That's never gonna happen again."

When Biggie came out of the elevator I said, "Yo biggie I need to speak to you." He rolls up on me and says, "Are you talking to me?" He's sweatin' and his pants fallin off his a★★ with four beautiful girls behind them. I said, "Yep I don't see anyone else name Biggie in the place. I'm never walking the stairs again. I pay 50 G's for this office and you think you can stroll in like you're somebody better than the rest of us? Fu*k you bro."

"The next time you want to come to my office, see that window over there? If your fat a★★ can fit through it, come up the fire escape and then you're welcome. You're never coming through my door again." He turns around and gestures to the girls to go out in the hall then slams the door as he exits. I never saw him again in my studio and I didn't give a sh★t.

Easy Mo Bee has been my friend over the years, and he was producing multiple artist like Biggie. Easy Mo Bee was the sh★ behind Biggie and many famous artist. He created great beats and produced mad stuff. Easy Mo Bee came to my house after Biggie died. We chilled about horror stories in hip hop. Most are better left unsaid. People do movies on hiphop stars such as Biggie, but the good sh★t is left out. You learn street sense makes sense. Sometimes you find straight up people who aren't willing to sell their soul to the Devil for the love of fame. There are times I shake my head how society made some of these people rich and famous.

Spolarized® Press Connection
Beneath the Hype in the
World of Entertainment
in Honor of the Late 2 Pac
and His Family

Mel, Easy Mo Bee and I stayed friends through the years. You couldn't get better dudes to befriend. Mel introduced me to DJ Rockstar P. The three of us laid down a year's worth of a TV series about the old days versus today and the industry. It is still in the can.

Busta Rhymes – Treach - Redman

I was invited VIP to Treach's birthday along with many superstars. I gazed over the balcony to watch the event from the VIP section. Sitting at the bar was Busta Rhymes who I had never met before. I sat down three seats away. He looked my way with attitude as if to say, 'who's this white b*tch?' but never uttered a word. I was going to say something but I'm damn glad I didn't. In a blink a dude walks over and slides his hand past the men surrounding him and taps Busta on the shoulder. The dude yells, "Oh yo Busta, I can't believe it's you. You're my idol, man." Busta turns around on the bar stool and looked at the dude and says, "You talking to me. Who invited you into my world?" Busta tells the two men to throw him the hell out. I couldn't believe it. I was flipping. The dude says, "Yo you got it twisted, I'm a fan yo." This dude had a VIP pass and dressed to kill. He was thrown out the door on his a★★. I was damn glad I didn't say hi to Busta. Treach greeted me with style.

He was happy as can be groovin with the people that came to celebrate his birthday. I knew one thing after that night, I'd never greet Busta unless he greeted me first. I learned from some of the people in the VIP room that when Busta's wasted, don't bother him cause he's in a zone of his own. When you want to know an artist that acts like the rest of us, it's Redman. Every time I have run into him he has been a gentleman. We can all benefit from listening to his work.

2 Pac's Investigation

I was befriended by a sergeant of the Gang Squad Investigation Department in Vegas. I'll call him DS. What went down with 2 Pac was hushed. I've seen movies and documentaries made about the life of 2 Pac and the way they think it went down. I know better that anyone that "Street Sense Makes Sense." Chillin' in Vegas year after year at conventions, after parties and casinos VIP rooms, you meet people who talk on a lee low. If you're always a VIP and meeting bigwigs you learn what's up. When you chill with gang members or hip-hop dudes or 2 Pac's family you hear sh*t on another level. When it comes to 2 Pac, many people want to gain fame by makin' up bullsh*t like he's alive. When I piece it all together along with the gang squad sergeant, I get a better feel about the drama that surrounded what really happened. Do you understand people get setup or take the wrap for someone else?

A setup to kill someone is usually for profit or gain. When you learn how the street operates you learn who to mess with and who not to mess with. You learn those with criminal records may not be as bad as those who have none. Keep an eye open on those who have a sly deceitful nature. Deception is the opposite of honesty. When a person is honest about who he is and the things he's done you know him. When a person is misleading he uses trickery, which is the practice of evil doers. I favor honest people who usually are bad-a★★es verses sweet talkin'. Why? Many times, "sweet talking" people are trying to persuade you or want

Legally Loaded Crew Workin' Together

you to believe them (Cambridge English Dictionary). I'm from the Concrete Jungle Philly and I'm straight up. The culprit to several murders is right in your mitts.

Eminem's – Shady Records

Eminem is my favorite rapper even though I rap. I know he's better. I can hold my ground rappin' and I've been in the game longer then Em. Perhaps when Em's my age (76) he won't be rapping like he's rapping now, and I know he doesn't drive a Ford. Hell, I got pros from Outkast who stood to their feet and shook my hand along wit many other famous rappers when they heard me.

I went to Miami to a conference where Shady Records was supposed to be lookin' for talent. I'll call the dude "R". He was brought in to talk to the artists about a record deal. He made a complete a★★ of himself. I'm just gonna give you dribs and drabs what his mouth said to the artists and musicians. I went there with Don from Universal and Robin. Personally, the whole event was a joke; a way to make money for the man running the show. I already had R's personal number. He doesn't give a damn about Shady Records. He's just eating off the label. Here's the lowdown. When it was time for R to speak he said, "I meet rappers on every block.

Everybody wants a record deal, and everybody thinks they're good. I get so much music thrown at me and people coming at me in the clubs or wherever I am. Record deals are far and between where the industry is right now." The young men in the audience we're disappointed. They were hoping R would just listen to their joint. R didn't give one sh★t about the artist; he was rude and cocky. Then he leaned over and said to the guy next to him, "did they miss what I said? I know one or two may be good in the audience but hell, I can get good on any block. We aren't signing sh★t these days." R didn't know his mic was still on. When he came off the stage I hit him up. I said, "Hey R do you ever pick up your f★ckin' phone?" He says, "Who the hell are you?" I said, "Ms Peggy. You're a disgrace to the industry and the game. Most of the artists questioned how Em could hire you." I assured the artists Em isn't in control of everything and the people he put in place to do things for him correctly aren't. I see it constantly with famous people. I learned this first hand watching, hearing, and seeing the actions of the homies surrounding DMX, Fifty, and Snoop.

Famous artists shouldn't take for granted the quality of loyalty from the people hangin' around them. If you have 5 true friends in life consider yourself lucky. I was disappointed because I anticipated Em would have had a better handle on the people around him and who he employs under his label especially in non-executive levels. I been trying to get wit Em on business with no luck. I've called Em's lawyer's office 10 times or more wit deals on the table and he doesn't return a call. It's like my mom said, "In life child to get to a better place then you were born you'll need one of three things. Know somebody or bl★w somebody or kiss somebody's a★★." Em's lawyer has no idea what I'm callin' about.

I want to believe without any facts that Em's lawyer makes Em's decisions and decides what to pass onto Em. Back in the days I befriended a label workin' with Michael Jackson in NYC. What a shame that was and a disaster. The guy was suckin' money while sittin' on his a★★. The difference is our corporation teaches our clients how to take hold of the rope and

In honor of my late engineer "Fly Eagle Fly" together we made music

become a business man. Don't let things go around you that you have no knowledge of. A CEO heads the rodeo, Yeehaw. This CEO drives a Ford.

In honor of my Belated Studio Engineer

I lost a 46-year-old engineer who worked for me 22 years. Not one day went by that this dude didn't text, email, or call me to play me a new lullaby. He and I had something in common: we were born to Rock. He was an over achiever, a skilled musician with a great ear for mastering.

He was better than any professional I've worked with. At his funeral, the father approached me, after my speech about my great engineer, and said, "It sounds like my son was a wonderful man, I feel sorry that I never got to know him." I was saddened as I looked across the church pews to see so many people there who knew nothing about the guy except maybe to learn from him or use him to record.

Some of the people knew him from his favorite bar and some of the people in the pews were relations. None really knew him. I was the one at his side who never gave up on him. I was the one he'd call when in trouble.

It was I who got him lawyers and bailed his a** out. It was I who went to his trials when no one else did. It was I who picked him up when he got out of jail. It was I who took him to rehab. It was I whom he shed his tears upon. It was I who believed in him and paid him so he could spend his life in a studio 24/7.

It was I who bought his studio equipment so he could create masterpieces. It was I who always answered the phone 3:00 AM in the morning to hear his new joint. It was I who answered the phone weekends when he'd leave the studio to get wasted.

He was a lonely guy who wanted something he couldn't seem to get, as in credibility in the entertainment world.

Many artists have their music stolen. It takes money to sue. Think how Santana would feel if his first blues band didn't get any recognition after playing an electrifying gig at Woodstock. My musical work was stolen, and the pain is indescribable. Especially when you hear it on the radio. I can't tell you how many times I told my engineer not to let other artists hear his joints. He was an accomplished instrumentalist who trusted other musicians and artists by letting them hear his joints. Are you kidding me? When you hear a joint enough the track stays in your head. He knew I'd tear up my multiple contracts and take the equipment if I ever learned he let people hear my artists' joints. To the best of my knowledge he knew I meant business when it comes to my sh*t.

He was a gifted man who had a sickness of drug and alcohol abuse and it killed him in the end. He never got over being a kid on the football field and being pulled off the field by his parent in front of the school and laughed at by his team mates. He quit the team but the name calling continued. He hit the streets and lived with his grandparents as a teen.

His mother stayed by his side the best she could as a single mother. He never got over not having a dad in his life to see his many achievements. All he longed for was those who said they loved him to recognize his great work.

He hated the fact that not one person gave a damn about his gift in music. As a teen he learned on his own how to make it happen for himself while everyone around him was busy

In 1959 Elvis made my heart zing.
He was signed to Sun Records making gold records.
In 1962 I was headed to Bandstand for my own record deal.
Sadly to say my gold hangs on another man's wall.

doing things of lesser worth. The people in the pew were faces who came to his aid way too late.

Memphis with Elvis and BB King

The Brooklyn warehouse dudes wouldn't last a night on Beale St. during Crossroads. That's where music emerged between Blues with BB King and Elvis with Rock-N-Roll. Been there, done that rodeo. Memphis helped me learn what hardcore is about. I was robbed three times in one day and I had three dudes live with me from Memphis who were bad a★★s.

I also befriended a Memphis dude named Na Na who was laying down his joints with his homies in my NYC studio. He has iron balls. Over the years I've gotten invites from many celebrates including BB King. Likewise, I got an invite to Elvis's estate. One of Elvis's last concerts I went to see. I sat next to the staff's family members on the side stage. She informed me about personal stuff I didn't know. He was a serious regular guy.

BB King also acted like the rest of us; a normal man who enjoys playing his music. The belated Elvis was a one of a kind; someone skilled and enjoyed conversation. I want to believe neither of them would pay payola in order to blow themselves up. I've met so many celebrities as Press and enjoy conversations with them.

Very few are what they seem when you're one on one. I take off my press badge and just chill with them. For some unknown reason people from all walks of life spill their guts about whatever is bothering them. For some unknown reason they feel like they can trust me. The part that is funny is that they almost always mention not to tell anyone after the fact. Hype vs. real, I guess.

Many stars stay at the Peabody Hotel. It's where I first met Aaron Neville opening the door of the elevator to let the ducks out. He greeted me as if we knew each other for years. He wasn't the type of artist who walks around thinkin' he's higher than those around him.

I was shocked that he acted like the rest of the people in the hotel. I was impressed. My neighbor Annette Grey introduced me to his version of the A·ve Ma·ri·a. I was impressed by his rendition which is slightly different than most. Three cheers to Barbara Streisand, Andrea Bocelli, Luciano Pavarotti, for their superb renditions as well. The Peabody Hotel is a place where live ducks walk freely and parade around the hotel including in and out the elevator; where you may get shit on your dress shoes. It made me think back to my mother-in-law who kept ducks in the bath tub. You best believe I never showered at her house.

The Bible says, the truth sets us free. How many people do you know who likes the truth, eh? I've learned over the years to say nothing when opinions without facts are voiced. What good does it do if a person doesn't have a practical understanding of the subject. When I agree with someone I say, Spolarized Dope A Mean. Meaning I agree with the person. Insight and common sense play a big part in making decisions. Awareness and familiarity along with experience is how we gain wisdom.

Being Catholic my family has heard the A·ve Ma·ri·a many times and laid flowers at the feet of the statue of the Blessed Mother. My daughter was the most beautiful bride I have ever seen twice around. She was married at the foot of the cross on the big rock where it sits on my estate. Beauty is in the eyes of the beholder and is created by the observer. I couldn't have asked for more that day. Money was well spent for a beautiful bride.

Bow Wow

I was asked to do a production for an act out of Florida where Bow Wow was going to be performing. A well-known manager for a major rapper I'll call J, asked me to do the shoot with him. I felt honored that I was asked. I didn't know he was takin' me for a ride. I had never met. I did everything in my power to do a great production knowing we were to split the money when the production was done along with my expenses. The manager said, "When we get back to NY I'll figure out what all is owed and the spilt for my services." I paid for the equipment rental, our accommodations and our air flight. I went along with the plan figuring I could trust somebody who's a well-known manager of a famous rapper. This dude proved untrustworthy. Hang wit thrash you become trash. The dude has been the famous rappers' manager since the get back in the 90's.

I got to film a little of Bow Wow on stage and go backstage. When Bow Wow was young and green in the industry, he was doing a good job. Backstage I hear Jermaine Dupri say to Bow Wow, "I told you not to be pulling on your crotch. You're too young to be doing that sh*t on stage. Where did you learn that?" Bow Wow says, "From the best... You." Jermaine kept it real and he turned and walked away with a smirk on his face holding back laughter. Most of us backstage were laughing. I'm thinkin' the kid's got it right. Jermaine is one of the best and the kid was following in his footsteps. I met a guy named Nasty who also was filming with us using his own camera and doing a kick-a** job. After the shoot was over I walked over to Nasty and said, "I'm supposed to give you a couple hundred dollars. J is supposed to reimburse me when we get back to New York." Nasty agreed he was also going to get more money once we got back to NY. We knew the money was real because we watched the act pay the manager hundreds of dollars in wrappers.

I wasn't as bold then as I am now. I was still somewhat green and really didn't know the cost of a video shoot. I questioned J about giving me a couple hundred dollars. He insisted the deal was to handle all the money once back in NY. I never got paid one damn cent nor did Nasty. It led me to believe that the major rapper could care less if his manager steals and lies. One good thing out of the whole story is I gained a friend over the last 20 years named Nasty.

Call me a bitch ain't that some sh*t. You need to walk through the wild weeds and find a violet so you can get on top your game and hear the A·ve Ma·ri·a."

Michael Sweet (Stryper)

One of my favorite Christian artists whose picture hangs in my office has always made my ♡ zing. He is an insane guitarist along with the band members who likewise have mastered their instruments with the ability to create great works. Michael's performances haven't

There is nothin' like layin' down a rhyme on roof tops

changed with age. He's as good today as yesterday. He has always been outrageous. Both Mylon LaFevre and Michael Sweet spread their message across the stage of ministries. Back in the days my favorite clothing line design they wore was the "The Yellow and Black Attack" wardrobe. There was no mistaking who the band was much like Kiss. There was never a time that Michael didn't show his fans love. Whenever you're down or when I was down, I'd jump in my car and pop in the song "Calling on You" and drive around.

It made me realize there was a side of me no one seems to understand. Yet for years I held on believing sunshine will enter my life. Little did I know that one day I'd trademark the word Spolarized with the design of the sun dotting the i in the word. Living where they claim the sun shines the least is where I discovered the sun shines the most. The creation of the word along with the sun and its design happened back in the 80's in my driveway. The word represents the ability to rise above your obstacles and shine the star that you are, Spolarized out of the polarity in which you sit. Rize Energized Spolarized® and Rock with the Sun!

Rooftops

I met a girl who I'll call K who had an office in NYC and an apartment out of the city. We became friends. I was in the game to learn about my past. Whenever I hear the song "We will Rock You/We are the Champions" by Queen, my thoughts go back in time remembering on the Streets of Philly many years ago a team of people who came together much like the Eagles and beat the odds to save three lives. K introduced me to the rooftop and multiple clubs throughout NYC where weed was flowin'. DJ's began to realize an older Caucasian woman was befriended by the urban community named Ms. Peggy. Those years taught me "Street Sense Made Sense."

I learned something wicked cool about the city. On the high-rise buildings people enjoyed climbing out their windows onto rooftops. Even homeless knew to climb the fire escapes onto rooftops. Unbeknown to the city, many renters of top floor apartments climb out their window's enjoying their rooftop. The homeless didn't seem to mine that their skin was ripped off from the tarpaper. I suppose it's not that much different than those who live on the block frozen to the concrete.

The homeless made the best out of the life given to them as children left on the block. It made me wonder why our churches are locked. Jesus is on the block yo and on the rooftops; he's not above.. he's among. People say they believe in Jesus, yet they walk pass him daily never takin' one homeless home with them. In speaking with rooftop and concrete homeless people, they never seem to complain about their living quarters. Many speak about being thrown to the street as children by their parents who thought begging on the block would give them some form of food. How sad is that?

Those who are wealthy in our country perhaps should put money on the streets they trot. Various types of people are waiting outside the shelters. I had no problem bringing home the homeless and cleaning them up. It bothered my husband to some degree, but he accepted the fact I wasn't going to stop. Somewhere around fifty-six people from the block came through my door. I was a nominee for the Humanitarian Award at the African American Music Awards.

New York in the House

RIHANNA'S FATHER RON IS AN ACTIVE, VIBRANT, AND A HELL OF A NICE GUY!

RIHANNA'S FATHER RON IS AN ACTIVE, VIBRANT, AND A HELL OF A NICE GUY!

RIHANNA'S FATHER RON IS AN ACTIVE, VIBRANT, AND A HELL OF A NICE GUY!

I learned nearly every city has people on rooftops. In speaking with the homeless you get a side of knowledge to think about. They look at the apostles as old men who eventually became senile. Some believe their gift is street knowledge. Some actually know we have found bones from Dinosaurs from 200 million years ago but haven't found bones from biblical characters such as the Apostles that were supposed to have been on earth 4,000 years ago. The homeless believe it's all questionable; therefore, they're happy to spend their life on a rooftop or on the block waiting to see what happens. Hmmm… It was amazing to hear them speak about ministers, priests, the rabbi's, etc. They speak about clergy who don't know any more than the rest of us, who get to live in furnished houses with medical insurance, food and clothing, a TV and money. The people in the pews work at McDonald's, sweatshops, grocery stores. Clergy in every denomination tryin' to teach us what's up and how to live. Hmmm…

Homeless Musician

You read how I washed toilets and cleaned homes for the wealthy as an extra when the regular employed housekeeper couldn't. I would take the money offered me and give it to the poor. After I got done cleaning I'd ride the streets handing out the money I received to homeless on the block while singing to music on my radio. It felt so good. When people ask me for money I take it as an insult. The first question I'd ask them is if they're still smoking cigarettes or weed? Their answer was always yeah. My answer back was perhaps you should give up your habits and find a violet.

One day I took a shortcut and drove behind a group of stores where the dumpsters are. I discovered a young man digging in the dumpster. I stopped the car and invited him to go with me to lunch. He didn't know me, so he said, "I'll walk to the diner out front and meet you there." We sat and had a nice lunch. I explained to him my money comes from scrubbing the toilets of successful people.

He enjoyed the lunch and was thankful. The following week I got a call to clean a home. I went to the basement looking for a mop when I heard a person coughing. I shouted hello, who's there? Out from behind the heater came the guy I took to lunch from the dumpster. I ask him, "What are you doing in someone's home in the dark basement." He said, "They have no idea that I climb in the cellar window to sleep nights." I questioned how long he has been doing this and his reply was years. He explained that he doesn't have a job and had nowhere to live. He confessed when they're not home he goes in the refrigerator and takes a little bit of food.

Then he asked me to keep the secret. Wow… The following week the same people asked could I come and serve their Jewish holiday dinner to their family and friends. I knew it would be quite an experience cuz I'm not Jewish. The day of Yom Kipper I arrived and prepared the table for the dinner. As the doorbell rang the husband would greet the quest and announce them. The doorbell rang and there stood the guy from the dumpster who lives in the basement dressed in a suit. I was shocked. The parents introduced him as their wonderful son who works on the west coast who flew in for the holiday. When the moment was right I whispered to him, what's up? "I'm their good for nothing son who hides in the basement who they are ashamed of. They don't want their friends to know about me."

SPOLARIZED® PRESS CONNECTION
BENEATH THE HYPE IN THE
WORLD OF ENTERTAINMENT...

The parents liked me so much they asked me to clean the following week. When I arrived, I headed for the basement. I invited the boy to come upstairs and chat with me while I cleaned the house. He answered by saying, "I can do better than that for you. While you're cleaning I will serenade you on my parent's piano and you can buzz around with the mop and the dust rag." Unbeknown to anyone he was a fabulous piano player. What I learned was they had no use for a son who wanted to be a musician.

Oprah, Stedman, and Ellen DeGeneres

As Press I never had the opportunity to meet Oprah. It has always puzzled me why society only seems to recognize Oprah as being a mogul with fame in the entertainment world. Society knows she helps those less fortunate. Somewhere society missed the boat by not recognizing and talking more about the personal side of her. A woman who has her act together in a relationship. A woman who has stuck it out with one man, Stedman Graham. We see constantly in the media how many Rich and Famous float in and out of relationships and marriages and how money changes them. Oprah hasn't changed who she is over the years.

She is faithful to who she is and never let money control her. Of course, I'd recognize this attribute it's one of my traits. Oprah knows a relationship is a bond between two people who strengthen each other. Stedman and Oprah have proved that two highly involved individuals can endure. Stedman is a man who understands what it's like to be a businessman and be in a relationship with someone who is at the top of her game. Three cheers to Oprah and Stedman for showing us what it means to be stronger together. I am equally pleased by Ellen DeGeneres's rise to the top. She excels on all the demonstrated skills she possesses, while being true to herself. She is selfless and giving and another example of how good people doing good things can win.

Bill Gates · Bill Maher – Howard Stern – Steve Harvey

There's something to be said about "Street Sense Make Sense." There're some people who just can't seem to get the rodeo right. When you're smart and savvy you open your eyes and ears and learn how business interacts with the ghetto and street. There's plenty of rich people like Bill Gates who put effort into being somebody by learning, studying, listening and struggling to get to the top and be a winner in life.

Bill Gates is a man who didn't let money rule him. He stayed faithful to humanity.

I often thought how fantastic it would be if I could hook up with Bill and he took hold of my trade secrets in technology. We all have the right to dream, eh...

Bill Maher is a man that is killa on speaking gut-wrenching statements on-point, which most people wouldn't have the balls to say. It's obvious Bill and Bill didn't sit in their own self-pity or they wouldn't be where they are today. I want to believe they were Spolarized® without knowing it. Shining the Star, they should be by brushing themselves off. I dreamed Bill Maher walked up to me at a venue and said, "I heard that you're a white bitch crazy. I am glad to meet you." The dream was so real that I sat up in my bed. Bill understands the term keepin' it real.

Nothing like a Ford and the Like Dat Generation Crew

Over the years he has stayed faithful to his moral qualities and beliefs whether they're right or wrong. He has his standard of who he is. Much like Howard Stern who likewise stays faithful to his ways and beliefs. My children knew growing up they couldn't use certain words till they were my age because they would get pepper on their tongue. Listening to Howard on the car radio the kids said, "Howard must be your age Mommy cause he uses the bad words we can't." I lied, shaking my head yep. We all know Steve Harvey from TV and the like. What I recognize in his character is he defends his decisions regardless of the backlash. Part of his character is seeing how people react and he knows how to apologize for his behavior when he feels he's wrong. How many people can do that eh?

Brooklyn Warehouse and a Ford

I've been told time and time again by those who feel they are above me that I needed to roll up in an expensive car if I wanted to be taken seriously in the entertainment world. A meeting was set up to meet in Brooklyn on airplay for my clients by a radio DJ at WBLS. I would take any radio station like Hot 97, Power 105.1, 103.9, Wired 96.5, or Power 99 out of my city Philly. Any radio station willing to give me airplay. My joints aren't just in Hip-Hop. I also have bad a** metal tracks with an artist that would blow most metal joints out the ballpark.

I weakened and let Mark B convince me that if I didn't roll up in a high-end Benz or Mercedes, I would be disrespected. We rolled up in Mark B's fancy car and were disrespected. I was told I need payola. Money is what I needed for airplay and with no guarantee. At that moment I thought back to 2 Pac "All Eyez On Me" you mothers. Who you think you're fu★kin' wit? Philly's in the house.

The dudes in Brooklyn workin' for the DJ had no idea about my background and the ghetto side of me. I have plenty of homies in Brooklyn who know not to ask for payola. I think of the song by Fifty, "In Da Club." People feel my buzz and yell Spolarized Legally Loaded® in the house when I walk in a club where the DJ knows me. I often wonder why Fifty hasn't stumbled onto to me. I'm from the concrete jungle Philly, tough like the role he plays. Payola hits a nerve in me.

People who don't know me don't understand how deep and far back Fords run in my veins. My grandmother Mary didn't drive but her first husband had a Ford. He died of TB and left my grandmother a Ford. She treasured it sittin' in the yard.

Her second husband Papa Joe is the grandfather I grew up knowing and loving. He didn't drive. They would call my father to take them places. Papa Joe was like a kid in a candy shop riding in my father's spotless shiny Ford. My father ungraded his Ford every 2 years. Papa Joe died of cancer and my grandmother Mary married her third husband who had a Ford. He died of TB and left her a Ford. You would have thought she would have learned to drive. Nope... My father's father drove a Ford.

Can you believe I married a man with a Ford? His father drove a Ford. I got my driver's license at 16. Tom bought a 1964 Mustang and I got to drive it. He had a shiny red Ford truck he used for work. On weekends he raced the Mustang at Langhorne Race Track. He dropped the tranny at 90 out the gate at one of the races. He replaced the tranny. He won, whoopde-do. The kids enjoyed screaming from the bleachers. When the boys were old enough to drive they got a Ford. One year our family bought 4 Ford Tempo's. My dad taught you don't

My parents passed driving a Ford onto me.
Many have felt my a** slid in and out along wit my family.

Fords Have Always Been Our Workhorse

Nothin' Like Enjoying A Beer With Two Real Cowboys...

trade a Ford in till it leaks water. That would be a person who would put their parent into a nursing home before they need diapers. Why I let Mark B talk me out of rollin' up with my Ford in Brooklyn I can't explain. It's so not me. I am who I am and that's a fact. The dudes in Brooklyn had no idea what they were dealing with nor did Mark B. When it comes to fu*kin' wit me, I become a warrior from the concrete jungle. This white bitch crazy... Philly Grown...

The dudes in Brooklyn thought they could play me and intimidate me. Wrong... There was a basketball hoop on the wall and those dudes were playing. I grabbed the basketball. Everyone stopped. I said, "Now that I have your attention, shut the fu*k up and open that fu*kin' door now." A few of the dudes said, "Who's the white bitch? Who does she think she is?" At that moment I shouted out loud, "Shut the fu*k up. Tell your DJ I don't pay payola." Once we were outside I turned to Mark B and said, "So how's your theory work about a fancy car verse my Ford?" If you been in Philly then you should know Philly bitches are No.1 who don't tolerate sh*t. They stand to their feet like masterpieces. This Philly girl is proud to drive a Ford.

Shadowbrook Resort

Thirty miles from our estate is a club called Shadowbrook Resort where our family would go every Saturday night to dance. I can't tell you how proud I was as a mother to see my children dancing on the dance floor high on Coca-Cola. We are all good dancers and dominated the dance floor. The DJ would spin the songs he knew we liked. He knew we kept the place poppin' and were the floor show. Songs like C&C Music Factory "Gonna Make You Sweat." We made up our own lyrics to "Mony Mony" and sang out loud. They went like this, "Hey say what good girls don't fu*k." We went crazy on a lot of songs. Songs like, "Keep your hands to yourself." We would put our hands up and push back as we sing along.

Dire Straits song "Walk of Life" in 1985 we'd walk by each other like hot stuff using our creative dance moves. In 89 Technotronic hit wit "Move This" off the album "Pump up the Jam" which talked about likin' it in the raw. You could actually see new dance patterns on the dance floor. The Disco years offered smooth mixes which made it easy to stay on time on the dance floor. Swinging your hips in a circular move with thrusting offered freedom to dance without a partner showing off your creative skills. Of course, my family loved it. Haddaways "What is Love" and 4 Non Blondes "What's Up" moved you in da club.

A German group called Snap released the song "The Power" which had a great hook. It also offered the listener the feeling of being in power. Three cheers to an insane track and production. Snap was killa and the lyrics off the hook. We as family have stepped to the beat our whole life. We enjoyed Joan Jetta and the Blackheart "Can't Help Myself for Loving You." Together we enjoyed dancing with the seeds we planted that grew into trees spread across our 90-acre estate.

Tom and I understood we were opposites from the get-go. One thing we had in common was we both love to dance. Tom hardly missed a day that he didn't climb in the playpen with his beer and dance with the boys. Tom was in his glory with two cowboys at his side. Our daughter who was a 3-year old would dance and sing on the outside of the playpen with me. Had the song "Halo" by Beyoncé been out I'd have played it even though I knew damn well my children wouldn't grow up with Halos over their head.

DJ Stylze Up and Ms Peggy to the flow Legally Loaded

I've had my share of correcting my children and their children. All in all, my children are a blessing. Forget pouting over wanting a marriage made in heaven. I knew damn well it wasn't going to happen. My mistake was letting Tom repeat over and over things to the children a** backwards due to being under the influence of alcohol. The sad part is the children were programed. They grew up believing bullsh*t stories. There wasn't a day that we didn't fight. Fighting over drinking and driving or fighting over something he did that was serious enough to argue about.

I let the stories he told the children ride that weren't reality. Now that I'm older and wiser I realize the damage it did. There's no way to change the minds of grown adults who believe the stories told to them weren't true. Tom was the luckiest man I know. He never got a DWI. Perhaps, it's all the rosaries I did that saved his a**. My sons wore scapulars through junior high school and my daughter wore a cross. By senior high my daughter and her brother were on dance floors winning awards.

The Bee Gee's had it going on in "Stayin' Alive" in 77. Music like the Bee Gee's hit dance floors the same time as my children's feet. Their early playpen days surely set them apart from the rest of the dancers. Shadowbrook Resort's dance floor was replaced by owning my own bar with a dance floor. Do you remember the song "What is Love" by Haddaway in 93? The song made people explosive on the dance floor.

Take note when Tom's little cowboys in the playpen were grown they were into AC/DC "Shoot to Thrill." They became inventors of the "Bad Dog" sight holder shooting bullseyes with bow and arrow and they did have horses on our estate.

Music from the Past

It's not just about who's popular today. It's about music from the past that brought us to today. Thinkin' back as far as the 50's or '69 with Woodstock. Back then music offered us live instruments and multiple musicians performing. Let's not forget the music people got high on dancing in a barn or a local bar such as mine. Together as a family we turned a little local bar in to the hottest place in the county. People drove for miles to the Friendsville Inn just to enjoy a stellar night with the touch of Philly in house.

Looking back, I wish I could have had Finger Eleven's song "Paralyzer." A song created by a band with a twist between grunge, metal, and alternative. It would have been nice if Flo Rida and Kesta's "Right Round" was around. A song that makes you want to sing along. My client Olivia's style is much like Evanescence. Olivia's metal is above and beyond most writers and her skills are insane along with her vocals. Sadly, to say, all the record deals offered to my record label were meant to fu*k the artist much like the Superstars contacts I've read.

Metal, Rock, along with Rock and Roll is where my roots began. Like Dat and Easy Moby Bee got me poppin' rap. I had introduced my clients, Stuff and Storm, to my metal engineer and what he accomplished with my clients was a different creative style. When it came to metal with Olivia together they were phenomenal. It was shocking to take my rap artist Olivia and place her in metal bringing forth such greatness in a completely opposite genres of music. In '09 T.I. and Justine Timberlake came up with Dead and Gone. The lyrics and the feeling it offered you is what made the song stronger. Listening to the artist Chingy

Livin' on the ridge is mighty rough. Livin' on the ridge you got to be tough. I got my swag and I got my hustle. With a mic in my hand I blow it on the flow yo... I took the fall for you all so why break me? When you made me...

back in '03 with "Right Thurr" lyrics and beat forced DJ's to play the song in clubs over and over.

It had the same effect as "Party Up" by DMX in '00. I practically lived in my studio in the NYC. I remember when Snow Patrol with "Chasing Cars" came out how it offered such a buildup that you almost believe you could lay in a garden. It made me think about on the way to my garden and pickin' a rose. The tear from the rose plucked me.

Entering the broccoli patch I woke from a dismal state learning a song I wrote was platinum. Being ripped off isn't an easy thing to ingest. Music, beats and movie scripts are still being stolen today. The TV series Empire has had its share of lawsuits coming at them. Kanye West with "Heartless" which proved an artist's greatness can be beyond their vocals. Say what you want about Kanya, but one thing is for sure the man knows his sh★t when recording.

We should agree Cardi B has rap down and has had a few breaks in the industry by merging her with artists like Maroon 5. You win some and like me you lose some. My gold on another man's wall is a hard thing to absorb. Litigation in the game never stops.

Look at Pharrell Williams lawsuit for "Blurred Lines." I wouldn't have thought with all his skill and experience Pharrell would have wrote a song like "Happy."

It made money for sure but most of his songs seem repetitive and tiresome. Take an artist like Aerosmith and the song "I Don't Want to Miss a Thing" where you hear creative skill and ability to lay out a good piece of work. I've been conducting analysis of music for years. Generations of musical work over the years has been created with artistic skill involved along with live instruments.

Technologies in the game took us to a new places. I took my client Olivia and placed her in 3 genres of music, and she killed them all. She is a fabulous writer and artist. We can go all the way back to 93 when pop culture hit the scene with Culture Beat and "Mr. Vain."

A new style of music created for dance moves and a beat that made you high without a drink. Technology allowed my engineer to play his guitar and turn what he played into a musical organ keyboard from his computer. He brought platinum out of a cellar studio. Years later I was still getting great work out of cellars and attics; it is said that Biggie got platinum out of a bedroom.

Talent Pound has a BBQ for you when you are done in the studio. I remember back in 03 when Kid Rock and Sheryl Crow hit the stage with "Picture." Their music was a calm easy mix. Even though it wasn't my type of music it sold well. People were happy with strumming loops and simple. My grandkids Rocky and Luke, both have guitars. Without any prior instructions, these two young boys began strumming to the beat hittin' cords equal to the music playing on their boombox.

How hard can strumming be? That is the reason why as an analyst I don't enjoy music that doesn't have creative abilities and skill involved. My engineer was much like Carlos Santana. Mastering the art of how to make a guitar scream notes. My parents were at the first Woodstock in 69 and saw Carlos Montana perform. You must admit that's talent. Great talent.

An Old Soul Legally Loaded

I'm old as the soul on your home stereo. Oh, cheerio you know why I want to go gold. I go back as far as Haley's Comets. I been doing this sh*t like Metamucil®. It has been hard opening my ♡ to society writing this book. My bodyguard Dr. Mark VIP hears my cries on a daily. Every day since I awoke from my dismal state back in the late eighties has been rough. When I first heard my song on the radio while driving unbeknown to me that the gold/platinum song I was listening to was mine. I began to tremble and shut it off. I pulled to the side of the road and cried. I had no idea what the hell just happen to me.

The following day is when I saw the vision of my baby on my chest and blood everywhere. Since that day when my parents sat me on the porch swing and told me what happened to me, I fear every day that I might hear my song played or see the vision of my baby.

The song has been remixed twice by other artists. Sadly, to say it has been used in a TV commercial and now and then it plays on radio stations. How dare someone ask me what song and make more money and fame for thieves. Each time it causes emotional pain to my soul and the shoe I'm standing in. It is why I turned to rap and hip-hop so I can spit out my feelings in a rhyme. Every day I hope I don't see someone in a store or on TV who looks similar to my sons and wonder if it could be my missing triplet. I'm yesterday, today and tomorrow Philly Grown faithful to who I be. I hope you're ready to "Rock the Block" with me east to west "Legally Loaded®" and help stop fraud and corruption.

Shootin' from the Hip Hoobastank

Hoobastank's song in 04 "The Reason" offered a musical work that people can relate to along with the track seated perfectly. The gritty vocals make the listener want to hear it again. The track is a sequence of musical notes that are satisfying to the composition. The song affected me enough to take my cell phone and play the song to my husband Tom.

When the song ended I tearfully read him a letter I wrote. I said, "Hon I hope you can understand I'm sorry if I hurt you and couldn't be the wife you wanted me to be the past 57 years. There's a side of me you didn't want to recognize, I am who I am. I wouldn't have been a strong woman without tough parents who handed me over to you as a child… I stayed focus on the mountain peak where you transplanted me.

Unbeknown to me my mother brought some "Leaves" to comfort me from my childhood playground the forest on the edge of Philly. I understand neither of us are perfect. It's clear we've never been on the same page with our lifestyle. You taught me how to stand tall and take the flak when things went wrong and find a fix, so you didn't look bad. Over the years I've been bombarded with your criticism. Without you I may have fallen but with you I became a warrior without sores able to step onward triumphantly. The blessing of being with you is together we planted seeds that will grow for generations to come. They represent us in the universe. They'll start anew and play among the "Leaves" left behind and amend our mistakes."

The Soul and the Shoe

Perhaps the soul is our Breath and the Shoe that walks the steps we take through life. The muscular part of our body takes in air through the lungs which then exhales it through relaxation. When we breathe in and out, we take in what is around us including smell and the vision of what we saw. Breath absorbs color as the message is sent to the brain. The Soul gasps color as we exhale and claims or avoids the color.

Through breath we exhale feelings and emotion within the Soul. Through breath the Soul feels temperature too. Sitting in a room that's cold, the Soul allows us to see our breath and clue us in. Through Breath the Soul feels attitude of people in a room by their breathing pattern. Sitting in a room that is too warm, the Soul begins to sweat and pant short breaths. Sitting in a room with anger or hostility the Soul begins to breathe without slack, tightness in the muscles. The Soul through breath knows to exit uncomfortable surroundings. A person's steps in life are better if the Shoe is comfortable versus those who have no shoes or those who have shoes that don't fit right.

The Shoe we wear doesn't stop our Step forward or onward. Perhaps those who get ahead in life is due to the Shoe they wear. They inhale and exhale properly through life. They've utilized the air learning what's up, what's not. Perhaps listening and trotting in tune, the Shoe will fit better, and the Soul will become genuine and great. A person needs a bona fide character with mental and moral qualities inhaling and exhaling knowing the surrounding around them and the Soul will breathe their worth.

Together We Made It Happen

CHECK

ONE

CHECK

TWO

I met a man named Lee
among this crowd who told
me in this game blondie you
better be on a low.

I never forgot those words
as the lights went
out a few seconds later.
I been on a Lee Low ever since.

Please Don't Ever Be Intimidated By What I Say. Be Inspired And Perhaps Learn Something You Never Knew...

Spolarized Entertainment Press Connection
Musical Analysis Section

You have surely guessed by now that music is my passion. Back in time I carried a Bible with a tablet in it jotting down things I learned from street. Today I'm a Baka, Diva, Jima, a music analysis and a mentor to the entertainment industry and the Stars. People send people to me who want to get it right saying, 'This White Bitch Crazy.' Over the years I've been in and out studios and learned chord progression, the sections, number of layers, effects, interludes, laying down vocals, mixing, mastering, and what is worthy of platinum. The finished product is a collection of multiple things, a good engineer, a good beatmaker, a great writer, and a good artist to lay the joint down. Lastly, ownership of the copyright of the finished product. As an analysis I enjoy hearing a riff as an ostinato figure repeating a progression riff that

I can still hear in my brain once the song ends. I want the musical composition to be worth letting it bore into my soul. A song that if I hum a few bars the person next to me would know the song. Over time I've seen musicians adopt techniques from other musicians. Being an artist and musician myself from age 14 and become an analysis over the last 50 years is almost like hearing and seeing a blueprint repeating itself. A copy of showmanship, style, engineering, rhythmic along with melodies, have been the backbone of "All in one Life Beneath the Hype."

Have you ever heard a song and ask yourself how the hell it went platinum? Millions of market money. After you hear the song enough you begin to think it's good and convince yourself the artist must be good because they are platinum. Sometimes, it's dirty money along with payola. Artists sometimes gain fame from being on a joint with a famous artist. It took years and years of pushing, yelling, and screaming in studios to get engineers, artists, and beatmakers to give me a finished product that is worthy of my name, Ms. Peggy.

Runnin' My Mouth as a Musical Analysis

It's time to run my mouth freestyle so get ready. I've been in the game so damn long I sat back and took my music background to the next level forming Spolarized® Press Connection. As a Personal Business Manager, I work on contracts along with being an analyst of artist musical work. An artist who executes a rhyme successfully is DMX. An example is "Party Up" in 00. All praise due for the video and rhythm "Ruff Ryders' Anthem" Those were the days of old school rap with Coolio (feat. L.V.) and "Gangsta's Paradise." Standing in a gangsta's life is no paradise.

Trust me. I've been around a lot of gangsta's over the last 76 years. Let's not forget gangsta's took me down when I was 19. Don't be surprised that I met with Frank Lucus's son Frank Jr and his people moons ago. I took his crew of 4 out to dinner. They were cordial and could have eaten at the president's house. They wanted my opinion on a joint. I told them what I thought. They were shocked that I was being totally honest but that's what they wanted. Listening to the song by Black Eyed Peas "Where is the Love." I thought it would've taken us to a better place in the world. Will.i.am is not only creative in the use of his name, he's a sweet pea who will give you his time of day. Nelly's cousins Big Sean and Yomi kicked a** to make it happen for Nelly. Once Nelly was rollin' in dough he didn't need them any-

SPOLARIZED™ PRESS CONNECTION
BENEATH THE HYPE IN THE WORLD
OF ENTERTAINMENT...

Spolarized Crew was featured on Billboards and in Magazines

159

Proof that fairytales are true. "Make a wish it may come true" is what my mother taught me. Over the years many rainbows appeared across the mountain side. The leaves soak up the sunlight as rain droplets fall from the sky. I would make a wish.

more. His songs and production are so-so. On another note regardless of the out-burst at times from Kanye West his joint "Gold Digger" is outrageous.

The way Kanye presents the lyrics is killa along with Jamie Fox and the track. It was originally done by Ray Charles and Renald Richard. Pitbull is a performer who never goes out of his zone. Pitbull's best song is "Give me Everything." When an artist does a song that's familiar to your ear like Akon did on "Lonely" with co-writers, the artist isn't really comin' out the gate with original work. I'm guilty of switchin' stations to hear a great musical work worthy of my praise receiving top honors from Spolarized® Press Connections.

When I met Outkast they were dressed like flower power from my old days. Happy-go-lucky greeting people at their booth at the Magic Convention, they were as crazy in person as they were in there video "Hey Ya". I met with them in a private area of the booth. Two sweet peas were smiling and greeted me with, "what's up?" I told them I spit. They said, "Spit something for us." I spit one of my joints free style and they both stood to their feet and shook my hand with the words that it was insane. I replied, I've been in the game forever; I'm in my 50's.

When I met Ice T he was soft spoken and smiling. It was hard to believe he once rapped hardcore. Finally, I met up with Stevie Wonder surrounded by his staff. I was new to the staff and even though I had a Press badge, the staff assured me Stevie wouldn't care and would brush me off. His staff informed me he only talks to people in meetings or those already in his camp. I shared a few minutes with his hair stylist. I walked away thinking it is Stevie's loss not mine.

If you want to know an artist that enjoys playing live with talent; you'd think of Santana and Wyclef and "Maria Maria." Metallica gives it to us with a slightly different touch in "Nothing Else Matters." Who can forget Eric Clapton or Led Zeppelin, Pink Floyd or Rolling Stones, Aerosmith or The Who, and Creedence Clearwater? All gifted musicians who knew what it took to put out a piece of music with creative appeal. The Eagles give us a different creative touch in their recording "Life in the Fast Lane" showing creative skill and a mindset that boost the listeners mood. Of course, Rolling Stones music also captured a lot of quarters in a jukebox.

R.E.M.'s track on the song "Losing My Religion" is insane. An A++. Back in time you had artists like Glenn Campbell, Johnny Denver, Frank Sinatra, and Dean Martin, when music wasn't as complex. Just hang on a beat and fans are basically happy. Artist like Blake Shelton understands what is sellable in the marketplace.

"Somewhere Over the Rainbow" by "IZ" is done so well you believe gumdrops will fall from the sky. Over the years many "Rainbows" have appeared in my yard and have appeared where I've had my office. Whenever I see a rainbow I immediately begin to sing the song. You can believe a story is just that or you can believe fairytales are real. Just like in a fairytale there have been times in my life when I mention I've seen a rainbow and instantly men began to sing the song to me. Believe it or not Mel Montana, Richard Zakka, Dr. Mark VIP, Mark Levy ESQ and my mother. What a surprising experience. The song also touched me by an unknown caller announcing there was a rainbow on a phone book ad of my corporation.

A rainbow is the reflection of sunlight in water droplets. The Sun is something I claimed long ago in my yard among the grandchildren, calling it Spolarized. The Sun is what makes

the colors. It is considered a phenomenon. For me it has been just that. John Legend who came up by being back up to famous artists made it on his own through skill. Although I like the song "All of Me" his voice is proof he isn't Elton John or Billy Joel or the many artist who hold platinum. He had help from Toby Gad on the song who is a fabulous writer. The song is a Grammy winner. Being honest, there's thousands of artist on every block and in churches who are good. They don't need to quickly change falsettos. They don't sing slightly under the correct pitch or cut short. I'll give headz up to anyone who stays faithful to the game and brings home a platinum. Green Bay doesn't have energy yet went Platinum.

Most singers modestly hold a two-octaves range. Some can accomplish more like Freddie Mercury of Queen or Axl Rose of Guns and Roses. The world's record of 10 octaves is held by Tim Storms. Sometimes lyrics, a hook, or the beat, magically brings home the gold. Willie Nelson is another old school singer who could teach us something about weed. Who would of thought Willie would have passed on his gifted talent to his son who contributed to the soundtrack of the movie "A Star is Born?" Over the years we've had natural comedy with Robin Williams and many others. Howard Stern over the years has offered a bolder look into things as a radio character and host. I can't tell you how many conversations I've had with the late Aaron Braunstein over Howard Stern. Aaron's desire was being live on radio. Aaron is another part of my world Beneath the Hype. Back in the days his so-called button business was around the corner from my office on 38th and Broad.

He had a hide away on the second floor few knew about. It was where the real business was handled. There were times when he'd say stay away from my office for the day. It made me curious, so I'd take in a coffee at the end of the block and watch to see who pulls up. Shockin' at times! I knew he was protecting me. In his home he was likewise protective of who he let into his world. I questioned who he was since he carried a piece (gun) in NYC. He knew some of the very people most people think are OK. Really... Think again... Now that we have Donald Trump as our President some of the very same people who I realize were Aaron's so-called associates are likewise Donald Trumps. Aaron's known for the first boxing match in Israel, however he was heavy into investing into the sport. He befriended some of the same people in the boxing world who I knew. Aaron's world let me see a side no one realizes exist. Something I knew to block out of my head. He loved his children and was proud of who he was. When I think about the entertainment world and all the avenues I've been involved in, I think of Irene Cara. She showed off natural aptitude along with chemistry in "Flashdance/What a Feeling" making a dance floor come to life. A Great Big World proved they could touch fans with "Say Something" scoring a home run. When I met Kid Rock he was soft acting and nothin' like I thought he'd be. His production "All Summer Long" hit home for his fans.

Alabama was his best work hittin' with a killa track. Rock being my base from childhood who could forget Journey and their hits like "Separate Ways." Their music and performances superb. I can't tell you how many times the song "Hot Blooded" by Foreigner was player in my bar. The song had what it took to make people actually believe they were Hot. They had it together as a band. Music beats insane. The lead guitarist hit the riffs that drove home along with the other members of the band. It is great guitarists and bands like Jimi Hendrix, Led Zeppelin, Phill Collen (Def Leppard) and the like, that took rock to another level. How

Tom was a 5 Time State Champion who taught his skill to his wife and sons. Shooting in the Pro Class Gregory took 10th in the country. Mike took 1st in the Double A Class in New York State and I was Queen of the Bow.

many can say their artist is so f★ckin' good that she kills it in rap and metal? Me. Spolarized Records owns all its master. My people don't screw each other.

I'd like to say in some sorta way Ted Nugent's style became his trademark. My husband Tom, my sons, and I shot archery crossing paths with Ted. His performances seemed to always reflect that of a warrior. Hard to beat and more than likely could kick my a★★ on the archery course even though I was queen of the bow. He may however have a rough time beating my son Gregory who's a champion bullseye archer. My sons patented the sight holder to stop the movement of the site on a bow, called Bad Dog. Thinkin' back on old school music which opened the door for emerging genres like rock, blues, jazz, country, soul, funk, and hip-hop has changed over time significantly. There's never been an artist that doesn't think he's the bomb. It's a common thread I hear every time I'm asked to analyze a musical work. Macklemore & Ryan Lewis came out the gate wit a hook that really did hook you. A clean clear piece of musical work that anyone could relate to.

There are tons of musical works worthy of my praise such as ZZ Top's "Gimme All Your Movin'" or The Dream-Cranberries with "What's Up?" or Linkin Park with "Numb." Back in '99 we had NSYNC pop/rock. Backstreet with "Larger Than Life" offered disco along with lyrics that made you think you could reach your potential. In '79 I'm analyzing Rod Stewart's "Do You Think You Can Dance." What I realized about the song was the lyrics offered a way to feel comfortable on the dance floor riding a bootie in time with the groove. Many times, his work is about phrases that grab hold of you. In '79 Sister Sledge creativity came up with "We Are Family." Lyrically the song will last forever. In '77 country people were enjoying the song by Jimmy Buffet "Margaritaville." I'm not much of a country fan but my customers at the bar played it a lot making me money.

If they knew anything about music they'd know it's not much different from other country songs. An ostinato repeated chord progression pattern. The song by UB40 with "Red Red Wine" back in '83 was a song like most of the others with a drag on melody of rhythmic instruments. As strange as it may seem no one in my bar ever requested me to add Dolly Parton to the jukebox. If people knew anything they'd know she helps people and has maintained her image. In '93 when the song came out "What is Love" by Haddaway I couldn't get enough of the track. The lyrics and vocals are superb. The song made you want to dance under a disco ball.

Bee Gees with "Stayin' Alive" in '77 gives you a beat and vocals hittin' perfectly in time. Mixed to perfection. Vanilla Ice had a repetitive beat along with a repetitive hook "Ice Ice Baby" which took the song to the top. Over time he fell away. Once an artist hits they got to take it to the next level. Example: Bruno Mars, Michael Jackson, Eminem, Prince, and Drake knew to keep switchin' it up. When artists stay in the old school groove such as KRS-One, Wu tang and the like, it leaves openings in the marketplace for up comin' talent to hit the chart. When a rock artist hits with a song that's over the top lyrically and has a killa track it plays in rotations for years. Artists in hip-hop have cocky attitudes' which gets in the way of their music and many times causes them to drop. It's not easy being an analyst because you can't be bias. I've learned not to slack on judgement and how to take emotion out of the equation and not let it affect my decision of the musical work. I listen to how the keys and guitar is slamin' along with the bass and drums.

SPOLARIZED® PRESS CONNECTION
BENEATH THE HYPE IN THE WORLD OF
ENTERTAINMENT...

The lyrics need to be hittin' along with an insane hook. I look for vocals in key mixed and mastered to perfection. The song "Uptown Funk" used multiple hands in the mix like Jeff Bhasker, Philip Lawrence, Brono Mars, and Mark Ronson, along with producers and writers and months in the makin'. The presentation of the pop culture song which hit the charts was a hard act to follow with 3.33 billion views. Bryan Adams was killa with "Have You Ever Loved A Woman" and "Everything I Do I Do For You." Bryan structures his music to speak to the soul. Plenty of good talent comes from Canada like Nickelback with "Rock Star" which offered us a flow different than other artists. The song "Free Fallin'" by Tom Petty hit radio stations forcing me to get opinions of the song and why we're lovin' it. T.I. (feat. Justin Timberlake) in "Dead NS Gone" harmony was awesome. Props go out to Afrojack/Eve Simons with an insane track on the song "Take Over Control."

The song 'Uprizing" by Muse in 09 was ahead of time with lyrics not knowing that by the year 2018 we must stand up for our rights. Power can't control us. Talking about great are the Bee Gees in "Stayin' Alive." Production is perfection at its best. Most people think of Prince as an artist with talent, that's true. His flare and style helped his musical abilities. His Echo's on vocals and space between lyrics' help make my decision that I've heard better artists. We should all be thankful for those who service us like the McDonald worker, the Shoemaker, the Carpenter, the Bricklayers and Labors, the Farmer, the Manufacturers, the Dress Designers and Tailors, the Engineers, the Truck Drivers, the Gardeners, and the Housekeeper, without them where would we be eh? There would be no one to buy the music. Will the real Russel Simmons step forward? Russel greets people but doesn't go beyond that unless there's something in it for him. Unlike Wyclef who's wicked cool. I once got an invite to an event on Mother's Day weekend with a VIP badge by Wyclef right up front. Excitedly I told my kids I wouldn't be around for Mother's Day. My kids said, "Who the hell is Wyclef that you would miss Mother's Day with your children?" I said, "Come on its Wyclef." I didn't get any flowers or a card from my kids. Jay Z is a little of this and that, good today and who knows what tomorrow. It depends on what block you're on in NY. I can tell you that my people blew up Rockawear on billboards and in the streets. We were given all the Rockawear free we wanted. My clients were in full page magazine ads blowin' Jay's clothing line up.

I'm thinkin' somewhere over the years Jay Z changed by stumbling through enough wild weeds and found a Violet.

The late Dan H. was a beatmaker back in the days for a blink with a few signed artists on major labels. His oldest son was headed for fame, but Dan killed the deal by being crooked. His son was killed for the love of the game a few months later. As for me Dan stole $8,000 worth of brand-new equipment along with a $3,000 brand new keyboard. The case was pending

Spolarized Press Connection

in the court house when he died. He was racking in cash money making beats with my equipment and moved around town so I couldn't catch up with him for the money owed. You win some and you lose some in the world of entertainment. It was me on a lee low who discovered that LA Reid had a thief employed scamming artist out of money.

Back in the days I was a learner blowin' up clothing labels like Rockawear and FUBU by having my peeps wear it. Over time I befriended Carl Brown and Daymond John. Two completely different characters way different than Keith Perrin and Alex Martin. All I can say is you got to know them before you can judge them. Likewise, L A Reid. Back in the days LaFace was the sh★t with artists hittin' in the charts. Let's not forget Dr. Dre was the touch that gave famous rappers what they needed like Eminem. Curtis Young has music in his blood much like his dad. Now and then I've had the opportunity to speak with Curtis and his wife.

This story could rock your socks, so you might as well slide them off and sit down. I saw first-hand Kiss; Gene Simmons slide his tongue between a girl's tatas at Magic after asking her permission. The best part is the girl didn't know who he was. Everybody gathered around and started yelling Gene's still got it, laughing, taking pictures as Gene slid his tongue deep into her cleavage. The girl turns and says, "who are you anyway?" What dumba★★ woman would let somebody slide their tongue between their tatas? She's somebody's daughter and I feel sorry for her parents.

My father taught me to hang with people of Jewish decent cuz they're intelligent and smart. I guess that includes Gene. When I got older and wiser I told my dad I'm a little bit of this and that and I don't give a damn, I am who I am and that's a fact. I'm alive. Who wouldn't love Madonna? It only took her a blink to get her act together. In 1996 the movie Evita came out based on the work of Andrew Lloyd Webber and Tim Rice. I've seen the movie 40 times or more with my bodyguard. We sing the song "Don't Cry for Me Argentina" as a weekly matinee. The movie depicts a woman who was a poor nothing and becomes something. The script, the acting, and production of the movie were superb. Madonna was sumptuous gold. The movie portrayed how anyone, a homeless person, a prostitute's, a McDonald worker, a laborer, is a soul and a shoe of someone who is spectacular. Madonna is glorious as an actress wit killa vocals.

We should all agree Madonna saw a violet beneath the wild weeds as a young woman. She heard the A·ve Ma·ri·a and was blessed with multiple gifts and talents.

Another artist/actress worthy of praise is Jennifer Lopez who is noble and became a spectacular star with endless talent. Jennifer has the ability to enter into multiple characters and capture her audience. Pink is the next icon to keep an eye on. She's an artist who is polished with off the chart performances. Vocals that exercise the power of lyrics with attitude.

SPOLARIZED™ PRESS CONNECTION BENEATH THE HYPE IN THE WORLD OF ENTERTAINMENT...

I'm forever grateful for the life and gift of Whitney Houston and her incredible talent. The song "I will Always Love You" is breath taking. Female artists like Adele, Celine Dion, and Rihanna, Janet Jackson, Lady Gaga, Olivia Alive, and Kelly Clarkson, Taylor Swift, Katy Perry, Carrie Underwood, Alicia Keys, Miley Cyrus, Joan Jetta, Jennifer Hudson, and Aretha Franklin capture their fans as well. They've got incredible vocals along with execution of artistic skill and unmeasurable talent. In 2004 Kelly Clarkson's song "Because of You" was hard to listen to because the lyrics hit home for me.

Her vocals are amazing. When I was young in the game Cher was the ticket in "Believe." In the late 80's I was chillin' in studios after hours listening to the newest music gonna hit the marketplace in R&B and Rap. Queen Latifah was hittin' an bustin' a slightly different flow. Unbeknown and without recognition I had a hand in the mastering of many artist's musical work. Credit wasn't needed. I was a victim to the system for the love of music. Vitamin C's "Graduation" song forever friends is superb. The production, track and vocals are magnificent.

I've seen Birdman of Cash Money many times in VIP lounges. During one of them, I walked up to introduce myself. Damon Dash nodded for him to walk away and come over where he was standing. I thought perhaps Lil Wayne was a way to get to Cash Money and reached out on line to him. I get a message back, "What does a white woman know about rap?" I laughed thinking what the hell does Wayne know about business? He signed with Cash Money and is in a beef after Cash Money blew him up. I hit him back with one verse I wrote in script format. At the end of it I use the word bro. Wayne hit me back asking why I use the word bro? Really dude. I hit him back wit, "cuz I hang with Italians yo." Of course, I cc'd Birdman. I'm not stupid enough to leave him out of the picture. What happened after that is better left under the rug. You be the judge if I'm telling the truth or not.

When you want to know a hard-a** in the game you'd want to know Na Na from Memphis. I've seen Na Na go into Beacon Center in Harlem to body build and challenge men twice his size. Best not to open your mouth because Na Na be comin' at you wit, "put your money where your mouth is and will see what's up n*gga." It doesn't matter if I'm interviewing celebrities as Press or just chillin' at VIP parties, coast to coast people talk bullsh*t. Let's not forget how T.I., Flo Rida and T Pain showed love and brought it together on a joint.

Likewise, Philly dudes like Beanie Sigel, and Meek Mills had a way to give it to us with a sharp edge different than Will Smith who chose a softer blade approach. Will Smith killed it in 97 with the song "Men in Black." Beanie Sigel has had his highs and lows, but then who hasn't? Whenever, I have been at a venue where he has been he seem to always act respectable. Hot DJ's spin tunes to please their audience. Dudes like Louie G, DJ Scratch, Mr. Cee, DJ Ace, DJ Jazz, and DJ Clue. There's nothin' like a good DJ. I've seen my share over the years. The list is endless. DJ Rock Star P is the dude who spins on my estate and in clubs throughout the NYC. In an attic studio in Philly is where I got a natural high from an engineer named RX bustin' a** on a joint. I think back to the days when Big Daddy Kane and KRS-One were hot. I've been around DJ Kool Herk enough to see his ups and downs for the love of the game. Sometimes it's cuz of the company you keep, and some people never

SPOLARIZED® PRESS CONNECTION BENEATH THE HYPE IN THE WORLD OF ENTERTAINMENT...

learn. DJ Kid Capri was a hot in the 90's with a manager who didn't return calls. Swizz Beatz always switchin' it up.

Damon Dash takes the cake on thinkin' he knows what's up. In reality he's always learning. He sucks up and at times he's fu*ked up. When you want to be a businessman you put the shoe on and wear it, bro. Jay Z and Beyonce are artists, performers and into a lot of things including business. Jay Z finally stepped out of his old self and became a successful businessman. I've been VIP to Jay's parties and observed him during Magic. Yet I also stumbled onto a different side of business while seeking DJ's in clubs to spin my client's joints. I learned I needed to meet with the stock holders before the DJ could spin my joints. The DJ assured me his play list had to be approved by the stock holders. I walked because payola isn't my game.

My NYC office was set up with 50 G's from a "Beautific Man" with a killa studio. I met a guy named Darrell who told a fabricated story that he worked for Warner Brothers and like a stupid a** I believed him. He seated himself in my office at one of the multiple desks and claimed it. I was green at the time and thought he was the way into Warner Brothers. Darrell ended up a liar and a thief. He stole money and my masters and actually thought he'd get away with it.

I called my homie Stuff and he came through the office door ready to kill Darrell. He had Darrell by the throat ready to throw him out the 14th floor window. I'm screaming at Stuff to let him go.. it's not worth it. Stuff didn't give up. Darryl yells "don't kill me yo, the money's gone, I spent it on bitches, but you can have your masters." Stuff lowers Darrell back to the floor. I noticed my top draws was slightly open at my desk. I opened the draw, and someone put a $100.000 in cash in my desk drawer with a note use it wisely. To this day I have no idea who it was. As for Darrell, he became a minister.

Through the book you 've seen pictures of superstars, NFL players and different people; know that I took all the pics. Many of them have the old-fashioned negatives. I have a collection of cameras along with a lot of film equipment back when George Lucas was using the Canon XL. I learned a lot from a well-known photographer, producer, film director in LA, named Marino. When it comes to motion pictures and photography he was one of the very best. He learned of my desire to learn film and took me under his wing. I lived in his home and he was always a gentleman and made great cappuccino. He taught me some of the hardest lessons one could learn about film and how you can be a winner or a loser so easily. When it came to film and teaching me something about script writing a motion picture, one could say he was a pain in my a**. Marino demanded flawless work. When the movie James and the Giant Peach came out in 96 we went to see it because he wanted me to learn live action and animation. Three cheers to a great teacher...We think of Michael Jackson in today's time, however, back when I was growing up it was about Elvis. TV was fairly new and not everyone had one.

We were middle class but had enough money to buy a TV. My twin cousins along with some of the neighbor's kids would sit in front of the TV watching Bandstand back with Bob Horn. Who'd of thought I'd grow up and go to Bandstand? Who would have thought I'd become prey for the love of music? As children watching Bandstand we'd sing and giggle and sometimes jitterbug across my mom's floors. The Ed Sullivan Show in 56 was featuring Elvis

Spolarized Press Connection
Beneath The Hype
In The World of Entertainment

Presley. His debut featured him singing "Hound Dog." He began to move around and then start thrusting from the waist down something no one had ever seen. My father got up from the kitchen table walked in and turned the TV off. I stood up and yell Daddy, "What are you doing? He's spectacular; wow did you see those moves?" He was shouting out you shouldn't be thrilled seeing that, and then he turns to my mother and said, "Mother Mary you know when I call you Mother Mary it's time to listen up.

Did you see the actions on that man?" My mother who loved music as much as I did say to Daddy, "The world is very different now. You know how I preach we must move with time. The sound of his voice is absolutely incredible, and I don't mind his moves at all. Over time new forms of dancing will happen beyond the Jitterbug and I'm ready to learn." It was rare to see my mother stand up to my dad. Years later in '61 Elvis came out with "Can't Help Falling in Love" which offered fans not just a performer with skill, but a musical work that touched the soul with multiple talented composers who dated back as far as 1784. The song became one of her favorites. Who would have thought I'd grow up to be a Music Analyst? Many times, artists are just performers with good vocals. Over time artists learned that as long as they add something to the creation of the musical work they would be included as a writer. I write my sh*t and its melodies yet I'm still unknown.

Several record deals crossed my desk to sign me or one of my clients. The deal was about how to cheat us out of money. Who'd of thought years later I'd be visiting Sun Records and an invite to visit Elvis's estate to see his gold records. The writers for Elvis were top notch along with the producers. It was impressive seeing Elvis's Gold Records all over the walls. In '82 I was married with 3 kids when the song came out by The Police "Every Breath You Take." The Police offer an outstanding production. They have a smooth slickness to their music that makes you want to hear more of their work. That's what it's about… When you want to enjoy good musical work, a good production along with a great presentation; you think of Guns and Roses. The song "Patience" is probably my most favorite.

My son-in-law can sing exactly like Guns and Roses to the point that if you heard him you'd think it was Guns N Roses. Axl Rose was a songwriter, an artist, a musician, and a performer. Using the violin in "November Rain" brought forth a masterpiece. When it came to "Patients" it took more than one writer. Three cheers to "Guns N Roses" one of my favorite acts… Thinkin' back to my days, it was Chuck Berry and let me hear some of that Rock N Roll music. Back then music was laid down with real musicians and real instruments with multiple writers who never got credit nor did the people in the studio chillin'. Those were the good old days when the band actually performed in the club and the audience hit the dance floor jitterbugging. Dj's would spin 33's. What made Chuck Berry successful were lyrics focused on the here and now and teens lovin' it. Words cannot describe the height Queen reached in the production of Bohemian Rhapsody. A composition lyrically and musically flawless. Perfection. What more can I say being a football Eagles fan about the song "We Are the Champions."? Years and years waiting for the Eagles to be Champions and years of Rocky movies.

Imagine a large family who loves music and also happens to be Eagle fans echoing across the mountain "We Are the Champions" by Queen in rotation along with other favorites, 24 hours a day to keep the wild life at bay. It's a way to let the animals know "We Will Rock You"

SPOLARIZED PRESS CONNECTION
BENEATH THE HYPE IN THE WORLD
OF ENTERTAINMENT...

with blood on your face and we're ready to put you in your place. You're a free loader who's got it easy. In order for us to live on earth we need to pay taxes. I asked you who wouldn't love the song "Somebody to Love?" Don't we all want somebody to love us? Queen got a lot of attention in our house with insane masterpieces. What do you expect when we are all rockers? Three cheers to Queen and it's production team. Queen is a hard act to follow... The movie Bohemian Rhapsody was insane. My children were finally grown and old enough to hit the clubs. When the song by AC/DC came on "You Shook Me All Night Long" we' hit the dance floor. We're a hard act to follow. We dominated the dance floor singing out every song playing air guitars with grooves. Great White's song "Once Bitten Twice Shy" gave you a lyrics and a beat with a groove that made hips move.

People actually sat back and enjoyed watching us even though some of them were dancers. They actually felt intimidated. Our high was Coca-Cola. At that point in my life I felt so fortunate to get out every Saturday night with my children. Talk about musicians like AC/DC hitting the stage strumming on those guitars. Those were the 70s when British bands were kickin' a★★. When the DJ played "Walk of Life" by Dire Strait we hit the dance floor with swagger. We all know that Bruce Springsteen is a wonderful performer, an American singer and a songwriter who plays guitar and is from Jersey. Most people can say they like the song "Born in the U.S.A." but for me it's "Dancing in the Dark." My children danced as toddlers in their playpen. A dance in ruffled crinolines set a spark on fire with my father.

A dance turned me Catholic and got me a marriage license. When you're the Press you can get into concerts and meet with lots of artists. When you've been in studios with famous artists along with those who aren't, you learn which artist is good like Santana and which artist is so so. You learn which artist writes their own lyrics. You learn which artist uses a team of writers and which artist uses a ghostwriter under contract. Standing in my shoe you will know if the engineer knows how to mix and master. What I found I like most in Bruce was his energy and his ability to bring a crowd together. Leaving his concerts, you always feel like you got your money's worth. When I think back to Bill Haley's Comets I think of Joey Welz's and how he stands playing piano and belts out tune after tune never missing a key or lookin' down. I think of Liberace and how much flair he had as a musician while playing piano or Elton John. As Press I traveled coast to coast interviewing artists. When I listen to Billy Joel I hear an accomplished singer, a composer and pianist who touches the soul through song. Two of my favorite songs by Joel is "Rebel." and "Only the Good Die Young." When my family went dancing weekends at Shadowbrook Resort and the DJ spun Billy, we'd belt out the lyrics. We'd get in a circle formation screaming more more more.

I asked you who wouldn't like "Piano Man" or how about Rod Stewart? Both are pop-rock singers, song writers, and performers who have sold over a hundred million records worldwide. When I was studying to be a songwriter and producer myself I studied Rod Steward's productions and his skills. Over the years he's been signed by many major labels. It made me wonder why. I've been in the game since 1994 and read enough contracts of major labels with my IP lawyer to know they favor the label versus the artist. When it comes to lyrics you should know the track and the lyrics are what's most important and that the engineer knew what he was doing when he mixed the finished product. "Forever Young." Three

SPOLARIZED® PRESS CONNECTION
BENEATH THE HYPE ENTERTAINMENT

cheers to Rod for writing about true life experience when he wrote the song "Maggie May". Rod's "Forever Young" hits me where it hurts. Jay Z's rendition of "Forever Young and Mr Hudson" is equally worthy of praise. I once went to a Meat Loaf concert that grabbed you from above. The lights went out for a minute and in that moment of darkness a huge Bat from above hovered over screeching as the band began the song "Bat Out of Hell." What a surprise. Much like other artists, Bob Dylan also shared some of the same similar melody and lyrics and shared royalties.

Jay Z's rendition is a remix or copy of another artists work. Both renditions make me think how beautiful my children, their children, and their children are. A picture-perfect life isn't life. Jay's version is more in tune with reality of things of today. He may not be my favorite rapper but on this joint he scores an A+, perfect. Jay Z's song "Big Pimpin'" is killa on production, lyrics and beat. It took multiple hands to compose such a great piece of work. All praise do to Jay Z and UGK and those who worked on the joint. I stayed faithful to the way I was raised Forever Young. It's one thing for me to love the talent, the music, and the quality of perfection, it's another thing when you have a son-in-law who can sing like Bon Jovi. When my son-in-law performs songs of certain artists, he sounds exactly like the artist. He is truly an amazing performer. I asked you who wouldn't love the song "Blaze of Glory?" When it comes to one of my favorite choices, it is "It's My Life." Bon Jovi is one killa artist who mastered the art. I've never known anybody who's went through as much as I've went through; there's enough left out to write another book. I could lay a few more incidents where tragedy came upon me and my family but what does it matter? The me-too movement talks about different women that were rape victims or did things they didn't really want to do but were forced to.

I feel sad for every person who is forced to do something against their will. That includes children who break my ♡ seeing parents push them around. I've been struggling my whole life in the game. Studying other musicians work, reading their contracts, and mixing with their engineers over the years on a lee-low, I worked in vein helping people trying to gain fame without recognition. Likewise, Mel Love (Like 2 Link) busted a★★ for Bad Boy. I've seen artists walk away from those who got them to the top without feeling guilty. Joel Johnson helped his fam get a major record deal. Yomi and Big Sean helped their cousin reach fame. What did these young men get for their work? Kicked to the curb like me yo... Rap hit the marketplace with hardcore lyrics about life. I sat back and let rhyme after rhyme flow through me inhaling and exhaling and analyzing this new form of musical composition. Incredible flavor applied to a beat with words that made the soles of my feet tap Boom Boom. The urban community found a way to get beyond ghetto life and struggle. I heard drama laid on a beat inhaling and exhaling of souls. Wow.

Eminem isn't just my favorite because he's good and can rhyme. It's because he had balls to step to the plate and show off his skill. Eminem let the urban community know they're not the only ones that had a rough life. Mel and I would head for the Tunnel in NYC; a totally hardcore ghetto hangout club that excepted me. A place to learn what is expected of a musical work in order for the DJ to spin it. Fifty wit "In the Club" from the get let everyone know straight up he's not a p★ssy. Even as an actor he's lettin' you know he's hood. I've tried

Spolarized® Press Connection
in the World of Entertainment

over the years to get wit G-Unit without luck. There was a time I chilled with Fat Joe's crew at Magic and Ruff Ryders enjoying Eve. DJ Kali would see me at Magic and give me a hug. He'd say, "So what's up Ma?" We'd chill a blink and talk about what Joe was doin'. If I sat in a pity party all these years I would have never been where I am today.

Whenever you have a pity party day look in the mirror and "Shine the Star that you are Spolarized Legally Loaded®." I continued analyzing different genres of music. Elton John has everything an artist needs to create a musical work of art and a rolodex to prove it. The competition in the marketplace is overloaded with artists. Artists like Evanescence with "Bring me to Life" are worthy of praise. Their vocal abilities are crazy along with the track. When I heard the song by Nickleback "Rockstar" I thought the lyrics are right in tune with where we're at. Hang out with a blonde, a wanta bee rock star, and have a drug dealer on speed dial. Everyone can relate to the lyrics. Makin' a hit you need marketing cheddar and a loop that's hot.

Put a few heavy weights on the joint like Usher, Ludacris, and Lil' Jon with "Yeah" and it's a recipe for success. One Direction's song "Story of My Life" lyrically grabs you along with the upbeat track. Maroon 5 hasn't had a tune that would make me what to rip down the road out of control when I hear it. I give respect to Maroon 5 for good productions. Adam Levine is not only a good performer but a professional entertainer on "The Voice." There's plenty of rappers I consider typical. The list is endless. It's not that they're good or bad.

B.O.B. in his song with "Nothin' on You" with Bruno Mars was on beat with harmony and a hook that was catchy. I was in New Orleans for the Superbowl and met up with B.O.B. and began rhyming. He gave me props by saying "hey listen to this white woman." Sadly, to say, I wish he wouldn't have noticed my color, but his people gathered around. He had no idea I was 71 years old. His head DOG pushed through the circle of homies gathered round and yanked my arm and said, "What the f★ck you doing stepping up on my man, white bitch? What ya know about rap? Move on, you hear me." My peeps saw what happen and came to bust a★★ but I said, "Let it go." My question is if B.O.B. hangs with this piece of sh★t racist dude what is that saying eh? I been in the game when these dudes were in grammar school and like most homies they chill with the rich and famous thinkin' they're somebody. I got news for ya, we need the shoemaker and the dress designer's like Franklin Rowe. B.O.B, needs to ditch his head DOG and enlighten himself that we all count. Shame on him. Music like Maroon 5 with Carli B.'s "Girls Like You" in tune with harmony hittin' on the beat lets you know women like me are not p★ssy's that can rap too. The level of competition and talent is very competitive. Look at the talent that's out there. Artist like Bruno Mars, Ed Sheeran, and Snow Patrol. Acts like 2 Doorsdown, and Daughtry. Let's not forget the late John Lennon with the song "Imagine."

The song "Chasing Cars" by Snow Patrol lyrics and production awesome. I admire Master P for having a smart lawyer on top his game with Edwin Hawkins. When Edwin left him, P dropped in the marketplace. New people will always jump in and replace the old. It was Edwin who spoke about Master P and the work it took to get P on Forbes list. Edwin let me know that nothin' in life comes easy. Just ask P.

Blessed Mother's Surprise Studio Visit

Blessed Mother's Surprise Studio Visit

I searched the web and found an engineer/beatmaker two hours away. I got behind the mic ready to lay down my first joint since childhood "Break Any Ribbon" on his beat. I found myself shaken and ready to collapse on the floor. Having the mic in front of me in a studio brought flashbacks of me in the alley at Bandstand. The pop screen on the mic became the reel-to-reel recording of my master and the vision through the filter became the vision of blood in my hair and a man biting the umbilical cord of my baby laying on my chest. I was horrified.

The engineer had no idea the zone I was in. I said to him, "I want this and you're going to have to help me so I can lay down my first musical work." He said, "Ms Peggy, you need something that will make you lighten up like tea, coffee, soda. a shot or a beer.

Whatever it is that would make you feel comfortable so you're able to lay down the rhyme you wrote on my beat." I said, "McDonald's vanilla sugar free iced coffee." He laughed and said, "It's not good for your vocal's but if it's the way to accomplish this so be it." We jumped in the car and grabbed the coffee and back to the studio. I was able to lay it down. I was determined to make it happen. Three cheers to McDonald's. My favorite coffee on the go.

When we were done it was wee hours into the night. The engineer insisted I stay over on the sofa within the studio area. Believe the following as factual or choose to not believe. His girlfriend had a blanket gifted to her when she left her country and she said, "Ms Peggy I'm going to set up the sofa ready for you to sleep."

Around 3:00 AM we called it a night. The engineer turned off the lights and I headed for the sofa. It was dark, and his girlfriend had already made the bed with her special never used blanket. I felt my way onto the sofa and laid down feeling good about my accomplishment. I looked towards a light peeking through the venetian blind on the ceiling with my hands in prayer filled with tears of joy and said, "I did it."

Within moments my back started to feel heat so hot it was burning me from head to toe. I jumped up and switched on a light. Before my eyes was the girlfriend's blanket and a picture of the Blessed Mother. I was awed and scared and fell to my knees not believing my eyes and headed for the engineer's chair on the other side of the room. When the engineer came in the studio the next morning I was sleeping in his chair in front of the keyboard.

He wondered why I wasn't on the sofa. I asked him if he had seen the blanket before. He said, "Not really. I can't say for sure, she's had it wrapped up because it is special to her. She came to this country with it." I felt the Blessed Mother was the sign I needed to believe I could finish my work. Later that day when they were both in the studio I asked if they knew the picture on the blanket. Both shock their heads no. I told them the picture is the Blessed Mother.

Rap brought me back to my feet spittin' on the mic. Rap is about life. Rap is about all the people who have made me insane. A fairytale of a "Beautific Man" gave me the steppin' stones. My first musical work hittin' the mic "Break Any Ribbon" about a Philly girl who's a warrior.

Violets and the A·ve Ma·ri·a

Papa Joe was known to walk the train tracks with a pick and shovel over his shoulder singin' on the way to work to dig a grave. On the way home he'd pick me wild weeds. He knew by my expression that I thought they were ugly. He said, "Child if you believe one day you'll see violets beneath the wild weeds and if you listen you'll hear the A·ve Ma·ri·a." Every spring I saw the violets beneath the wild weeds and sure enough I would hear my grandparents sing the A·ve Ma·ri·a

Question for Platinum Artist

How many platinum artists can claim their album is being sold for over $2,000 per CD in the marketplace? How many platinum artists can claim their used CD is being sold for over $130.00? I can claim that I pressed 500 CDs and they are still being sold to this day for that amount of money on line. Of course, a major Corporation in the marketplace was told to shut it down and of course most artists think of the company as being good. However, it still can be bought today (2019) at that price. Not one famous platinum artist like Michael Jackson, Elton John, nobody, can claim their CD sold for over $2,000. Hell were talkin' about an unknown artist here. How is it possible to sell even one at any price when I only pressed 500 CD? Better yet I still have 365 still sitting in my office. I have never seen one dollar from any that were ever sold. Not one penny. I bought one myself to make sure this major player in the industry was actually rippin' me off.

Yet millions of artists and labels deal with this Corporation. Let me refresh your memory that this stellar album being sold for an astronomical price isn't my stolen master at Bandstand that went gold with my money in someone else's pocket. I'm still waiting 30 years for a real deal from a major player in the industry. I want "My Country Tis of Thee" to be better than it is. The reason I wrote this book is to help educate people with truth. You be the judge if I'm telling the truth or not.

Perhaps, reading the life I lived you'll somehow understand how 30 years I've served the entertainment world as press with the hope no one will go through what I went through "For the Love of Music." 'Get Legally Loaded' is about makin' a better world regardless of race, religion, or social status. We all must "Rize Energized Spolarized" to the highest degree and Shine the Star we should be Legally Loaded with education. Once you're Legally Loaded® on our website your name gets registered in the "SpolarizedSmart™ Book of Knowledge" that you stand against fraud, corruption and discrimination. Step forward with me and Rock the Block and Get Legally Loaded. People are critical of me. Walk a mile with me and see if you can fill my shoes. In my Christian Life and Christian walk, I didn't use any swear words. Did that mean I didn't think in my mind the word damn it, when sh*t happens? Of course, I did. Words can't explain my first time on the mic layin' down a rhyme and how hard it was to overcome my last experience.

This time the song was about my life called "Break Any Ribbon" and how to ride the waves. I finally own my own publishing company, Spolarized® Music BMI. My first rap joint ends with, "Rap is about Life and all the People in it Who Made Me Insane." Song is available for sale on the website "Get Legally Loaded."

I think back when I was a child what Papa Joe would say, "Life is full of wild weeds but if you search beneath the wild weeds you'll find the beautiful violets and hear the A·ve Ma·ri·a. It is what makes a person get legal." Little did Papa Joe know I'd grow up and claim the Sun as the mark above the trademark Spolarized® teaching people to shine the star that they are. He would be proud knowing I've served society straight up Legally Loaded®.

Spolarized Press Connection Sports Has Been Interviewing Multiple Professional Athletes Since 1994

Three Cheers To The Teams That Won The Vince Lombardi Trophy

Spolarized® Press Connection Sports Beneath the Hype

There's something about living in the street where "Street Sense Makes Sense" where you meet all kinds of people. For years I lived on a lee low. The rich and famous were continually crossing my door along with many a★★holes. The Bible I carried was full of pages that I glued in place of the ones I pulled out of the apostles. In 1994 I started the Spolarized® Press Connection traveling from coast to coast, convention after convention, interviewing the rich and famous from nearly every country. For some unknown reason I had some kind of karma that drew people to me like glue. Regardless of what you may think of me or regardless of what I think of you, I am who I am. I laid it out in a rhyme called "Philly Grown" found on the website "Get Legally Loaded." I think about back to how much I enjoyed Whoopi Goldberg in Sister Act and 8 Mile which I've seen over and over and how both movies kept it real. There're still things that give me a chill which is reality and living in it. Those two movies make you think about the world we live in.

When I think about keepin' it real and the news, I think of CNN anchors and reporters give you both sides of the story with less fake news. Most of the anchors and reporters also speak from their ♡ which makes some people uneasy. I ask you is that bad? Would you rather have a person who's self-doubting who can't stand their ground and sides with whomever they're with? I know plenty of people who are wish-washy and are much like watered down tea. At my table "If You're not my Cup of Tea I'll never be your Coffee." I'm sure you understand people are allowed their opinion and it can differ from yours. Three cheers to Whoopi, Oprah, Eminem, Joy Behar, Ellen DeGeneres, Howard Stern, and Bill Maher who speak their mind and aren't wishy washy. I listen to Sanjay Gupta who keeps us up dated on what is new in the world of health. Cheers to CNN for givin' it to us straight up.

I spit in my rhyme, "Educate Your Mind One Time One Time". I get both sides verses other networks which give you their side. I been a Dem since the day I could vote. I try and keep in mind the 50% rule. 50% of us does sh★t that isn't cool. The other 50% is the good things we do. It's not so bad to speak your mind. If you hung around the rich and famous or with athletes you'd realize many of them swear, may seem rude, even crude, but living in their shoe isn't easy. It's not like those who are famous can walk to the grocery store, go to the movies or walk the mall. It's not like they can walk the streets in New York or Philly, LA or Chicago or Las Vegas.

Sometimes we should give compassion or slack on those who make us happy at the box office, or those who beat up their bodies playing sports so we can enjoy a good game, or those who give us our favorite TV series. Let's not forget our news media. CNN is my favorite news station. SLN, TMZ, VH1, MTV and BET are likewise' worthy of my time. I enjoy Kevin Hart and Tracy Morgan. When I can't sleep I take in watchin' Conan O'Brien, Jimmy Kimmel, or James Cordon. It's so easy for us to be critical of people who are busting a★★ to give us enjoyment. In my days the TV turned off at 12:00 midnight. Perhaps you remember when the National Anthem also played across the network. My parents would stand with respect as the flag waved across the TV. The song is to honor history and the struggle of its people.

Philly Grown

Philadelphia the City of Brotherly Love
held together by its surface and roots
where people respect thy neighbor's unique flava

parlayin' nationalities and cultures as one...
Stars comin' at you Spolarized like the Sun!

My classmate throughout high school was Harry Schuh. Everyday I'd hear him say "I'm gonna be a football player for the NFL." Sure, enough he got his wish. I've been interviewing NFL football players since 1994. When I first met Terry Bradshaw in the booth at a convention signing autographs, I stood back and thought how gracious he was to autograph footballs of men standing in line to meet him regardless of how long it took. Another player I recall who signed autographs until the line ended was Herschel Walker. Of course, I wanted to share with Herschel because I'm an Eagle fan and at that point so was he. There are a lot of other players who stayed to honor their fans by photographing and autographing footballs. I often wondered how their hands ever held up. I enjoyed Randall Cunningham and Brain Westbrook enough to wear their jersey.

I took note that one quarterback during the Super Show always had an excuse to exit after a few autographs. He sure in hell wasn't an Eagle. The head rep in the booth would come out and say he's sorry but he had to run. Reality was that he was tired of standing signing autographs and being cordial. It happened almost every time with this dude. Perhaps you took note of a different quarterback with attitude who walked off the field without shaking the Eagles quarterback's hand when the Eagles won the Championship? There is no excuse a quarterback could give us fans except, if he'd be willing enough to say he f*cked up not just to the Eagles but to the fans who watched him do it. My family is two generations of athletes and if any of them screwed up they'd admit it. When I screw up I say I screwed up yo and you won't see me Ridin' that Rodeo again... Fifty-Seven years fans believed in the Eagles and they never thought for one moment that the "Underdogs" couldn't win.

It shouldn't surprise anyone that the game of football comes with a lot of pain. My husband believed you needed to hit the guy coming at you back as hard as he's going to hit you. At least you'll both be in pain. It's not like he didn't know what he was talking about. He was a coach for a Catholic School. He played Sandlot football as a first-string RB and a third string QB. In the Army he was a first-string RB. He was a baseball pitcher who was offered a scholarship for college along with a scholarship in football. My parents were diehard Eagle fans. I was screaming for the Eagles from the day I was born because my parents never missed a season.

My first words were daddy, second word Eagles, then mommy and eventually I learned to scream the word Phillies. Being married to my husband was a pleasure during football season because he was an Eagles fan. Of course, we raised our kids to be Eagle fans and of course our grandchildren were raised to be Eagle fans and likewise our great-grandchildren are being raised as Eagle fans. Four generation hoping our team would one day win. We were taught it's about being a die-hard fan and pushing yourself to never give up on the dream that one day your team will win the Super Bowl. Our family gathers at one of the four homes on the homestead to watch the games. We scream at the TV so the players can hear us and our extended family all the way to Philly. If you want to see nutzo's, be in a bar or club in Philly during a game. You'll be exhausted from duckin' people on top the bar and tables spillin' shots and beer about the room every touchdown. On their ride home red light to red light, block after block people are blowing horns and yellin' Fly Eagles Fly. Who would have known Sylvester would be wearing a shirt of his own, eh?

SPOLARIZED™ PRESS CONNECTION SPORTS
BENEATH THE HYPE SINCE 1994

If you know anything about football you would know that the Eagles sell the most paraphernalia of any football team. If you want any paraphernalia don't bother to go to Dick's unless you're perhaps in PA or a surrounding state over the boarder a few miles. Dick's carry the products for the teams in each state. Perhaps it's about products that may or may not sell if it's a team other than the team of that state. What about donations of product not sold or discounted? When it comes to shopping out of state for your team you're more than likely sh*t out of luck. When I moved on my estate out of Philly the nearest town was 12 miles away. It's where the first Dick's store began with Richard Stack who later gave the franchise to his son Edward. Edward opened more Dick's Sporting Goods stores. So much for daddy's dream to pass on to the son; the original store has had very little makeover.

Wouldn't it be nice if all of us had a daddy who could pass on a business? There's also something to be said about a son who takes his father's dream to the max. I've never let money ruin my life. Anyone who knows me can tell you that. I can claim I had the willingness to do for others before Oprah since I'm 11 years older. lol! Philly fans are generations of diehard fans never givin' up the dream to fly.

When you're in Philly and the surrounding areas during a game win or lose your ♡ is pumpin', not just for the sport but with Brotherly Love of the city comin' together as one. Eagle fans teach their toddlers to put their arms out while yelling at the TV, Fly Eagles Fly as the theme song plays. My husband worked on some of the beautiful buildings throughout the city. Philly isn't just about the Eagles and the players or the bald eagle. If you know anything about football you would know that the city of Philadelphia is a City of Brotherly Love. It is a city beyond its sport teams. It's a city of multiple cultures that strives to be strong. It's the city where I was born and learned to survive the many obstacles that came my way in the world of entertainment. I took the fall for y'all on the streets of Philly of criminal activity happening within the city walls. The city where as a child my soul trotted the pavements with the sole of my shoe pitching pennies to the beggars. Years later the beggars from the city of Brotherly Love returned the favor by saving my life and my sons. Dishonesty is in every city along with bribery and betrayal. Philly has a way to reboot its people by knowing if you spread your wings you will fly like the eagle capturing the touch of brotherly love on "The Streets of Gold Live in the Soul." The first song I wrote and laid down in a cellar studio upon awakening out of a dismal state with the artist Harmony Jams.

Spolarized® Press Connection Sports Grand Nationals 4-Wheeler Race

My twin boys (Greg and Mike) rode four-wheelers with their father as young kids and by 10 years old their kids rode four wheelers. We rode as a family. We'd ride at least 15 miles oneway stoppin' at every bar so Tom (my husband) could grab a beer and greet his bar buddies. We'd return home after midnight. It would be pitch-dark riding through the forest following Tom's tail lights over creek and dale. Eventually, the boys made a track on the top of our mountain. They used our Cat Dozer to make jumps 15 to 20 feet high. It was a bit scary at first, but I finally got used to them ruff neckin'. Once in a while a few of their buddies with four wheelers and the neighbor boy Paul would come over and hit the jumps.

WHAT'S IT LIKE TO HAVE TWIN BOYS
RACING 4 WHEELERS AND SNOWMOBILES?
IT'S LEARNING HOW TO SUCK IT UP SINCE
EVERYONE IN THE FAMILY IS A RIDER...

One weekend without telling us our boys pulled up in the driveway with their wives and the babies and began loading the truck with four wheelers. They continued packin' up grabbing a tool box, a couple extra tires and gas cans. Tom and I ran out asking, "What the hell are you boys doing?" They said, "We're leaving for West Virginia to race in the Grand Nationals." Tom and I looked at each other and in the blink of an eye we knew damn well there was no stopping them; we were gone with them. I called my daughter and said, "Will pick you up in 10 minutes, grab what you can and the camera, we're headed out the door following your brothers to a 4-wheeler race. Don't ask what the fu*k they're doing or why; there doing it. It's gonna be the ride of our life and by the way they've lost their minds" They stopped at the corner of the dirt road to pick up the neighbor boy Paul who had never been away from home or on a vacation. We knew our boys never bullsh*t and this was for real. On the trip to Virginia I'm asking Tom over and over like a broken record the same questions, "What the hell do they know about racing? They've never raced on a track. They spin around the property and through the woods. Can't you stop them? This is crazy!" His answer was "boys will be boys, they'll be fine" while he's sippin' on a beer driving. I was scared to death...

We're off to the Grand Nationals which will be televised. Lucky for me I had a pair of rosaries hangin' from the car mirror. In today's time it's against the law in most states to hang anything from the windshield mirror. I thought perhaps saying the rosaries will help save my children so I could take both boys home after the race in one piece. How stupid is that, eh! When we arrived, we rented one hotel room for the nine adults and 3 kids. The first day was qualifying to see who's in the finals. Coming out of the gate there was so much dust and so many four wheelers hitting the turns you only could see the color of the machines. Intents... The jumps were so high you only saw the bottom of the 4-wheelers and the riders couldn't see if there was an accident on the other side of the jump. I had rosaries wrapped around my hands and relied on my daughter shouting out what's happening. "Mom Mike made that turn. Mom Greg made that jump." Both boys qualified. The second day my daughter continued to shout out how the boys were doing. All of a sudden I heard, "oh no! Greg's gonna crash!" He was in mid-air and couldn't see there was a big accident on the other side of the jump. He landed on top the crash.

One of the riders was air lifted unconscious and ended up paralyzed. Greg got up and grabbed his ribs. He flipped the bike back up and jumped back on and continued to race. Greg knew he was hurt but he wouldn't stop. His four-wheeler began leaking gas and had to be shut down from the crash. His brother said, "Use my machine." Greg would pull into the gate and Mike would jump on the machine and out the gate. No time to check anything or a pit stop. I want to believe my twin boys are the only riders who have ever placed in the Grand Nationals using one machine shared by two riders with no back up machine, tires, tools or extra engine.

This is one example of love for another. Self-sacrifice to share the machine with your brother was more important than the win, (John 15:13 Greater love hath no man than to lay down his life for another). We were so full of dust our faces looked like mud. The hotel room had two double beds that meant some had to sleep in the car. The babies got showers first then the adults went by age to shower sharing the towels. The tub was full of mud. Paul

MY PARENTS BELONG TO THE PHILADELPHIA RAMBLERS MOTORCYCLE CLUB AND THEY RODE A HARLEY EVERY WEEKEND. THEY RODE THEIR BIKE TO THE FIRST WOODSTOCK ALONG WITH SOME OF THE MEMBERS OF THE CLUB.

was beside himself and was never gonna tell his parents about his vacation other then it was a blast. Paul was the youngest so by time he got his shower to remove the mud the tub was not only muddy, but all the towels were wet. We told him it could be worse. We could be camping without water. Paul was basically a quiet kind of guy unless you ruffle his feathers. We were a family that doesn't sit back listening to bullsh*t. We step to the plate with input. This trip was one that you don't go home bragging about unless you place in the top 10 and receive an award. Greg was in severe pain from the accident.

My husband told him, "Suck it Up." One can only imagine Greg had broken ribs since he flew in the air and landed on a machine. We taped Greg's ribs and he sucked it up. I should be used to Tom thinkin' everything is OK by now. When the boys were hurt with broken bones he'd shake his head mumbling to himself. They could see his disappointment in his actions and knew they better suck it up. The final race was Sunday of Mother's Day. Towards the end I hear my daughter screaming and jumpin' up and down yelling Mom Mike's gonna take a win; 10th Place. I'm tripping in the dugout jumpin' up and down. Live video was rollin' televised. The boys were happy, and I thought to myself this is gonna be the death of me if my sons continue this sport. It's one thing to watch racing on TV. It's another if the one racing is your family. The fans are the opposite they enjoy seeing the crashes hoping it's not the one they want to win. They came over to me and said, "Mom Happy Mother's Day. We want you to know we will never race at the Grand National's again." So much for the saying boys will be boys. They didn't race four wheelers again, instead they raced snowmobiles. As the years passed their children were like father like son, riding and racing 4 wheelers. My thoughts were all this for a trophy. Yet I love football so much that I yell at the TV screen words not fit for kids. My kids are used to swear words and know they're only used by adults.

Spolarized® Press Connection Sports Harley's at Woodstock

My parents drove a Harley and rode with the Philadelphia Ramblers. Unbeknown to most people, many of the Philadelphia Ramblers where cops including undercovers cops. My parents went to the first Woodstock in '69 with the Philadelphia Ramblers. My parents taught me the difference between gangs and those who call themselves thugs and those who really are thugs or hoodlum. My parents and I had many discussions on multiple subjects throughout my life. They explained that whenever there is a group of people with titles there's always going to be bad a**s and good a**es among them regardless of their title. When there's a group or gathering of people they usually give themselves a title. A title is a just a title. No two people are alike. People think's independently. A person who thinks independently usually is self-confident and doesn't let criticism, get to them. They taught me about the 50% rule. 50% of the time a person will do good things and 50% of the time they'll do bad things because no one is born perfect. They spoke about how sin has no weight and that no man's sin is greater than the next man's sin. The one thing my parents forgot to mention was people can be programed to believe a certain way. That is exactly what I let happen by letting my husband Tom tell stories with discrepancies to my children. He let a doctor take away my "Golden Note" by putting me in a trance-like state. Hell, my head injury was enough. Yet with that said my husband was kind, thoughtful of others, and basically an over-all a good person. He even saved a life in a burning fire when firemen wouldn't. He enjoyed my

To Whom It May Concern:

I am writing this letter regarding my affiliation with Spolar Inc. I must say on their behalf that this is a very professional organization and I am pleased with the relationship being built at this time. Peggy Spolar and her staff are very sincere and honest people who are on a mission. The vision of central focus that she has, in my opinion, will change the lives of many people, especially the children. I have no reservation at all regarding joining forces with her on this and every other project that may evolve. My plans are to totally commit with dedication and complete support in every aspect needed. I believe in Spolar because Spolar believes in me.

In closing I would like to thank you in advance for all of your support on behalf of Spolar Inc. and myself, David Lang former running back for the Dallas Cowboys.

Sincerely,

David Lang
Formerly of Dallas Cowboys

A Letter from the late David Lang...

father's company enough to buy a motorcycle. Excited he rolled up on the front yard with an "Indian Motorcycle. My father said, "Get that sh*it off my grass. I only rock with a Harley, kid." Tom came in the house and said, "I think I pi**ed off your father buying a cycle that wasn't his brand. I'll return it tomorrow. I don't want to fu*k with my father-in-law." This is an example of the good side of Tom. He understood being friends with my parents was what was important. Riding an Indian cycle among Harley cycles wasn't a smart move. When I went in business working with major players contracts I could care less what they have done in the past. I'm brought in on a lee low to oversee contracts of major players, celebrities and athletes to explain the contract or find a loophole out of a messed-up contract. Aside from business, I don't give a damn how they live their personal life.

I figure everyone's entitled to live the way they choose and pay the consequences for their actions. My list of clients includes motorcycle gangs and bike riders like Vestal Cycle Club. Most of the groups/gangs are some of the nicest dudes you'll ever meet. I gave Geoffrey and Wade from Ruff Ryders the heads up coming to my estate. It was just as strange for them as it was for me to truck through Yonkers. I gave them headz up when they get off the highway to call me, and I'll truck them through; don't get out of the car. Unlike Philly, a city of multi colors and Brotherly Love, in my PA community black is not especially socially accepted and hot cars have a way of being stripped. Every city coast to coast has its own code of ethics and bylaws. My parents would be very proud of me because I never got on a Harley. My family bought four-wheelers and snowmobiles and travel across hillsides. Since there's so many of us I suppose we could be titled a gang.

Spolarized® Press Connection the Late David Lang & Johnny Unitas

I met David through a girl named Sophie. We connected instantly and David asked me if I'd work with him on a lee low. I had already been going to the Super Show and the Tailgate Show meeting with many athletes as Press. Having David as a client, a Dallas Cowboy RB, got me into places where I couldn't get on my own with a Press badge. I went to many private parties where I got introduced to the NFL players who learned what I did and asked me to work with them on a lee low. As always, I'd sit back and listen to what's up on the back end of the NFL. Johnny Unitas enjoyed a getaway now and then and would sneak away to my estate on a lee low when he was in my area to sign autographs at a car dealership. I would kid him about The Golden Arm. I wanted him to be in a movie I was shooting. Johnny refused and wanted me to use his son Joe who was in "Any Given Sunday." Johnny loved his family and didn't want any of them to play football. Johnny was right. Joe was easy to work with, took the script as his own and killed it on screen. David on the other hand loved football so much that he wanted to help every kid that he could who showed an interest in football. On one of my visits to David's house we had a long discussion about walking around with his Super Bowl ring and welcoming young adults interested in football to his home. The end results are that he lost his life when his ring was stolen. Whatever you see on TV about athletes is different behind the scene when you're Press like me. David was a sweet pea. Having a client who's a Dallas Cowboy wasn't easy when I'm an Eagles fan my whole life.

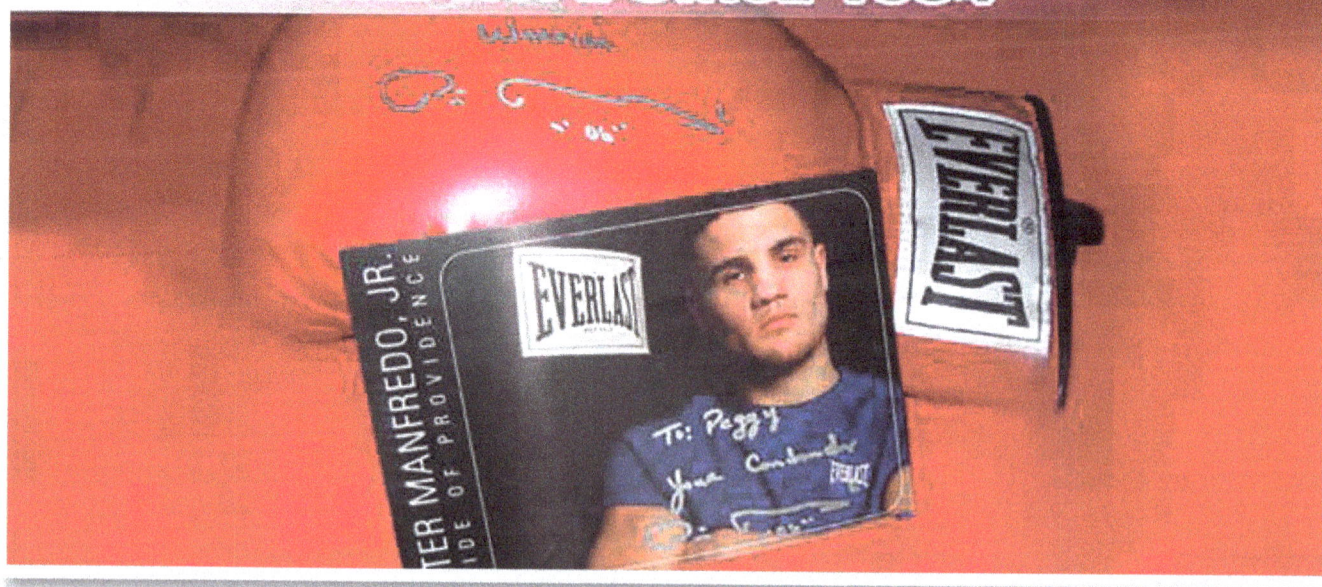

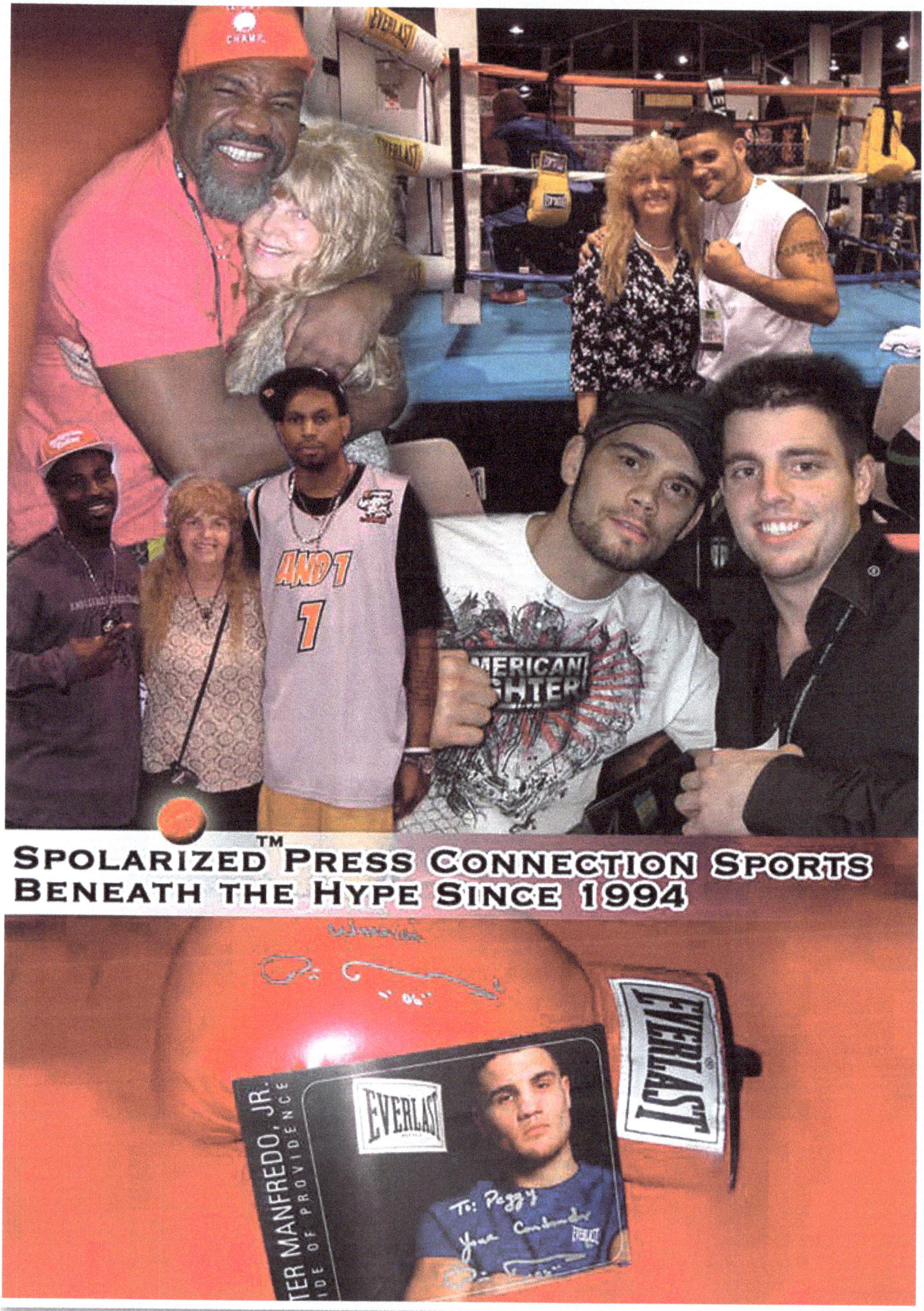
SPOLARIZED™ PRESS CONNECTION SPORTS
BENEATH THE HYPE SINCE 1994
EVERLAST
AND1
1
EVERLAST
EVERLAST
TER MANFREDO, JR.
IDE OF PROVIDENCE
To: Peggy

Spolarized® Press Connection Sports Beneath the Hype in Boxing

If you were a mouse in the corner you would have been able to hear the back end of the fight between Buster Douglas and Mike Tyson. Ahead of the fight you would have known that one didn't practice while the other did. You would have known where the bets were on and off. At this point in my life I was new to boxing so I sat back and watched how it's played. In the back of my mind I knew the boxing world was a sport in which you keep your ears and eyes open. If you are asked anything answer, "I see nothing." It's a sport where I follow my father's advice, if asked about something, plead the 5th Amendment or exercise freedom of speech and say nothing. Years later I met up with Larry Holmes and his team and had the opportunity to work on a product and have it created in China for him. All my efforts and work were in vain. Larry wanted what he wanted and that's not how the marketplace works. Try explaining to someone with power you can't always have what you want. Someone else claimed the idea ahead of Larry and he would be second in the marketplace. The public would see Larry as a follower not a leader, plus the product was already successful in the marketplace and turning money. Regardless what I knew as facts about marketing a new product or licensing, Larry seemed clueless to what it means or what it takes to creating a new product or the ability to copyright and patent the product. I met Larry many times at conventions and sat with him and his people. I saw how genuine his ♡ was and how he had hoped together we could successfully pull off a business deal. I learned from my multiple clients that you win some and you lose some and if you just keep moving forward something will finally work.

Spolarized® Press Connection Sports - Two Awesome NFL Players

Perhaps you don't want to believe me and perhaps you have a different opinion and that's ok. At a sport convention I got to meet Jason Babin. Oh, what a sweet pea... You would have thought we knew each other for years. He was honest and spoke about how his family has always been the most important thing in his life. We chilled and laughed and discussed multiple things about football. One of the highlights we discussed was the personal life of football players and one of my most favorite quarterback's Michael Vick. Not because I'm an Eagles fan but because he was a great quarterback. He got out of the pocket even though he was short and found the opening and threw the football for touchdown after touchdown. He took a hell of a beating getting sacked at the end of his NFL career. The line didn't seem to protect him the way they should have. It's just through the eyes of the beholder, which is me, watching a great quarterback go down sack after sack after his episode with dogs. If your mama didn't teach you then let me be your teacher. Every man (meaning human) has done bullsh*t stuff they're not proud of. We are born 50% good and 50% bad that's because there is no perfect person. One man's bad is no different than the next man's bad nor is good any better than good.

What I learned from Jason Babin was that Vick is one hell of a good person and that he is a man who loves his family and a man who is faithful to his wife. I also learned from Jason that he too is a straight shooter like Vick. Jason Babin made my ♡ zing when he spoke about Vick being a dude worth knowing. NFL, boxing, UFC, baseball, golf, wrestling and drag racing took me to a zone unlike hip-hop with my mouth and my attitude over the top about

I'm a Spolairo from head to toe. I'm the last days comin' at you like the Sun. Are you ready to rock the block east and west, livin' the dream who we be? Spolarized Legally Loaded like the Sun...

sports. I've met many players and coaches along with the money men at parties and conventions and have seen them in rare form. Music and sports go hand and hand. Investments into artists sometimes come from athletes. It's nothing to see money crossing hands on a side bet on games and who's gonna win. I befriended Barry Goldstein years ago when his daughters were young. Aside from being on the cover of Golf Magazines as a professional instructor, he has the six best tips in golf. I knew Barry when he was raising his daughters. He put them before golf and dating. He wasn't vain even though his picture was plastered on golf magazines. Fatherhood was No.1 in his life. Most parents want to believe their family and their kids are No.1 but many times they're not. Sport, business, money, and hobbies sometimes comes first without a person realizing it. Even in my case my husband, who loved his family and sports, drinking with his buddies took up a lot of his time. I became a transplant out of Philly put into a new world I knew nothing about. It forced me to learn many things. There are times I'm grateful that my husband forced the move because I more than likely wouldn't have been a hunter, gardener, or a farmer.

I wouldn't have drove a 4-wheeler or my Arctic Cat snowmobile over creeks and dales. I surely wouldn't have been a lay minister. When I sit back and watch famous athletes I understand how lost in the sport they can become. That's why it was refreshing to learn Vick had his priorities in order. Likewise, many times artist get so wrapped up in the game they miss what is right in front of them, their family. Then there's people like me who are the fans who scream at the TV and yell swear words during the game on the bleachers (mostly at the refs) and dress in teams' products. When my kids and the grandkids were in sports I was so bad on the bleachers none of them would admit we were related. Funny though when they needed me to step up then I was OK. My sons' high school football coach thought my son's hair was to long because you could see hair out the back of the helmet.

So, in front of the team he said, "if you boys don't get a hair cut I'll cut your hair myself. Best have it cut by the next game? Got it?" When they told me, I called the school to see if it was in the rule book. When I found out it wasn't, I went up to the coach before practice and said, "if you touch my son's hair or bench them I'll shave your head bald in front of the team. Got it? Trust me bro. I'm from the Concrete Jungle where people live and die in the jungle yo." After that the team started growing their hair. Years later my grandson was playing football on the same high school field with a future NFL player Chris Snee. The coach had no problem with my grandson's hair out the back of the helmet or any other kid who had long hair.

The legend of our 'discussion' lasted. During the NFL football season, I'm not only screaming "Fly Eagles Fly" I'm screaming at the blind refs who many times determine the games. They get paid enough so they should be able to see. The coach should be allowed to challenge all the bad calls. For instance, in 2019 when a ref declined to flag the Rams for 2 violations (on the same play) the Saints were denied the opportunity to run out the clock and prevent any overtime. I'm not only an Eagle fan I'm also a Phillies fan who also watches the Yankees when I can't get a Phillies game. Since Chris Snee was picked up by the Giants and played football with my grandson, it created one Giants fan in the family verses the family team of the Eagles. This led me to likewise follow the Giants' games. A-Rod seems like a gem like Michael Vick. Family first...

SPOLARIZED PRESS CONNECTION
SPORTS BENEATH THE HYPE

SEES THIS PLAYER AS
THE BEST SMILE IN THE LEAGUE

SPOLARIZED® PRESS CONNECTION SPORTS
BENEATH THE HYPE SINCE 1994

SPOLARIZED PRESS CONNECTION SPORTS
BENEATH THE HYPE SINCE 1994

SPOLARIZED PRESS CONNECTION SPORTS
BENEATH THE HYPE SINCE 1994

My bodyguard Dr. Mark VIP likes the Giants and the Yankees. In Florida there's a bar for just Eagles fans called Buckets. If you're not an Eagle fan you're not welcome. I'm not kidding. My children and their children knew our family has rules. Even if I use the word fu★k, they knew they're not allow to say that word till they're my age. They know I'm as old as my home stereo and been screaming "Fly Eagles Fly" since the age of one. They know when Hip-Hop began rhymes, it included the word fu★k bleeped. In 1998 while driving with the grandkids listening to the radio and DMX's song "Get At Me Dog" they ask, "Baka, does DMX think he's fooling us kids bleeping the bad word we can't say? Is he your age Baka?" I laughed and said, "He's using the word so he must be" knowing damn well I lied. Not good yo. After that every song that used the word fu★k bleeped on the radio the grandkids would say, "There's another rapper your age Baka." I'd laugh. My day finally came when I put a CD in the car radio of my own joint using the word fu★k bleeped. My grandkids said, "Who the heck is that Baka?" I said, "Me silly. Philly Grown from the Concrete Jungle. A Spolaro Legally Loaded. Perhaps one day you'll understand what it was like for me to be a Baka Diva."

SPOLARIZED DOPE A MEAN SECTION

Spolarized Dope A Mean - Means you agree with someone. Shout out "Spolarized Dope A Mean" every time you agree with someone. When you're out with someone and they say something you agree with, shout out "Spolarized Dope A Mean." Say nothing if you disagree because you'll end up on their sh★t list. It's an awesome way to let people know that you agree with what they're saying. It's a way to let people know you're on their side. As you know opposites attract but they almost never get along. You've also probably heard that if you hang with trash you become trash.

Reading my book, you've read about my Grandma Mary who not only taught me about "Human Ducks" but started a revival of a human condition that existed and needed fixing. It was her way of teaching me to learn to speak out about things that I see so I didn't fall weak agreeing with things I really disagree with. As I grew older I learned she was right. There were things that I absolutely thought were ridiculous and there have been times when I asked myself why people do what they do. Grandma Mary taught me if you question it, you learn from it.

Don't hate me for what I say. Perhaps, learn something from what I say. I remember my mother Mary telling me how I grew to be older and wiser and I learned to surprise her. The following are questions I've asked myself. Perhaps while reading them you will also ask yourself why people do what they do. It is time for us to start cleaning up the things that we can and make a better place for all mankind.

If you agree with me you'll shout out "Spolarized Dope A Mean. "Here we go... Here we go... Like an old time, record on your stereo playing a tune that offers you Legally Loaded® headz up.

True friends tell you things about yourself you don't want to hear. Can I Get A Spolarized Dope A Mean?

Did you ever wonder why people just kick their shoes off inside the door? Wouldn't it make more sense if they took them off left to right? Can I Get A Spolarized Dope A Mean?

Do you agree that your house should always be in order in case someone knocks to visit? Can I Get A Spolarized Dope A Mean?

Do you dislike when people sit on the arms of your sofa or chairs which are not made for a★★es? Can I Get A Spolarized Dope A Mean?

Our country including our hospitals are full of staph infections. It can be deadly. Do you agree that sucking your fingers while eating spreads germs and bacteria to others? Practice at home by not sucking your fingers and you more than likely will remember not to do it when you're out. There're a few dishes, snacks and the like where sucking your fingers is socially acceptable. One such food is chicken wings. However, as you know you need a hand wipe when you're done. Do you agree that not sucking your fingers is a habit we all should learn? Can I Get A Spolarized Dope A Mean?

Do you agree that you shouldn't touch things in a person's house that are not yours without permission? Can I Get A Spolarized Dope A Mean?

Do you agree drivers going the speed should be on the right and shouldn't be camping out in the passing lane? Can I Get A Spolarized Dope A Mean?

Do you agree that some people forgot that they have hair on the back of their head and forgot to comb it? Can I Get A Spolarized Dope A Mean?

Do you agree that people shouldn't talk with food in their mouth and should wait until they're done chewing before they speak? Can I Get A Spolarized Dope A Mean?

When it came to my mother Mary and my grandma Mary there was a reason they taught about the way toilet paper was placed on the roller. Growing up grandma Mary had an outhouse. Something as simple as an outhouse can teach you a lot about how much people respect where they sh*t. Our 90-acre estate came with a few outhouses. I suppose it was in case the farmer needed to go while he was on the tractor. We still use them during the Annual Pig Roast to remember our great grandparents and the old timers who once lived on the estate. It is a reminder how far we've come with flush toilets. I was taught the "Toilet Paper Rule" and what it stood for. The proper way to place toilet paper on the roller is to have it roll over the top away from the wall, so your fingers stop touching the wall where few people clean. The "Toilet Paper Rule" shows the person who properly placed the toilet paper roll knows there is more to life than just wiping their a★★ clean.

It likewise pertains to being tidy. The word tidy means: neat, orderly, or trim, as in appearance of dress; a person that's clearly organized. After sitting in many of bathrooms I learned what was taught to me is probably right. Once people know the "Toilet Paper Rule" my grandmother created, they realize how tidy or not they really are. Do you agree that the "Toilet Paper Rule" can help people to be tidier? Can I Get A Spolarized Dope A Mean?

Do you believe that weed should be legalized so that we can stop filling jails with people smoking pot and giving them a criminal record making it harder for them to get a job? Our jails are full. This means hardcore criminal needs to be released early to put a person smoking pot in a cell. Can I Get A Spolarized Dope A Mean?

I'm assuming everyone knows that your feet were created to stand on. Have you noticed how many people lean on your walls, your woodwork, marking it up, scuffing it up, and leave their handprints behind? One of my pet peeves is how many people lean on the walls. When my children were growing up I could be pretty rude to their friends. What the hell, it's my house so respect it. I've been known to ask their friends if their mother taught them to stand on their feet. They would look at me funny and say yeah. I'd say then can you stop leaning on my wall and stand on your feet. Once my children got homes of their own they thought a lot more like their mother.

Better yet, why is this guy's a★★ leaning against my hutch scratching it up? It wasn't made for a★★es. I don't want their fingerprints or their dirty clothes on my walls. Most walls are not as washable as you think. I don't need their residue left behind. I would say it's acceptable only if I needed their DNA. Do you agree that people should stand on their feet and not lay against your walls? Can I Get A Spolarized Dope A Mean?

This is a toughie to write but sometimes straight up and being tough is what it takes in order for some people to get it. This is about ADHD or ODD and some of the other letters in the alphabetical are used. When a child is a little hyper or doesn't want to sit and behave or doesn't want to listen they title him. Call it what you want but in the old days' parents didn't have children on drugs because their children didn't behave. What did mother's in the old days do with their children that didn't want to sit down in the class and behave? They more than likely gave them a smack and they got the message instantly. As in 'those that don't listen will feel.' Things have changed in today's time. Let's step it up to where we are today. My great-grandchildren have tablets and play games; however, they know how to behave. If they don't behave, no tablet. Sure, enough they get the message. If they don't sit down and behave they'll lose their tablet for 30 minutes. Do it again and it will be an hour.

In today's time usually both parents work. Children are placed with a nanny or a babysitter or put into preschool. Did you know one of the three things is needed in order to diagnose a child with ADHD or ODD? Talking to the parents, perhaps a teacher, or perhaps the babysitters. WOW… The parent seeks out a child behavior specialist describing the behavior habits of the child. The doctor goes on what is being told to him and secures the child as a patient. The doctor observes the child in order to feel justified classifying the child by seeing something in the child's behavior like he doesn't sit still. Forget that the child doesn't understand what the hell is happening here.

The child may even be silently thinking, "does this doctor know my parents have their own behavior problems and little time for me?" This is one hard subject to write about, but I think it is a good subject. I think we have to agree there are too many children with these types of disorders. But is it really a disorder? The only proof is someone describing how the child acts out. Doctors are making thousands of dollars on parents and prescription medicine for children who have no say or knowledge of what's being done to them. So, they may be a little hyper in class than the next child. Perhaps, they weren't taught to behave in the manor of what is sociably accepted. This doesn't seem fair to a child if he wasn't taught from the get-go right and wrong actions and what is acceptable. It's truly not his fault.

Should he be given drugs and be classified that there's something wrong with him? Usually that cuts team sports out of activities at school. The school assumes he can't take orders. It makes the child feel different and not accepted by other students. Does any of this seem fair? In writing this section it puts me in a zone where either you're with me or truly against facts. Do you think for one minute my children and their children weren't hyped up at times? Think again. Rules are what works.

I ask you what parent likes criticism? Let's talk about my children and their children and their children, three generations wide. When they did something wrong there was a price to pay. Yes, this is a tough subject to write about and my feelings are that the truth is what really should set us all free. THERE IS NO TRUE DIAGNOSIS... there are however behavioral problems. Don't all parents deal with behavioral problems? The difference between one verses the other is some parents take time to enforce to their kids there are rules in life, and they must be followed even for mommy and daddy. There are parents that don't feed drugs to their children for behavioral problems. Some parents are smart enough to get to the root of the problem, how the child got to this point. Lack of parenting skills.

Put yourself in the child's place. Children are placed on drugs which may make them slow down, feel calm, probably less sharp, due to lack of the proper supervision from those in charge of the child's daily life. Sad...

Do you agree that too many children are being classified with ADHD/ODD/and the like? Do you agree to many children are being placed on prescription drugs when there's no PROVEN TRUE DIAGNOSIS other than a parent's verifying the child's behavior is out of control? Can I Get A Spolarized Dope A Mean?

Do you agree all Wal-Mart stores need new carts? Wal-Mart has the worst carts of any chain store. Can I Get A Spolarized Dope A Mean?

How many times have you seen people kiss people on the lips? More than likely many times. Parents kissing their children is more frequent than most adults kissing on the lips. A better habit is cheek to cheek. Kissing on the lips passes germs, viruses, you name it, yet parents continue to kiss their children on the lips. Perhaps some of the parents should take some notes that kissing on the lips transmits more than germs. It can cause cold sores, glandular fever and tooth decay. Take note that saliva can transmit various diseases. It is an easy fix if you learn to say remember cheek to cheek. Can I Get A Spolarized Dope A Mean?

Do you plop when you sit? Do you slide off the chair to get up? Both are wrong. It's not nice to give the spine a quick snap nor is it a good thing to plop on the couch after work. The majority of microbial species, viruses, bacteria and fungus can be found on your clothing.

Think about your clothing having the ability to shed 37 million microorganisms every hour. It's not thought a big deal unless you come in contact with somebody who has a staph infection which can be found on the skin. Who would know better than me? I had two grandchildren who came in contact with it. It can be deadly. Just drop a little blood on the wrestling mat or just have a small cut and sit in the same booth with someone who had staph. People with staph are not quarantined to stay home yo.

Not all furniture is made strong enough to plop. Over time the cushions and the fibers in them along with the springs decline. Over time your guests, family and friends, will know you're a plopper by your sofa showing wear and tear. Getting up out of a chair is just as important as sitting down. Your hands on the arm and lifting yourself out of the chair is proper. Sitting down in a chair by putting your hand on an arms of a chair to lay your butt upon it is the proper way. It's amazing how many people never learned the proper way to sit down and get up.

Of course, when you speak to the manufacturers who own the factories (usually in other countries) they say there're glad that there's ploppers because people end up buying more sofas and chairs. Going to all types of conventions the past 30 years and learning what is acceptable and what is not acceptable using their products was a learning process I've endured. I'm giving you headz up the things that are left out when purchasing products.

I always loved it when I went to Magic, the world's largest textile shows, where you learn about clothing. You get to meet the manufacturers of other countries and you learn who is the actual manufacturer of the tees and clothing for major trademarks like Nike, New Balance, and such. The t-shirt can be the same t-shirt however the logo tells you it's a different ticket price than the identical one next to it on the shelf. The tag price for the trademark logo is the only difference.

My question has always been if I'm going to wear your product, then I want to know what you are doing for my country? I studied different companies like Coca-Cola, McDonald's, and some of the major chains by going to major corporation meetings with executives. I learned why they're No. 1. I learned all the rest are just followers trying to look like they're doing a good job when in reality they're trying to catch up. I support companies that come out the gate giving to communities' verses giving just to their wallet. Now that you've learned a few reasons why plopping isn't good for you, the furniture and the many germs left behind, do you agree it is better to sit than plop on furniture? And to carefully read the clothing labels? Can I Get A Spolarized Dope A Mean?

Are you a person who double dips when eating chip and hors d'oeuvres passing your germs and bacteria onto others? No one wants to leave and get sick from your nasty habit at a gathering. Put chips and veggies on a plate along with a spoonful of salsa. Shame on those who don't give a damn. Can I Get A Spolarized Dope A Mean?

Did you ever wonder why there's two toilet tops for one toilet? One is to sit your butt on, and the lid is to stop germs from entering the air in the room when you flush. Surprise... Another reason dudes should pick up both seats to take a leak is, so they don't leave their piss and germs on the seat where ladies sit. Just think if you sat down on piss when you went to take a poop; real nasty eh... Do dudes really care about cleanliness and being sanitary? It is a proven fact that during flushing bacteria such as feces-borne, salmonella, streptococcus as well as viruses and hepatitis A and E. Germs can spread to nearby locations causing diarrhea.

It seems like a lot to ask of us to put the lid down when you're done but not when you know the facts. Here's the next tip when you're done peeing and putting down the toilet seat wash your hands. We pass bacteria from fecal contamination on our hands on to our food and surfaces. Help by cleaning yourself up, yo. Do you agree it is better to put the seat down then leave it up? Can I Get A Spolarized Dope A Mean?

Do you agree Aldi Markets has the best prices over all other food markets in its service areas? Don't forget I raised my own beef and chickens, eggs and veggies. Regardless of how our cows/bulls were fed or their names, when they reached 1000 lbs. they went to market. Likewise, herds from farmers and ranchers get trucked to the auction. The auction is where the big buyers come to buy beef at a fair market price. The cows are on parade. They're killed and shipped to the marketplace. Remember labels are just that. An orange is an orange and milk comes from a cow. Do you agree Aldi's has the best prices? Can I Get A Spolarized Dope A Mean?

Don't you just love it when people visit you and touch your things, even open your drawers. What are they lookin' for eh? I put a note inside my drawers. "Did you know you're a snoop?" Call me a bitch ain't that some sh★t. The note also reads:" you need to walk through the wild weeds and find a violet so you can get on top your game and hear the A·ve Ma·ri·a." Do you agree people shouldn't snoop around your house? Can I Get A Spolarized Dope A Mean?

Do you watch that you don't hit the car next to you when you get out of your car in a parking lot? Do you lean on other people's cars? Do you agree we should respect another person's property? Can I Get A Spolarized Dope A Mean?

Do you know lemons in a restaurant, bar, or public places are rarely washed? Their handled multiple times during wedging by multiple people rarely wearing gloves. Lemon wedges are usually placed in containers under or over the lemons not used. Believe it or not the waitress, waiter, bus boy, or whoever makes your drink will grab a lemon wedge for your drink with dirty hands. 70% of lemon wedges are covered with 25 different types of germs. Forget the E-Coli along with the contamination. Enjoy your lemon but don't think you're clean. Lemons absorb germs. An old lemon can cause food poisoning. However, lemons are good for you if you can get a clean lemon for your drink. Do you agree that lemons used for drinks in public places can be unhealthy and nasty? Can I Get A Spolarized Dope A Mean?

Next time you're sitting in a restaurant take note that the waitress or busboy cleaning the table goes from one table to the next while wiping the chairs with the same rag. It spreads germs, bacteria, staph, and viruses. The rag used from table to table and wiping chairs spreads microorganisms. My family works construction where lime and cement is likely to be on their work pants. Wiping a chair after them and then the next table will put cement which is almost impossible the see on the table top. Cement has lime in it. Inside the body it can cause internal burning due to heat of hydration. It will also begin to harden. There's plenty of construction workers beside my family who eat in restaurants. What is happening to society to accept such bad health habits? Including sucking your fingers. Both are Nasty… I ask you where is our health board and fines? Where are we to not step up and demand better. What about the future generations not being taught healthier habits? If you love your children then you teach them to be better then you. Can I Get a Spolarized Dope A Mean?

Did you know your bed sheets are to be washed every 7 to 10 days? It will keep the habitat bacteria and skin infections out, including lice and bed bugs. If you're the type of person who likes a clean bed, then you will agree washing your sheets is a good habit. It gets rid of oils, dead skin, and bodily fluids that collect. Washing your sheets also helps to eliminate every day health issues like flu and cold viruses. Can I Get a Spolarized Dope A Mean?

Next time you're traveling to town look at how people cut their yard. I could care less about how they live or cut their yard. Really… I'm just amazed how they think. Do they think they've cut the grass but don't need to weed whack? Don't they know without weed whacking the job isn't finished. Could it be they don't take pride in their work? One way or another do you agree that mowing your yard and not weed whacking is doing a half a** job? Can I Get a Spolarized Dope A Mean?

When someone throwing trash out their car window do you agree they can't love "My Country Tis of Thee?" When someone throws gum on the sideway do you agree they careless about the sole of your shoe where you trot? Can I Get a Spolarized Dope A Mean?

The next time someone says something you agree with; I hope you'll shout out "Spolarized Dope A Mean". Let people know you're educated to the highest degree registered in the SpolarizedSmart™ Book of Knowledge and you're Legally Loaded®.

I hope you've enjoyed reading my book. I wanted to learn German because at times that's what my grandma spoke. She said, "I want you to speak English." I learned slang from the street and wrote this book without an edit. I've givin' you Ms Peggy in the raw. Please take a moment and go on my website www.getlegallyloaded.com for a buck and Get Downloaded Coded Legally Loaded® against Fraud, Corruption and Discrimination. If you have purchased the book go to the website and click on the book box and receive a download of the song "Philly Grown." The song has already been paid for through your purchase of the book. Just follow the instructions and enjoy. Thank You, Ms. Peggy

Together We Made It Happen.

214

THE RICH AND THE POOR WHO CROSS YOUR DOOR AND ALL THE A**HOLES IN BETWEEN ARE THE STEPPING STONES THAT HELPED YOU ALONG LIFE'S WAY...

AUTOGRAPH PAGE

A Collection Of The Rich And Poor Who Crossed My Door Along With Friends And Family

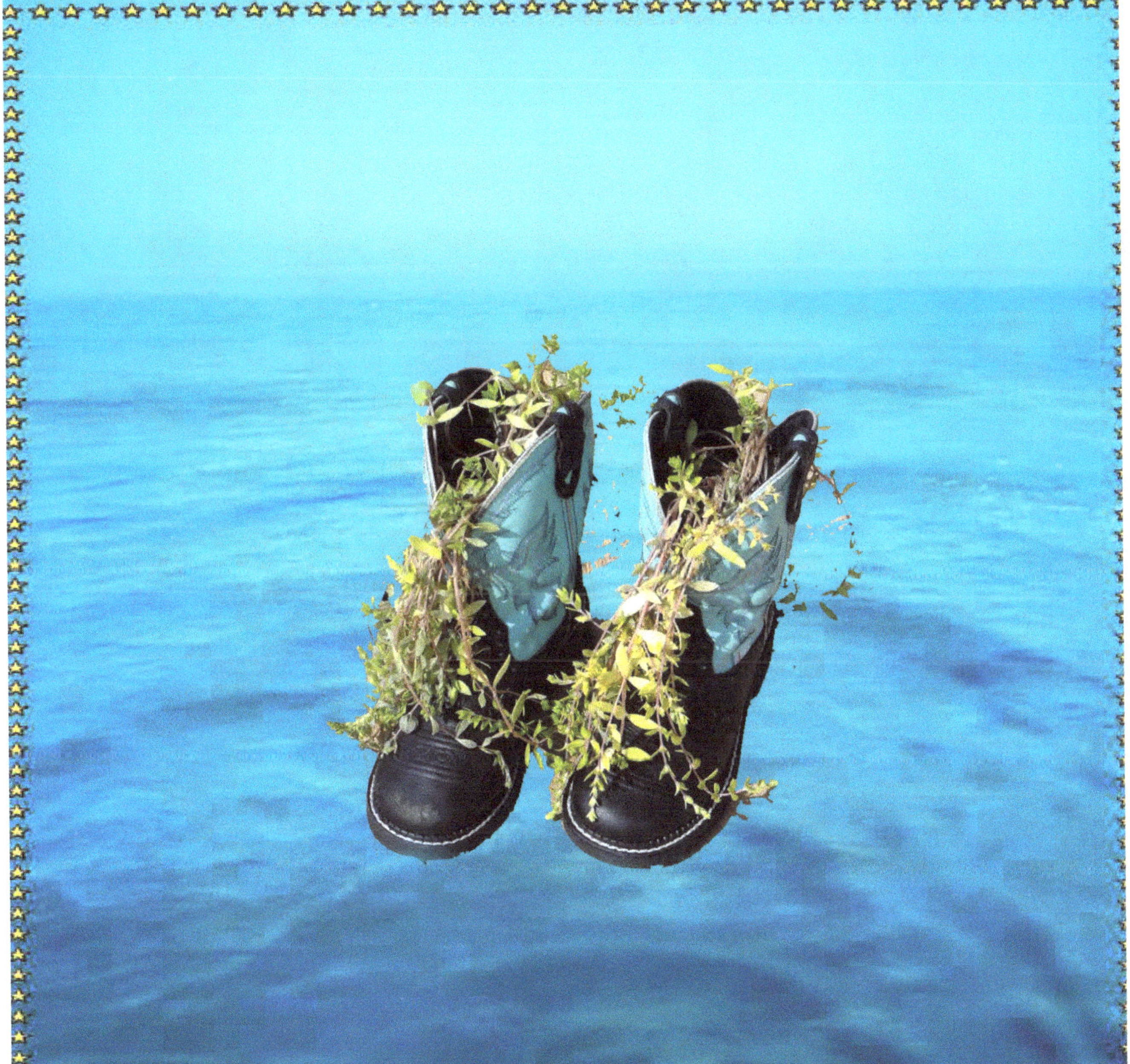

Those were the days back in the 90's with

Olivia Alive

World

Karen

It was truly

A Legally Loaded Spolarized Experience.

Shine the Spolarized Star that you are legally loaded. ~ MS. Peggy